THE LIVING OF
CHARLOTTE PERKINS GILMAN

*the text of this book is printed
on 100% recycled paper*

CHARLOTTE PERKINS GILMAN

THE LIVING OF
CHARLOTTE PERKINS GILMAN

AN AUTOBIOGRAPHY by
CHARLOTTE PERKINS GILMAN

Foreword by
ZONA GALE

HARPER COLOPHON BOOKS
Harper & Row, Publishers
New York, Evanston, San Francisco, London

First HARPER COLOPHON edition published 1975

STANDARD BOOK NUMBER: 06-090422-4

75 76 77 78 10 9 8 7 6 5 4 3 2 1

TO MY DEAR DAUGHTER

*whose ceaseless devotion and good
cheer have made me happy to the
end; and to my beloved grandchildren*

DOROTHY S. CHAMBERLIN

making me poems and pictures, and

WALTER S. CHAMBERLIN

*whose loving companionship and
genuine interest in my work have
been so deep a comfort*

THIS BOOK IS DEDICATED

AUTHOR'S NOTE

MANY a foreword gives thanks to various authorities for help in writing the book.

I wish to offer gratitude, deep and warm and true, to those whose warmly expressed affection has made this closing year a happiness; to my more than sister, Grace Ellery Channing-Stetson; to my cousin, Lyman Beecher Stowe and his wife, Hilda Stowe, whose loving kindness and generous care have shouldered so much of the burden I was unable to lift; to Zona Gale, whose affectionate intent promoted this publication; to Amy Wellington, keen but gentle critic, who has arranged my second book of poems, *Here Also;*

And to those close and tender friends, Martha Bensley Bruere and Robert Bruere; Dr. Edmund P. Shelby and his wife, Gertrude M. Shelby; to three generations of the family of Judge Charles Amidon; to Mary Hutchinson Page and her family; to Alexander Black and Mrs. Black, to the Reverend Alexander Abbott and Mrs. Abbott, to Mr. Edwin Higgins, whose extraordinary kindness and legal ability have cared for me so ably— I cannot give a list of the friends of a lifetime; but these, and more, have helped me through sudden widowhood and long illness to the end.

CONTENTS

FOREWORD

In the long, slow development of our social consciousness, Charlotte Perkins Gilman has flamed like a torch.
This seems the right simile, for she has burned her
way about the world, one message blazing from her
spoken and written words, and from her living:
"Life is growth."
Anything which hampers or thwarts the growth, the
expanding consciousness, the increasing coöperation of
The Social Body, that Unit of Life, has been to her
the sin not so much unpardonable as incredible. For life
is growth. That is the brilliant common sense of her
enormous awareness of the human scene.

Set against the simple tragedy, the simple ambition,
even the simple aspiration of the individual life, this
interpretation of hers raised living to new riches. It's
not new to us now. We know about it. But when
Charlotte Perkins began to understand it, most ethical
concepts in America still had to do with individual mo-
rality and the hope of personal reward after death.

In the 1870's Arnold Toynbee had not yet begun
to preach his "self-identification with the oppressed"
in London, and Toynbee Hall, forerunner of Hull
House, was not yet opened. But even if she had heard
of this doctrine, it is doubtful whether it would have
interested Charlotte Perkins. "What are you about,
sitting there all oppressed?" she might have said.
"Stand up and realize that you belong to the human

race. And as for you who know better and live better, and are nothing loath to see or even to be oppressors, open your eyes! You belong to the human race, too. What are you going to do about it?"

Man not so much his brother's keeper as his brother's brother. It was as simple as that. But it was still revolutionary then—as it remains still unpractised now.

From Palestine, from Persia, from India, from China this word had filtered in, but who in the East was any longer burned up by it, and who in the West did not think that we had found a better way, in individual and family righteousness? Sane words from pulpits in New York and New England, to be sure; gentle centers like Brook Farm, foremarked for failure. But this girl's word was simple and more basic than any of them: "The purpose of life is growth." Test all things thus: Do they help or hinder growth? Never mind doctrines, policies, politics, expedients, morals as you have conceived them; never mind your hesitant "doing good," your new-found philanthropies, your western caste system, your business sense, your economics even, if any of these accept anything which flaws human growth. It was extraordinary how many learned controversies dwindled before this rather crass test.

The old Franciscan devoir to Lady Poverty left her cold. "Not less life. More life. Oh, so you feel that Plenty causes death of spiritual living? What do you mean by a spiritual living that cannot stand up under cleanliness and decent living conditions and human co-operation and human *growth?* Greed is the only death —greed of goods, of power, of personal profit, personal salvation, personal anything which hinders corporate growth. For growth *is* life, life is growth. Not less life. More life. More growth!"

Especially the stunted development of women roused her passion and her pity and her protest. Women, "specialized to sex and to housework"; women, "confusing marriage with domestic service." She saw in women half the human race, mothers of all of it, cut off from their great work of world-raising by their position as private servants. "Every man," she stormed, "requires one whole woman to minister to him! There must be nothing left of her." And again: "What else can she do with her powers, her energies, her sense of social consciousness? No, for when he comes home, she must be *there!* And when they ask you to marry them they say: 'I need you so!'"

In the rich and shared living into which certain men and women have entered now, all this is a commonplace;—and in certain bizarre extremes of to-day, such a picture as she draws has long since passed. But in the 1870's this was heresy to which every sort of opprobrium was attached. The idea of any life for women besides that offered by sex and housework was then unthinkable, and the larger integration could not be visualized at all. That women had many another contribution to make which would enrich society and human growth; that women could be mothers to the race as well as to one family "around the evening lamp"; that unlimited child-bearing is immoral; that if a woman is equipped for, or specialized to creative work, then to do housework alone, even her own, is against even the Hebrew Bible's injunction on the subject of the talents; that women's share in living is as limitless as that of man—all this was new and heretical —as to-day it remains heretical to millions.

To her all this was but newly revealed interpretation of age-old facts, and her beliefs were rooted in the story of the race. Her correspondence files yield

important exchanges of comment. From Professor
Lester F. Ward of Brown University, whose Chapter XIV of his *Applied Sociology* had meant so much
to her, there came the following:

1464 R. I. Avenue
 Washington, D.C.
   April 10, 1904

MY DEAR MRS. GILMAN:

It cannot be denied that the great step from oviparous bird
to viviparous mammal was made through the gradual modi-
fication chiefly of female organs, and the classification of the
animal kingdom is based not only on the reproductive organs
but almost wholly on those of the female. The important steps
were bird, Monotreme, Marsupial, Mammal. You would find
nearly everything you want in Haeckel's History of Creation
and Evolution of Man (English translations). It is very easy
reading. You can judge of it by my extended review of these
books, made before they were translated, a copy of which I sent
you long ago. But you would do well to read Geddes and
Thompson's Evolution of Sex, and Havelock Ellis's Man and
Woman.

Mrs. Ward and I are now reading the most eye-opening
book I have met with from the human side. It is Le Tourneau's
Condition des Femmes dans les differentes Races (Giard et
Briere, 16 rue Soufflot, Paris), recently published and since
the author's death. He passes in review all the human races
from the standpoint of the condition of women, and it turns
out that there is no race that does not retain survivals of a
matriarchal stage in its history. I could have greatly strengthened this part of the argument if this book had been out when
I wrote Chap. XIV. Every woman ought to read that book.
Can't you find some one who will translate it into English?

...You will find Germany intensely androcentric and only
half civilized.

Sincerely
LESTER F. WARD

More than a quarter of a century later Dr. Edward A. Ross of Wisconsin University was writing to her as follows:

Madison, December 25, 1923

DEAR MRS. GILMAN:

This day reminds me of your comment on Santa a year ago and I bethink me that I have not acknowledged your splendid "His Religion and Hers" which came to me in the autumn. It is a wonderful book and your tracing of how religion bears the stamp of sex is most original—an imaginative *tour de force.* I don't know how it will jibe with the vast and overwhelming array of facts as to early religions which the folk lorists have brought together. I suppose some dry-as-dust will check up your "genial theories" with the accumulations of data and prove your theory right or acceptable in a modified form; while the naturalists all tell me we must reject Dr. Ward's doctrine of the priority and superiority of the female sex for nearly all his instances are drawn from the realms of insects which were never in the least degree ancestors of the mammalia. I am a feminist on other than genetic grounds. It is woman's *psyche* that makes the hit with me, for her maternal instinct is becoming more precious with every step in our social evolution whereas man's special endowment of pugnacity threatens to ruin civilization through war. The more I see of men and women the more I like women's reactions to the situations life offers and the more I am impressed with the defects of the male *psyche.* The fact is, I find women the more reasonable sex and some day I hope to get into one of the literary magazines an article on "The Reasonable Sex" which will surely flutter the dove cotes. I would like to mass a body of evidence which would give the pride of the he-men a heavy jolt. However that may have to wait quite a while yet, there is so much I have to do first. I hope you have seen my little book "The Social Trend" which contains a chapter "Women in a Man Made World" which will interest you. I got my start out of your "This Man Made World," but gathered evidence of my own. . . .

I brought out a book at the end of October entitled "The Russian Soviet Republic" which I want you to have if you would like it.

Your affectionate friend
EDWARD A. ROSS

This letter brought a spirited reply from Mrs. Gilman—two years later, but as if she were resuming a conversation momentarily interrupted.

380 Washington Street
Norwich Town, Conn.
July 6, 1925

O Eminent Sociologist,
    Effective and agreeable Writer
      and Excellent Friend,

Greetings! I don't know how long it is since I've written you, but just now I found on my desk among the "not immediates" yours of about two years ago, with kind words about my last book and most gratifying news. ... I have some new lectures I'd like you to hear; The Falsity of Freud; Americans and Non-Americans; and Standards and Programs.

Personally I am enjoying this old place in a country town increasingly, and have become a frantic devotee of gardening. The place used to occupy the entire time of a hired man; we cannot afford one, so Houghton and I do it ourselves. We have all kinds of vegetables and a big flower garden too. I am as brown as an Indian and husky—you'd be astonished.

As to real work, I have started in a feeble way on my Autobiography, but it does not interest me as much as it ought to. My real interest is in ideas, as you know. Here is one I think you will care for and can perhaps do something about. You know my suggestions about "Standardising Towns ... ? Did you ever see the little pamphlet William Ogburn of Reed College prepared on the strength of my lecture on that topic? It is Reed College Record, Number 27, Social Service Series no. 4—Dec. 1917.

Well—that has got to be done for Nations.

You know how we all love, honor and brag about our own

land? And it never occurs to us that nations vary in value to the world, some useful, some of small account, some deleterious. My proposition is to prepare some sort of list of "Points" in which different peoples visibly excel, as for instance, Art; Science; Music; Warfare; Invention; Discovery; Benevolence; Refinement; Honesty; Progressiveness; Political Development; points to be agreed upon by some competent authorities, and then a group of the principal nations classified under that list.

My suggestion to editors was to get an able man of each land to write the braggingest article he could on his own people's attainments, say twelve of 'em, publish them monthly, then have the facts checked off by an international group of historians—(fine fighting there!) and the whole bunch measured and rated.

I tried it in a loose tentative fashion, I don't know enough to undertake it seriously—something like the enclosed. Of course any list would be violently disagreed with, but instead of mere bragging and lying there would be in the popular mind *something to judge by.* You'll be amused by my estimate of Ireland's achievements, but, as a nation, what have they contributed to the world besides a few writers?

In thinking about this I was particularly struck by the difference between Ireland and Scotland, so nearly alike in environment and with so much in common in stock. Yet there was enough difference in that stock to make the one people unite the warring clans and build a kingdom, develop a freer religion, raise a group of real thinkers, and make literature which is world-literature and does not have to be "revived." Oh, there should be also a sort of fever chart arrangement, showing the period of greatness of Spain, Greece, etc., and that some peoples are rising, and some decadent. Then if we hear these Irish boasts of what they used to be in the sixth century the come-back is clear!

Did the Turks ever do *anything* good? I think of them as a purely predatory people, and an injury to the world.

How I would like to have a good talk with you! Don't you ever come this way with time enough for a glimpse of us? We'd love to have the two of you for a real visit.

I think your "naturalists" comment on Ward's Gynocentric theory extremely shallow. He gave instances enough from birds and quadrupeds, even in ordre mammalia, to rest the whole thing on. Except for the special decorations and fighting machinery of the male, and his seasonal pugnacity, the female is the equal in all race activities, and adds her increasing power as a race-builder. Of course it's her "psyche," if you wish to call it that. See what a nice thing I've got on Freud.... Sex is not the "Life Force." Life existed for ages, and reproduction went on, billion-fold, before sex was developed. It is not essential to life, nor to reproduction, but to the improvement of species. So there!

With cordial regards to Mrs. Ross, your old friend,

CHARLOTTE PERKINS GILMAN

But among her letters including those from distinguished people—Alfred Russell Wallace, H. G. Wells, W. D. Howells, Ethel Snowden, Edward Bellamy, and others—no letters could have been more stimulating to Mrs. Gilman than those received from countless women then unknown. For example, it is thrilling to come upon this letter from the late Marie Jenney Howe written in her young womanhood to Mrs. Gilman. She said:

1613 Rebecca Street
Sioux City, Iowa
August 12, 1899

Mrs. Charlotte Perkins Stetson:
DEAR MADAM,

I have read your book on "Women and Economics." It seems to me that I have waited all my life to read this book. It justifies my most cherished convictions. I have long believed that all women *ought* to be self-supporting. At the same time I have recognized that society, in its organization and its institutions, renders economic independence impossible to the women who marry. I therefore concluded that there existed an internecine warfare between this *ought* and this impossibility.

The only hope I held was that of a radical change in the
nature of men as husbands—a desperate hope indeed!

But you prove that society itself must alter. You show that
it is able so to alter, that it can adapt itself to new needs, that
this is practical, even inevitable.

I cannot sufficiently express to you my debt of gratitude.
You have helped me, helped my mental struggles, my efforts
to understand. To me your book is illumining. I have been
blundering along on these lines of study-reading which enabled me readily to receive your thought. My profession is
preaching. I confess that at present I am seized with the desire
to preach "Women and Economics."

Next winter I shall be in Des Moines, Iowa, as minister of
the Unitarian Church there, and I intend to give the substance of your book in a series of talks to the women's society
of the church, or to the Political Equality club.

It has been hard work to persuade a few women to care for
political freedom, it will be still harder to make them care for
economic freedom. Even unmarried women, who may support
themselves, do not seem to prize their independence. They are
not born economically free, they do not achieve it, it is thrust
upon them by the pressure of necessity.

I have been four years in a non-sectarian theological school,
and two years in the Liberal ministry. I have come to believe
that in time men and women will practice the same virtues.
In the interim I could wish that men and women might attend
separate churches. In the men's church I would have preached
the virtues of self-sacrifice and gentleness, while the women.
in their separate church, should be exhorted to self-reliance
and self development. As it is now, if a minister speaks of
self-sacrifice, the men think he is addressing the women; and
when he speaks of any strong virtue he calls it manliness,
and the women know it is meant for the men. I believe you
are a socialist. It seems to me that women are not ready for
socialism. The wave of individualism that swept over the civilized globe during the last century entered every phase of life
and work excepting the lives and the work of women. During
the present period of transition I believe it is wise to preach

individualism to women, and Christianity to men. Surely Jesus himself gives us the completed ideal, wherein no virtues are masculine and none are feminine. He is unique in that he is human. In him character has no sex bias. Just as Newton's discoveries and those of Galileo were thrown forward several generations, so this ethical ideal was thrown forward centuries ahead. It will perfectly fit the period of equality. It is not understood today. This example of Jesus I would use to illustrate the thought in your last chapter. Where I have been groping my way, the little light I have found helps me toward your larger vision. Indeed I fear that you have found a disciple, whether or no you so desire.

Women must be economically free. Social customs can and will be adjusted to this freedom. Of this I am sure. Since reading your book this belief has sunk into my mind as a deep conviction. I am glad you are in the world to spread this truth. If you will help me now, perhaps in the end I shall be able to help you also. (I am not yet thirty, and I am not married. This is an important item.)

I want you to tell me what to read. After Westermarck, Le Tourneau and those, I can find no others.

I want you to tell me what else you have written. Some time ago I came across "In This Our World." I sent to California for it.

I want you to write me. You will, won't you! Perhaps you are flooded with letters. Never mind. They don't care as I care. I have thought of all this for years. I had even dreamed of writing something myself. Now it isn't necessary, since your big book includes all that might have been in my little book. Drummond's "Ascent of Man" suggested a way to branch off into an ascent of woman, but it is all included in your book. I tell you all this to show how much it means to me that the book has been written, and that you are in the world. It is solitary to hold these views, especially here in the west. Surely you must understand. And if you understand you will write.

Gratefully yours,
MARIE HOFFENDAHL JENNY

To those who marvel at the vitality and one-pointedness of Mrs. Gilman's interest down the years, the obvious rejoinder is that this interest *was* her life. From the days of the '70's and '80's when she was a pioneer in America in this thinking, the integration of her ideas into her living and writing and talking never flagged.

One wonders where Charlotte Perkins got it. Even she does not know, though in her autobiography she tried to recall. Inherited wisdom explains something; and already the air was being charged for the new day. But her mind was one of the first in America to catch the fire. Incidentally, she never thought of suffrage for women as anything more than one iron in that fire. Useful, expectable, inevitable. That, of course. Then more, more! She had a thousand suggestions no less vital. Women must be released from drudgery. Human creatures they were, with the varied powers which are not those of "man's work" but of human work, half the world's ability—and they must be released from the individual kitchen. College education was just opening to women. But she longed for more. She longed for the release of the married through professionalized house service. No one could get decent ice-cream, pastry, preserves, tinned stuffs in that day, save through the individual kitchen, and the woman who stitched her own husband's shirt-bosoms was still more highly appraised than the one whose husband bought his shirts, as was possible even then. A public laundry was disdainfully regarded no matter how well the work was done. As for cooked food ever being served to the home instead of raw materials, or ready-made dresses worn—either was ridiculed. "But," Charlotte Perkins would say, "a man does not build all of his own house any more, or make his own shoes, or his own suits. Why should a woman...."

It took a long time. Even yet the cooked food service has but begun. Nor, though tractors and harvesting machinery are coöperatively owned and used, are realized her brigade of expert house-cleaners, to enter the home in spring and autumn, with proper equipment. Except, indeed, that in such beautiful apartment houses as those of the Sweringens in Cleveland and in some others, exactly this process of house-cleaning takes place, and is included in the rental price.

She was intensely sad about women, about their lost opportunities, their lost advantage and for the millions who had gone down to the breast of earth with no knowledge that they were not the inferiors of the men who had taught them so well that they were so. I remember waiting with her on the platform of a small railway town in Wisconsin. Beautiful red-and-green switch-lights shone out and great engines rushed back and forth. "All that," she said, "and women have had no part in it. Everything done by men, working together, while women worked on alone within their four walls!"

In the 1870's already she was as scornful of the woman who had to be "protected"—who dare not walk alone on the streets at night, as is the woman of to-day. And once, when she had refused a man's "escort" to her home, he cried, in bewilderment:

"But any man would be glad to protect a woman. Man is a woman's natural protector!"

And she asked him: "Against what?"

She was one of the first to stand for the use of her own name by the professional woman after marriage—or by any woman, if she so prefers; and one of the first to note that there exists no law whatever against this, but only a convention.

"The convention of the owner of a human being, giving that being his own name. As in slave days," she would say. Reminded that there might be some mystical significance to this custom—as in the Hebrew scriptures, Saul became Paul and Abraham Abram, after a great spiritual experience, she would say: "Perhaps. And then, remember women have always transfigured their conditions—when these didn't kill them, body or soul."

She has stood always for equality of the moral standard for both men and women—but she had expected that the level of the standard would be up, to where she believed that women stood, and not to a level which she believed to be down, where the lax and casual superseded the slow effort toward the understanding that life and its processes are probably more than that which we believe them to be. So that now, after all her prophetic thinking, it comes about that to-day Mrs. Gilman is regarded by many of the new generation as reactionary, because of her impatience at the useful bunglings of Freud, that husky bull in the Venetian-glass shop of certain still veiled equilibriums.

One of her greatest social contributions is her interpretation of the needs of childhood. In her youth, no one had ever heard of a nursery-school. Kindergartens had not long arrived in this country. The whole duty of a mother was to give entire *and ungraded* instruction to her children. How did she know enough to do this? Well, wasn't she a mother? Did not God-given wisdom in how to do these things arrive with the baby? And so on. It seems strange now, in the light of the enormous literature on child psychology, on understanding children, on their development—to realize that "train" and "discipline" were the two words then most often applied to the growth of children. Human growth again. This hope, always in her thought, taught her that children were everywhere misunderstood and lied to and inhibited and repressed and crippled in mind and in energy by the terrible impress of the adult upon a consciousness of which, in a large measure of cases, that adult knew next to nothing. Some children, Charlotte Perkins saw, came through by the grace of God and by the circumstance of wise and understanding and intelligent parents. But by far the majority, she held, in literal numbers, were crossed and stunted and flawed in their growth by parental unwisdom, parental selfishness, masking too often as parental love—and usually totally unself-conscious.

So she preached that a majority of children under school age were being ruined in their homes. At this women, of course, turned to rend her. She advocated great airy nurseries where small children could be taken and developed, taught to *grow,* by women specialized and trained in this wisdom. Women called her an unnatural creature. Now, in the days of pre-kindergarten care, of the books on "newer ways with children," of the definite knowledge that children may be mentally scarred for life before they are five years old, all this objection to child development takes its place with the old cry against college education for women.

"Natural enough, that cry. The threshers with flails stoned the first threshing-machines in England, remember," Charlotte Perkins said.

But she mourned the dead gifts, buried in the bodies of children.

"A child between two and three," she noticed, "stood with her mother at a window in London, watching a man sweep the crossing. 'See the nice man,' said the

child's mother, 'making the street clean for Maisie.'
'No, Mama,' replied the baby—'not for Maisie—for
all the mans!' The dead gifts, buried in the bodies of
little children, who never know, and whose parents
never know, that they had them! Women specialized
to piano, specialized to voice, specialized to cooking—
never to child-development. That 'comes with the
baby,' forsooth!"

At Tower Hill, Wisconsin, the Summer Colony
founded by Jenkin Lloyd Jones, she gave me a remembered rebuke. Mr. Jones, with his shock of silver
hair and his silver beard and ruddy face, came smiling
towards us, as we sat talking to a little girl. 'See,' I
said to the child, 'here comes Santa Claus!' The child's
eyes widened and deepened, and Mrs. Gilman touched
my arm. When she had my attention, she held me in
silence for a moment, and then she said, very low: "It
isn't true." A memorable moment.

Her passionate scorn of our half-way methods, in
muddling through to growth, shook many an audience.
"The purpose of food is to feed folks!" she would
cry. "Not to make money—to 'corner'—to destroy to
'keep up the market'—to limit. Food is to feed folks—
when shall we learn that?"

In a seminar in economics at the University of Wisconsin, the leader kept appealing to her, who was a
visitor there, for her opinions. At first refusing to
speak, then much pressed, she cried at last: "Well, if
you will poke me up, I don't think you are discussing
economics at all. I think you are talking about charity."

Emerging on that campus, the summer school students streaming over its green swell in the slanting late
afternoon sunlight, bright colored groups under the
trees, the university band playing, she said: "There's

heaven. There it is. What more do we mean? People, free to come together, and in beauty—*for growth.*"

She has been, all her life, a glorious companion to all who have known her. Her spirit, her zest ("zest—the last gift of the immortals," Edmund Clarence Stedman once said) are beyond the approach of most folk. Her physical energy, as a girl, was super-normal, super-natural, and her mental energy now, is the same. I can see her enunciating some new lines of attack on some horizon, and ceasing, and laughing: "I'm a mile high, and shining!" She was—she is.

Of the sudden vacuity, physical and mental, which fell upon her after her marriage to Charles Stetson, what shall be said? From an energy so extreme that she could exercise, lift, carry, endure beyond the strength of most women, she became, by her own account, first an invalid, lying, daylong on a couch and weeping, and then a nervous wreck, dangling a rag-doll from a door-knob, to play with. Over-training, perhaps, in her youth, one says—or lack of vitamins—or eye strain! But on her long absence in California, she recovered her strength and her energy, only to lose all again on her return home. After the divorce, she regained something, though never all of her former power. The inference, to which her autobiography does not allude, is that she was a woman not adapted to marriage as understood and practised in these immediate centuries. In this, too, she belonged to some future. Her work has analyses of the general situation of women "specialized to sex or housework," but she makes no particular reference. One fact appears, that if ever a nervous case was misunderstood by a nerve specialist, it was hers—with the recommendation to "rest and never touch a pen or brush for the duration of her life"! The "grinding misery" of those days is in her face, in the photographs subsequent to 1884, her marriage year.

"And I never had the faintest sympathy," she says, "during any of that time. Every one thought I was an unnatural wife, an unnatural mother. Perhaps, some-day...."

Her course after the divorce, when Mr. Stetson married her closest friend, Grace Ellery Channing, and they all remained as friends, was a course to be taken for granted now, though then it was regarded as the height of savage usage that they were not savage towards one another. Her daughter showed definite aptitudes for art, and Charlotte Perkins Stetson permitted her to go abroad to study with her artist father and his wife—and this decision also would be accepted today as sensible and—in her own phrase—as best ministering to the child's growth; but in that day, with its evident need for the food of feuds, this course was censored, editorially, from coast to coast. Though already, now, the reported heresy of her motherhood would be wisely interpreted; the earlier "heresy" of her marriage attitude still would be harder to handle and to apply because of general property and "support" difficulties to be met. "Economic independence" was the fundamental in her demands for the new soil for the growth of women; but for their "support," save while their children were little, her patience was small; and as for alimony, her scorn had no words. "The meanest money payments ever made," she would say.

She is direct, abrupt, blunt, devastating, as the need arises, and oblivious—as any Beecher ever was. Sleeping in a ground-floor room in a small town-house, a visiting wind-storm of tornado force failed to waken her. But towards daylight she was roused by voices—people moving about with lanterns and talking. After a

little while she spoke from the window—begging them
to postpone their conversation that she might sleep. In
the morning she learned that a large tree had been
blown over onto the house next door—whose occu-
pants were naturally interested! Now no matter if
Mrs. Gilman's doctrines should be accepted by men
and angels, never would that family believe in these
or in her! Nor would that magazine editor, who approached her for a contribution "from your pen, and,
our treasury being small, may we hope that you will
use our columns freely to spread your ideas, without
the check which we should like to send if we could."
Of this editor and his magazine she disposed with one
scratch. "You can't get material for nothing from me
like that," she wrote. "And you're dishonest to ask for
it in this way."

There is nothing of the formal saint in Charlotte
Perkins Gilman. But, essentially, what is a saint? One,
perhaps now as always, who would save the world.

She is wont to shrug a bit at the psychic, as is the
custom of those whose intellect fills up the frame. Yet
when she was a girl, this happened to her: Retiring
early, as was her habit, she woke with her usual sense
of a full night's rest and "time to get up." It was winter, when she usually arose before daylight, a street-
lamp being enough to dress by. Down she went to
start the fire for breakfast, noticing, as she passed, a
light in her brother's room. It was most unusual for
him to awake early. She knocked at the locked door—
was answered by a voice—but the light went out.

While "shaking down" the kitchen stove, her visiting
aunt thrust an astonished face from her bedroom door
and demanded, "What are you doing!" "Making the
fire, of course." "Do you know what time it is?" She
looked at the kitchen clock—just midnight!

So she went back to bed, puzzled but content enough, and slept the night out.

At breakfast her brother said, "Lucky you waked me last night!" and explained that he had been reading and had fallen asleep with his candle on the bed—and the door locked.

"I don't know anything about that," she said, "excepting that it happened."

Others might see her as a center of energy so intense that it could contact greater powers, greater awareness, then she ever divined.

I must not fail to record that, when the war came, in 1914, after having preached all her life the unity of man and the need for human growth, she sided unconditionally with the allies and spoke of the German nation as criminally insane. This was a surprise to most of those who knew her, an utter contradiction of thought. And like Kropotkin and Babuschka in Russia, she never has seen in the beginnings of the Russian economic revolution anything of the political or moral revolution for which, in a more gradual evolution, she had hoped. However, she saw then in nationalism a stage of development which, in her earlier thinking, she had been willing to omit in favor of "above all races is humanity." To those to whom the earlier ground would seem to be the more fertile, for human growth, she tolerantly allows their present faith in her own former conviction.

Women and Economics, probably her greatest book, acclaimed in England even more favorably than in America where it became a great textbook, will stand for many as the sum of her life-work. It lit to energy many thousands of the unaware, the indolent, the oblivious, and made of them socially-conscious beings. You cannot say for a book more than this, unless you can also say that it kindled a spiritual energy. And the book did both. It does both now, and will continue to do so. It is a clear call to all women to be "a mile high, and shining."

In This Our World, her poems published here and in England, shakes the complacence, the self-righteousness, the self-sufficiency of to-day, even as it did when it was published. If you want to be interpreted, like a dream, this book is your gentle Daniel—who bites, too, sometimes. *His Religion and Hers* performs for many a service like unto that of *The Green Pastures,* since it tells to a man and a woman his and her individual absurdities, while innocently imputing them to a type— or a race. All Mrs. Gilman's books are, for the greater part, of and for to-day. Like her quatrain aimed so laughingly at youth:

The Front Wave

The little front wave ran up on the sand
And frothed there, highly elated,
"I am the tide!" said the little front wave,
"The waves before me are dated!"

We shall hardly outgrow her in long, long lives to come. In time to come, they will be saying: "How She Knew!" and there is an epitaph.

Her greatest single achievement was the *writing* and publishing for seven years, of the *Forerunner,* a monthly magazine all of which she wrote herself. These seven volumes are a treasury of the advanced development of the social awareness of our own time. These are "Gilman, in seven volumes." Fiction, essay and poetry in the magazine were all written by her, and there was the serial use of several of her later books.

Two of her poems, "An Obstacle" and "Similar Cases" set forth her constant preoccupation:

An Obstacle

I was climbing up a mountain-path
   With many things to do,
Important business of my own,
   And other people's too,
When I ran against a Prejudice
   That quite cut off the view.

My work was such as could not wait,
   My path quite clearly showed,
My strength and time were limited,
   I carried quite a load;
And there that hulking Prejudice
   Sat all across the road.

So I spoke to him politely,
   For he was huge and high,
And begged that he would move a bit
   And let me travel by.
He smiled, but as for moving!—
   He didn't even try.

And then I reasoned quietly
   With that colossal mule:
My time was short—no other path—
   The mountain winds were cool.
I argued like a Solomon;
   He sat there like a fool.

Then I flew into a passion,
   I danced and howled and swore.
I pelted and belabored him
   Till I was stiff and sore;
He got as mad as I did—
   But he sat there as before.

And then I begged him on my knees;
   I might be kneeling still
If so I hoped to move that mass
   Of obdurate ill-will—
As well invite the monument
   To vacate Bunker Hill!

So I sat before him helpless,
   In an ecstasy of woe—
The mountain mists were rising fast,
   The sun was sinking slow—
When a sudden inspiration came,
   As sudden winds do blow.

I took my hat, I took my stick,
   My load I settled fair,
I approached that awful incubus
   With an absent-minded air—
And I walked directly through him,
   As if he wasn't there!

Similar Cases

There was once a little animal,
   No bigger than a fox,
And on five toes he scampered
   Over Tertiary rocks.
They called him Eohippus,
   And they called him very small,
And they thought him of no value—
   When they thought of him at all;
For the lumpish old Dinoceras
   And Coryphodon so slow
Were the heavy aristocracy
   In days of long ago.

Said the little Eohippus,
   "I am going to be a horse!
And on my middle finger-nails
   To run my earthly course!

I'm going to have a flowing tail!
  I'm going to have a mane!
I'm going to stand fourteen hands high
  On the psychozoic plain!"

The Coryphodon was horrified,
  The Dinoceras was shocked;
And they chased young Eohippus,
  But he skipped away and mocked.
Then they laughed enormous laughter,
  And they groaned enormous groans,
And they bade young Eohippus
  Go view his father's bones.
Said they, "You always were as small
  And mean as now we see,
And that's conclusive evidence
  That you're always going to be."

"What! Be a great, tall, handsome beast,
  With hoofs to gallop on?
Why! You'd have to change your nature!"
  Said the Loxolophodon.
They considered him disposed of,
  And retired with gait serene;
That was the way they argued
  In "the early Eocene."

There was once an Anthropoidal Ape,
  Far smarter than the rest,
And everything that they could do
  He always did the best;
So they naturally disliked him,
  And they gave him shoulders cool,
And when they had to mention him
  They said he was a fool.

Cried this pretentious Ape one day,
  "I'm going to be a Man!
And stand upright, and hunt, and fight,
  And conquer all I can!

I'm going to cut down forest trees,
   To make my houses higher!
I'm going to kill the Mastodon!
   I'm going to make a fire!"

Loud screamed the Anthropoidal Apes
   With laughter wild and gay;
They tried to catch that boastful one,
   But he always got away.
So they yelled at him in chorus,
   Which he minded not a whit;
And they pelted him with cocoanuts,
   Which didn't seem to hit.
And then they gave him reasons
   Which they thought of much avail,
To prove how his preposterous
   Attempt was sure to fail.

Said the sages, "In the first place,
   The thing cannot be done!
And, second, if it *could* be,
   It would not be any fun!
And, third, and most conclusive,
   And admitting no reply,
You would have to change your nature!
   We should like to see you try!"
They chuckled then triumphantly,
   These lean and hairy shapes,
For these things passed as arguments
   With the Anthropoidal Apes.

There was once a Neolithic Man,
   An enterprising wight,
Who made his chopping implements
   Unusually bright.
Unusually clever he,
   Unusually brave,
And he drew delightful Mammoths
   On the borders of his cave.

To his Neolithic neighbors,
   Who were startled and surprised,
Said he, "My friends, in course of time,
   We shall be civilized!
We are going to live in cities!
   We are going to fight in wars!
We are going to eat three times a day
   Without the natural cause!
We are going to turn life upside down
   About a thing called gold!
We are going to want the earth, and take
   As much as we can hold!
We are going to wear great piles of stuff
   Outside our proper skins!
We are going to have Diseases!
   And accomplishments!! And Sins!!!"

Then they all rose up in fury
   Against their boastful friend,
For prehistoric patience
   Cometh quickly to an end.
Said one, "This is chimerical!
   Utopian! Absurd!"
Said another, "What a stupid life!
   Too dull, upon my word!"
Cried all, "Before such things can come,
   You idiotic child,
You must alter Human Nature!"
   And they all sat back and smiled.
Thought they, "An answer to that last
   It will be hard to find!"
It was a clinching argument
   To the Neolithic Mind!

One of the great women of the two centuries, she has the supreme reward of standing, in the mind of to-day, for that for which she has striven. She has sought to give out the sovereign knowledge that life has meaning; and that human growth—which is to say, the current of awareness of brotherhood, resulting in conduct—is the chief flow of the spirit to awareness of what that meaning may be.

ZONA GALE

THE LIVING OF
CHARLOTTE PERKINS GILMAN

CHAPTER I

BACKGROUND

WHEN about fifteen years old I was told of our extremely remote connection with English royalty, and wrote eagerly to my learned father to inquire as to the facts—*was* I related to Queen Victoria? To which he solemnly replied, "It is quite true that you are related to Queen Victoria, but there are a great many persons between you and the throne and I should not advise you to look forward to it."

There are two tall yellow books in our public libraries, *American Families of Royal Descent;* almost any one who can trace back to England can hook onto a royal family or two, but I did not know this at the time and was much impressed by the genealogical outline he sent me. It was such fun to recognize names familiar in Scott; and faces sadly beautiful from Agnes Strickland's *Queens of England.*

We run up through a bunch of New Englanders, Perkins, Pitkin, Woodbridge, Wyllys, to Governor John Haynes of Connecticut, who was John Haynes of Copford Hall, England. "In Essex I think," says father's letter. Through this worthy, or rather his wife, up presently to one Catherine Fiennes, whose father was Thomas Fiennes, Lord Dacre of the South, and whose mother was daughter of Sir Humphrey Bourchier. Then the fun begins!

Up goes one long line of names, through two more Bourchiers to Thomas of Woodstock, Duke of Gloucester, son of Edward III and Phillippa of Hainault; then it streams off to that universal progenitor, William the Conqueror; to Malcolm Canmore III of Scotland; to Edmund Ironsides and his less attractive father, Ethelred the Unready.

Climbing another branch, through Edward II's wife, Isabella of France, "the She-wolf," it runs merrily on through Phillip the Fair and Phillip the Bold to Louis XIII and Alphonse of Castille; to Henry II, Duke of Brabant, Andrew II, of Hungary, and through his wife Yolande to her father, Peter de Courtenay, Emperor of Constantinople.

More pleasing to my young eyes was the name of Fair Rosamund—"Henry II and Rosamund Clifford." The Plantagenets are as thick as thieves, and there are whole rows of names out of novels and plays, Beauchamp, Neville, Le Zouch, Fitzhugh, Willoughby, Montecute, yes, and John of Gaunt—I do hope he was "Time-honored Lancaster."

Unfortunately, as one learns to lay out one's ancestors in concentric circles, doubling the number with each ring after the simple "Father and Mother" in the first, these glittering lines leading to far-off dignitaries shrink to mere isolated threads, and are overwhelmed by crowding multitudes of ordinary people—or worse. Looking only eleven generations back, to the worshipful Catherine Fiennes, we may count in her ring two thousand and forty-eight ancestors—unless reduced by inter-marriage of relatives. When we reach the kings, Edward III being in the seventeenth circle, there are 131,072 ancestors—and only one king!

Our nearer forebears, in this country, were mainly persons of piety and learning, with very many ministers; plenty to furnish standings among Daughters and Dames, but I have never bothered to find them all out, being glutted as it were, with this list of remote glories.

The immediate line I am really proud of is the Beecher family. Dr. Lyman Beecher was my father's grandfather, his twelve children were world-servers. It is the fashion of late among juveniles of quite different origins to contemptuously dismiss the settlers and builders of New England as "Puritanic." One needs more historical perspective than is possessed by these persons to appreciate the physical and moral courage of those Great Adventurers; their energy and endurance; their inventive progressiveness. The "Blue Laws" of Connecticut, so widely sneered at, were a great advance in liberality from the English laws behind them.

As characters broadened with the spread of the growing nation new thinkers appeared, the urge toward heaven was humanized in a widening current of social improvement, making New England a seed-bed of progressive movements, scientific, mechanical, educational, humanitarian as well as religious. Into this moving world the Beechers swung forward, the sons all ministers, the daughters as able. Harriet Beecher Stowe is best known, but Catherine Beecher, who so scandalized the German theologian by her answer to "Edwards on the Will," is still honored in the middle west for her wide influence in promoting the higher education of women; and Isabella Beecher Hooker was one of the able leaders in the demand for equal suffrage.

Mary Beecher, my grandmother, the only daughter not doing public work, married Thomas C. Perkins, a lawyer of Hartford, Connecticut, and had four children, Frederick, Emily, Charles and Katherine. Emily married Edward Everett Hale, the distinguished Unitarian divine, author and lecturer; Katherine married William C. Gilman; Charles followed his father's footsteps in the Hartford law office; and Frederick, the oldest, my father, took to books as a duck to water. He read them, he wrote them, he edited them, he criticized them, he became a librarian and classified them. Before he married he knew nine languages, and continued to learn others afterward.

As an editor he helped to found, or worked on, the *Independent,* the *Christian Union* (now the *Outlook*), the *Galaxy,* Old and New, and various other papers and magazines. As a librarian he introduced the decimal system of classification, and his reference book, *The Best Reading,* was for long the standard. When I first visited the British Museum, Dr. Garnett was most polite to me for my father's sake. In those days, when scholarship could still cover a large proportion of the world's good books, he covered them well. Uncle E. E. Hale told me that he never asked my father a question that he could not immediately answer, or tell him where to find the answer.

But—with all these abilities went certain marked characteristics which prevented assured success. While a student in Yale he thrashed a professor, who had, he said, insulted him; which exhibition of temper cut short his college attendance. He was keen to feel injustice and quick to resent it; impatient of any dictation, careless of consequences when aroused. In an Irish riot in New York, during the Civil War, a Negro was being chased through the streets by a mob. Down rushed Mr. Perkins from his office, dragged the Negro into the hallway and faced the mob, but was himself pulled into safety by friends. A courageous man and a good boxer, but unwise. He did not, be it noted, enlist. When about thirty-one he married Mary Fitch Westcott of Providence, Rhode Island, and they had three children in three years, of whom I was the third.

The doctor said that if my mother had another baby she would die. Presently my father left home. Whether the doctor's dictum was the reason or merely a reason I do not know. What I do know is that my childhood had no father. He was an occasional visitor, a writer of infrequent but always amusing letters with deliciously funny drawings, a sender of books, catalogues of books, lists of books to read, and also a purchaser of books with money sadly needed by his family.

Once I remember his holding me by the heels when I had casually swallowed a pin. "It *cannot* be a pin!" protested my mother, but I managed to explain that I had put it in the bread and milk myself—why, I cannot imagine.

Once he brought some black Hamburg grapes to mother, and would not let her give them to us as her heart desired. There was a game of chess at which I beat him, or thought I did—being but nine I now doubt the genuineness of that victory; one punishment, half-hearted, and never repeated, at the same age; and a visit some two years later, when we lived in the country and he brought my twelve-year-old brother a gun; these are the sum of my memories of my father in childish years.

There must have been other visits. I think he used to come at Christmas when possible, but nothing else has stayed in my mind. He made no official separation, said his work kept him elsewhere. No word of criticism did I ever hear, mother held him up to us as a great and admirable character. But he was a stranger, distant and little known. The word Father, in the sense of love, care, one to go to in trouble, means nothing to me, save indeed in advice about books and the care of them—which seems more the librarian than the father.

By heredity I owe him much; the Beecher urge to social service, the Beecher wit and gift of words and such small sense of art as I have; but his learning he could not bequeath, and far more than financial care I have missed the education it would have been to have grown up in his society.

A profound believer in the divine right of mothers once stated, in answer to some suggestion of mine as to the need of expert assistance in child-culture, that the mother was in any case the best person to bring up her children; if she was a good mother she was an example to be followed, if a bad one, an example to be avoided.

If unswerving love, tireless service, intense and efficient care, and the concentrated devotion of a lifetime that knew no other purpose make a good mother, mine was of the best. To appraise the story of that motherhood needs a background.

Her father, Henry Westcott, was descended from Stukely Westcott, one of Roger Williams's deacons and fellow-settler of "Providence Plantations" in days when being a Baptist took some courage, and he, my grandfather, was a Unitarian when being a Unitarian took even more. I remember him dimly, a mild, gray man, whom I horrified by crawling downstairs face foremost at an early age. Mother told me lovely tales of his tenderness and benevolence. He would start for home with a well-filled market-basket and give most of the contents to needy persons on the way. Grandmother's reaction she did not mention. In that characteristic bit of Irish rebellion, the Dorr War, grandfather had to stand guard with a musket, but he saw to it that it was not loaded—killed he might be, but he did not propose to kill any one else.

He was a widower with a little girl of four when he married Clarissa Fitch Perkins, a child of fifteen. A small child too; I have a little dress she made and wore, the softest finest muslin, scanty and short as some of our recent abbreviated garments, with a tiny Empire waistlet and short sleeves, mere shoulder-bits. Deeply embroidered is this frail garment, with inset lace in the big Persian pattern figures, all the work of those slim fingers.

At seventeen she had a baby, which died, and another at eighteen, Mary Fitch Westcott, my mother. I remember grandmother as up and about, visiting us, but before I was eight she became bedridden—of arthritis I suppose—and was the object of my childish prayers and sympathetic letters. She was cared for, almost to her death, by her mother, who was Clarissa Fitch, of Windham, Connecticut. Clarissa married Edward Perkins, cousin of my paternal grandfather. Great-grandma was a handsome stiff-backed old lady, wearing a brown "front" and a cap, and managing those about her with swift competence.

Mary Westcott, darling of an elderly father and a juvenile mother, petted, cossetted and indulged, grew up in frail health. She was "given up" by one physician, who said she had consumption and could not survive a date he set. She did, but he signified his displeasure by not recognizing her afterward. Delicate and beautiful, well educated, musical, and what was then termed "spiritual minded," she was femininely attractive in the highest degree.

Her adventures and sorrows in this field began when she was a school-girl of fifteen in pantalettes, and an admiring gentleman, named Wilder, asked permission

of the thirty-three-year-old mother to "pay his addresses" to her daughter. From that time there were
always lovers, various and successive. The still child-
like Mary, even at seventeen, used to excuse herself
from callers and go upstairs to put her dolls to bed.

Engagements were made, broken and renewed, and
re-broken. One sudden adorer proposed to her at first
sight. The penultimate engagement—with a Mr. Gla-
zier, a theological student in the strongly Baptist city
of Providence—was broken on account of his faith;
but he saw another light and became a Unitarian. They
were again betrothed, and he was visiting at the house
immediately before their approaching marriage, when
he contracted typhoid fever and died. Poor mother!

In course of time she met her mother's second
cousin, Frederick Beecher Perkins of Hartford. They
were engaged, that engagement also was broken, but
finally, at the extreme old maidenhood of twenty-nine,
she married him.

Of those three swiftly appearing babies the first died
from some malpractice at birth; the second, Thomas A.
Perkins, is still living, and in fourteen months I followed, on the afternoon of July third, 1860. If only
I'd been a little slower and made it the glorious Fourth!
This may be called the first misplay in a long game
that is full of them.

There now follows a long-drawn, triple tragedy,
quadruple perhaps, for my father may have suffered
too; but mother's life was one of the most painfully
thwarted I have ever known. After her idolized youth,
she was left neglected. After her flood of lovers, she
became a deserted wife. The most passionately domestic of home-worshiping housewives, she was forced to
move nineteen times in eighteen years, fourteen of
them from one city to another. After a long and thor-

ough musical education, developing unusual talent, she sold her piano when I was two, to pay the butcher's bill, and never owned another. She hated debt, and debts accumulated about her, driving her to these everlasting moves. Absolutely loyal, as loving as a spaniel which no ill treatment can alienate, she made no complaint, but picked up her children and her dwindling furniture and traveled to the next place. She lived with her husband's parents, with her own parents, with his aunts, in various houses here and there when he so installed her, fleeing again on account of debt.

My childish memories are thick with railroad journeys, mostly on the Hartford, Providence and Springfield; with occasional steamboats; with the smell of "hacks" and the funny noise the wheels made when little fingers were stuck in little ears and withdrawn again, alternately. And the things we had to wear! When I protested, mother said it was the easiest way to carry them. This I long resented, not in the least realizing how many things she must have had to carry, with two small children to convoy.

After some thirteen years of this life, mother, urged by friends, and thinking to set my father free to have another wife if he would not live with her, divorced him. This he bitterly resented, as did others of the family. So long as "Mary Fred" was a blameless victim they pitied her and did what they could to help, but a divorce was a disgrace. Divorced or not she loved him till her death, at sixty-three. She was with me in Oakland, California, at the time, and father was then a librarian in San Francisco, just across the bay. She longed, she asked, to see him before she died. As long as she was able to be up, she sat always at the window watching for that beloved face. He never came. That's where I get my implacable temper.

This tragic life carried another grief, almost equal to loss of home and husband—the perplexed distress of the hen who hatched ducks. My mother was a baby-worshiper, even in her own childhood, always devoted to them, and in her starved life her two little ones were literally all; all of duty, hope, ambition, love and joy. She reared them with unusual intelligence and effectiveness, using much of the then new Kindergarten method, and so training herself with medical books that the doctor said he could do no better by us.

But as these children grew they grew away from her, both of them. The special gift for baby-care did not apply so well to large youngsters; the excellent teaching in first steps could not cope with the needs of changing years; and the sublime devotion to duty, the unflinching severity of discipline made no allowance for the changing psychology of children whose characters were radically different from her own. She increasingly lost touch with them, wider and wider grew the gulf between; it reminds one of that merciless old text: "From him who hath not shall be taken away even that which he hath."

There is a complicated pathos in it, totally unnecessary. Having suffered so deeply in her own list of early love affairs, and still suffering for lack of a husband's love, she heroically determined that her baby daughter should not so suffer if she could help it. Her method was to deny the child all expression of affection as far as possible, so that she should not be used to it or long for it. "I used to put away your little hand from my cheek when you were a nursing baby," she told me in later years; "I did not want you to suffer as I had suffered." She would not let me caress her, and would not caress me, unless I was asleep. This I discovered at last, and then did my best to keep awake till she came to bed, even using pins to prevent dropping off, and sometimes succeeding. Then how carefully I pretended to be sound asleep, and how rapturously I enjoyed being gathered into her arms, held close and kissed.

If love, devotion to duty, sublime self-sacrifice, were enough in child-culture, mothers would achieve better results; but there is another requisite too often lacking —knowedge. Yet all the best she had, the best she knew, my mother gave, at any cost to herself.

Note. A fourth child was born some years later and died in infancy.

CHAPTER II

BEGINNINGS

OF infant achievements I have by hearsay this: at about three years old, being summoned to the parlor, I appeared with the announcement, "Here I come, doll in hand, to obey my mother's command." Further, evidently having heard tobacco condemned, and finding a visiting relative in the act of using it, the four-year-old reformer sternly remarked to him: "I disgust you, Uncle Charles!"

I taught myself to read during an illness of mother's, having been brought almost to that point by her, but remember much greater pride in putting the last touch on ability to dress myself by buttoning my little frock all up the back, at five.

Great-aunt Catherine Beecher visited us in the old house in Apponaug, Rhode Island, which fact I happen to remember because of a shock felt by the whole nation, by the world. The newspaper was outlined in black. Aunt Catherine, with her little gray curls, and my mother facing her, sat speechless—Lincoln was dead! They took me in town that day, to Providence, and the streets were hung with black.

Mother, to us children, was mainly the disciplinarian, but all her conscientious severity was unable to anticipate the varied mischief of two lively-minded youngsters without sufficient occupation. She taught us, admirably; *Object Lessons* were our delight, and Hooker's *Child's Book of Nature*.

We took *Our Young Folks,* in which some pleasant papers on natural science made an indelible impression on me, and one story, "Andy's Adventures," convinced me forever of the essential folly of lying. It occurred to me even then, that whereas mother taught us that lying was very wrong, evidently much more wrong than other misdemeanors, yet when it came to punishment we were whipped just as severely for less offenses—that this was unjust. Once, having done something for which whipping was due, I humbled my proud spirit and confessed, begging mother to forgive me. She said she would, but whipped me just the same. This gave me a moral "set-back" in the matter of forgiveness—I've never been good at it.

Often during life has the first waking hour brought ideas, percepts, often of wide reach, and even in those baby years I woke once with a vast concept my inadequate vocabulary utterly failed to describe. It only provoked laughter when I said: "It felt like having the whole world on my toes"...an enormous sense of social responsibility with power to handle it.

Our many movings we children took as a matter of course; to us the stays here and there seemed long, a six months' visit is a little lifetime to a child. We were most lovingly entertained by my father's aunts, Charlotte and Anna Perkins, for both of whom I was named. Those pious ladies, who used rags for handkerchiefs in order to send more to the missionaries, used to pick out the best from clothing contributed to give us children. They lived in Hartford in a square old house on the corner of Main Street and College— now Capitol Avenue.

Here mother had a little school for us, with some other children; she was a phenomenally good teacher for the very young. To one of those early schoolmates a tale belongs, funny enough to repeat. There were two little boys, let us call them Harry and Johnny Blake. Harry was a dark, handsome boy, and polite to me—a new experience. Mother took me to the Blakes' to dinner one day, a dinner so good I remember it yet—boiled salmon, egg sauce, green peas. Mrs. Blake was most kind, but the main attraction was Harry, a most courteous young host. So I gave my seven-year-old heart to Harry—and after that summer never saw him again for some fifty years. Then, in New York, joining some friends for a theater party, a tall, dark, handsome man was introduced to me as Mr. Blake, of Hartford. "Harry Blake!" I cried, unbelievingly, but he it was. We sat down together and dropped those fifty years completely, went back to 1868, my mother's little school, the other children, and I told him of that visit and how good his mother was to me. While completely immersed in childish reminiscences a tall, handsome, gray-haired lady was brought up and introduced to me as "Mrs. Blake." I sprang to my feet and greeted her with affectionate enthusiasm—"Harry's mother!" I cried ... and it was his wife....

I was taught to sew before five, little patchwork squares, in the tiniest of "over-and-over" stitches. When about eight, buttonhole-stitch was added to my accomplishments, and here occurred my first invention, genuine enough, though slight. As taught, the thread was looped about the needle before pulling it through, and I discovered that the same effect could be produced by pulling it through first and then picking up the thread in a certain way, with the advantage of being able to use up a shorter end.

We children were so violently well brought up that

we cherished an Ishmaelitish resentment against "grown-ups." Young women we called "proudies," and for young men I found a lovely name in a book—"fops." Of all the record of malicious mischief which distinguishes those early years the utter worst is this: we would roll our hoops in mud and trundle them against the voluminous crinolines of the period. When angry ladies turned on the aggressors they were met by such sweet-faced, polite apologies as abated their wrath instantly.

In a New York boarding-house, for description of which see Henry Alden's *Old New York*—he even mentions "little Charlotte Perkins"—we established a record for infant iniquity, but it lacked the Machiavellian quality of those apologies. In later school-life my brother remained a source of ingenious misdemeanors, while I was well behaved, so I truly think that he, the older, was mainly responsible for our pranks, but one crowning outrage there in New York was wholly mine. The house was one of those tall, narrow ones with a four-story staircase winding back and forth in pinched loops scarcely a foot wide. Down this slit one could look, or drop things, from the top floor to the basement. To Mrs. Swift, the landlady, doubtless a worthy soul, we imps had taken a dislike. She had reproved us as we well deserved, for our sins against the boarders. We objected also to her little red-eyed poodle, Pinky, and did horrid things to his food.

On one sad occasion I, looking over the banisters on the top floor, perceived Mrs. Swift similarly leaning over on the ground floor, directly below me. . . . If you were a mischievous child—she had the beginning of a bald spot on the crown of her head—what would you have done? Or at least wanted to do? I did it. It was too tempting— Down softly from story to story sailed the little white drop, and landed, spat! exactly on that bald spot. . . .

That was the time when a distracted mother insisted that my father, who happened to call that evening, should whip me. He did, with a small whip she had purchased for our chastisement.

"Hold out your hand!"

I held it out, as flatly stretched as I could make it.

He struck the little hand several times, told mother that he would never do that again, and never did.

Among our pleasantest visits were those at the new big house of Aunt Harriet Stowe in Hartford. She had built it, to suit her eager fancy, out of the proceeds of *Uncle Tom's Cabin*. There was a two-story conservatory in the rear, the great entrance hall opened on it, the back parlor, and the dining-room; upstairs a gallery on three sides allowed access from bedrooms and hall. Aunt Harriet used to sit at a small table in that back parlor, looking out on the flowers and ferns and little fountain while she painted in water-colors. From her dainty flower pictures I got my first desire to paint, and an eager love for Windsor & Newton's little china dishes.

One splendid memory of those years stands out above all others. We were with the aunts in Hartford, at the time of the Grant and Colfax election. There was a torch-light procession, houses were illuminated, much money was spent in decoration by those who had it to spend. We had not, but determined to make as good a show as we could. In every one of our tiny window-panes we stuck a candle, making a many-faceted glitter more effective than fewer lights in larger panes.

"The Stowe girls," Hattie and Eliza, came to help us. Across the front door we placed a large table, and behind the narrow windows on either side set a large lamp. In the full light of those lamps stood a Goddess of Liberty—eight years old! A white dress, a liberty cap, a liberty pole (which was a new mop-handle with a red-white-and-blue sash tied on it and a cornucopia of the same colors on its top), and a great flag draped around me—there I stood—Living. One crowded hour of glorious life, that was, to a motionless, glorified child.

The procession seemed to go on forever. I think it took at least an hour to pass a given point, but to that fixed little figure at one given point it was none too long. They were soldiers, real soldiers in uniform, who had been in the war but three years since, who cared passionately about the General they wished to elect. As each company passed a specially illuminated house the leader would turn and march backward, keeping time with his sword, and it was: "ONE! TWO! THREE! U! S! G! HURRAH!" ...

I can hear them now.

Might not our educators consider if such a soul-expanding experience is not of lasting value to a child; and if, some day, we may not learn how to accustom our children to large feelings instead of keeping them always among little ones....

If I was a pretty child no hint of it was allowed to enter my mind. Mother cut off the fat little brown curls at an early age, lest I should be vain—and kept them as long as she lived.

My passion for beauty dates far back; in picture books the one or two that were really beautiful; in the colors of the worsted mother used, loving some and hating others; in bits of silk and ribbon, buttons

—children used to collect strings of buttons in those days; I keenly recall my delight in specially beautiful things. There was a little cloak of purple velvet, deep pansy-purple, made over from something of mother's, that enraptured my soul.

Dolls were never lovely enough, most of them were mere babies, china heads and flat-jointed, sawdust-stuffed bodies; I wanted people, boy and man dolls as well as girls, and named my favorites Lady Geraldine, Lady Isabel, and so on. I wanted queens, and thrones to play with, murmuring a little jingle about "Burnished brass and polished glass"—I did not see why dolls could not be like the kings and princesses I read about. Their meager bodies especially distressed me. "Why don't they make them like little statues?" I demanded. Only once, calling somewhere with mother, did I find a girl who played as I did—an unforgetable pleasure. And once I conceived a devoted affection for a schoolmate, a pale, long-haired Sunday-schoolish child—Etta Talcott was her name. When we as usual moved away, I sent her a sacrificial offering, a box adorned with decalcomania which I thought lovely, and in it my dearest toys.

For real growth there were two notable steps during a brief school period, when I was eight—my total schooling covered four years, among seven different schools, ending when I was fifteen. This little patch was in a public school in Hartford, quite a big one it seemed to us. Floods of children I remember, going down some stairs, and beauty—a girl with a rich mane of wavy chestnut hair. There was a carrot-headed Irish boy who read in a halting sing-song about "the yellow catkins hanging on the willows in the spring," and gave a touching version of "Lo, the poor Indian's" speech thus: "Then came the timid whiteman, asking to lie down on the Indian's bare skin." We thought the white men far from timid.

I had reached long division, and learned how to prove the examples, a keen delight to the rational mind. Taking the slate to be marked by the teacher, she said, "This one is wrong." "I have proved it," I replied confidently. Then she showed me her book with the answers. "See, here is the answer, yours is wrong." To which I still replied, "But I have proved it." Then she did the example herself, and proved it, and I was right—the book was wrong! This was a great lesson; science, law, was more to be trusted than authority.

Then, one day when that big light room was quiet save for the soft buzz of many hushed voices muttering over their lessons, the speculative Charlotte said to herself: "I wonder why we all have to keep still. . . . I wonder what would happen if any one spoke out loud. . . . I'm going to find out." But I was cautious as well as experimental, and selected the shortest word I could think of. Across the low-murmuring room arose a clear, childish voice remarking, "It." "Who said that?" Up went my hand. "Come here." I went there. The teacher put her arm around me (my brother and I usually stood well with our teachers on account of general information and decorum). "Why did you do that?" she asked.

"I wanted to see what would happen," I truthfully replied.

Nothing happened. She said I must not do it again, for which indeed there was no occasion. So I learned another great lesson, long remembered and acted on— that things debarred may sometimes be done—in safety.

Of all those childish years the most important step was this, I learned the use of a constructive imagination. Under mother's careful regimen we children had a light and early supper, and then were read to for a while, too short a while, inexorably cut off by bedtime. The reading was interesting, sometimes thrilling, *Oliver Twist* for instance, to an eight-year-old. But that painfully early bed hour stopped the story, perhaps in the middle of a chapter; off we went, dumbly, but with inward rebellion.

You may lead a horse to water but you cannot make him drink. Bed is one thing, sleep is another. Exciting literature after supper is not the best digestive. Lying there, not a bit sleepy, full of eager interest in the unfinished chapter, following the broken adventure to possible developments, I learned the joy of brain-building. Balboa was not more uplifted by his new ocean.

Beauty and splendor were mine at last to pile and change at will. The stern restrictions, drab routine, unbending discipline that hemmed me in, became of no consequence. I could make a world to suit me. All that inner thirst for glorious loveliness could be gratified now, at will, unboundedly. Not all this was clear to me at the time, but one thing was—this was so delightful that it must be wrong.

Fine blunderers in ethics we are, so generally conveying to children the basic impression that pleasantness must be wrong, and right doing unpleasant!

I arranged it with my conscience thus: every night I would think only of pleasant things that really might happen; once a week I would think of lovelier, stranger things, once a month of wonders, and once a year of anything I wanted to! This program was probably soon forgotten, but it shows conscience wrestling with fancy at an early age.

The dream world grew apace. Sometimes it was "having my wishes." Here with sagacity I avoided all those foolish mistakes made by the misguided persons in the fairy-tales, who had their wishes and made a mess of them. My first one was: "I wish that everything I wish may be Right!" To be Right was the main thing in life.

Most of the wishing was childish pleasure in having things of glittering gorgeousness, but what comes up most clearly was the laying in of copious materials to work with, as paper, pencils, paints. There was a stationer's store in Hartford then, Geer & Pond's, wherein was a big sample case of Windsor & Newton's water-colors—I wished for the whole case! They had also a pen of unparalleled beauty, a gold pen with a handle of pink pearl—that never-attained pen lasted me for years as a type of beauty.

Soon, among the delights of having things, grew the greater delight of doing things. In the attic were piles of *Harper's Weeklys* with the powerful cartoons of Nast. I browsed among them, became deeply impressed with civic crime and the difficulty of stopping it, and when my schoolmates would crowd around me at recess and say "Let's tell," my preferred topic was the capture and punishment of Boss Tweed—this at about ten. I did not compose, make stories like Frances Hodgson in her childhood, but was already scheming to improve the world.

In 1870 we went to live in the country near Rehoboth, Massachusetts. After a summer with friends mother took a house by herself, and there we lived, for about three years, on what I do not know. Clothing was mostly given to us, though mother made the brown-checked gingham dresses and drawers in which I played untrammeled, and knitted long woolen stockings and mittens for us both. We ran barefoot in summer, reveled in snow-drifts in winter. My brother kept hens, from which he made enough to buy himself an overcoat, besides furnishing us with eggs and fowls to eat.

There were memorably delicious meals, new potatoes boiled in their jackets, all peeling and mealy, with a bowl of hot milk with butter and salt in it; and a whole dinner of "hasty pudding," first with milk, then with butter and molasses, then with milk again and so till we could no more. These were pure delight at the time, but now look strongly like bed-rock necessities.

Three years of this country life, healthy but barren. No playmates, save two children of the farmer who lived opposite. No school, though mother still gave us lessons, and once a school-teacher came—possibly boarded a while, and taught us some arithmetic. This letter (probably fall of 1872)—I was doubtless told to make a better copy—illuminates the period.

DEAR FATHER,
  Will you please send the money for July, August and September. You told me to remind you of The Princess and Goblin if you forgot it. My three kits are getting large and fat. Thomas drowned the old cat for she killed four chicks. Thomas has got a nice garden and furnishes us with potatoes, tomatoes, melons, corn, beans and squashes and pumpkins. We have apples and pears in plenty. Please write a real long letter to me. This morning Thomas found a chimney swallow in the dining room. He had come down the parlor chimney, the fireplace of which was open. I wish you would write to me often; Willie Judd and Thomas Lord write to Thomas and he to them but nobody writes to me but you. Thomas caught a little turtle about an inch big. Thomas has got his snares set again, and caught a partridge this morning. I inclose two pictures in hopes you will do the same. Your affectionately

with my little monogram for signature.
  My brother, with his garden, hens and hunting had

a somewhat fuller life, outside, but no one had a richer, more glorious life than I had, inside. It grew into fairy-tales, one I have yet; it spread to limitless ambitions. With "my wishes" I modestly chose to be the most beautiful, the wisest, the best person in the world; the most talented in music, painting, literature, sculpture—why not, when one was wishing?

But no personal wealth or glory satisfied me. Soon there developed a Prince and Princess of magic powers, who went about the world collecting unhappy children and taking them to a guarded Paradise in the South Seas. I had a boundless sympathy for children, feeling them to be suppressed, misunderstood.

It speaks volumes for the lack of happiness in my own actual life that I should so industriously construct it in imagination. I wanted affection, expressed affection. My brother was really very fond of me, but his teasing hid it from me entirely. Mother loved us desperately, but her tireless devotion was not the same thing as petting, her caresses were not given unless we were asleep, or she thought us so.

My dream world was no secret. I was but too ready to share it, but there were no sympathetic listeners. It was my life, but lived entirely alone. Then, influenced by a friend with a pre-Freudian mind, alarmed at what she was led to suppose this inner life might become, mother called on me to give it up. This was a command. According to all the ethics I knew I must obey, and I did. . . .

Just thirteen. This had been my chief happiness for five years. It was by far the largest, most active part of my mind. I was called upon to close off the main building as it were and live in the "L." No one could tell if I did it or not, it was an inner fortress, open only to me. . . .

But obedience was Right, the thing had to be done, and I did it. Night after night to shut the door on happiness, and hold it shut. Never, when dear, bright, glittering dreams pushed hard, to let them in. Just thirteen. . . .

CHAPTER III

THE END OF CHILDHOOD

Our next move, in the fall of 1873, was to Providence, Rhode Island, to a little house on Vernon Street where bedridden Grandma Westcott lived with Great-grandma Perkins, who still took care of her daughter. But the valiant old lady was over eighty, and died in December, leaving mother to care for the invalid. Only a little while, however, for grandma died in March. My brother had typhoid fever at the time, but when death came to the house the Irish servant promptly departed, leaving mother to get on as best she could.

Thomas recovered in due time. All I recall of that illness is that the doctor let him have ripe bananas as soon as he could eat anything. Thomas always "took" whatever disease came within reach, and had it severely. If unescapable I had it later and lighter, as when he had scarlet fever and lost the use of an ear, I followed with scarlatina only; when he nearly died with diphtheria I succeeded to it so lightly that I did not go to bed at all.

In June mother joined a "coöperative housekeeping" group, with Dr. and Mrs. Stevens whom she had previously visited in Rehoboth, Mrs. Isham and her two boys, with whom we had lived in Hartford, and a Mr. Wellman of Cambridge, Massachusetts. All of these people were Swedenborgians, mother presently joined that church, and had us children enter it also—an impermanent experience. There was a strong flavor of Spiritualism on the part of Mrs. Stevens, the dominant figure of the group.

Coöperative housekeeping is inherently doomed to failure. From early experience and later knowledge I thoroughly learned this fact, and have always proclaimed it. Yet such is the perversity of the average mind that my advocacy of the professionalizing of housework—having it done by the hour by specially trained persons, with the service of cooked meals to the home—has always been objected to as "coöperative housekeeping." Upton Sinclair's ill-fated Helicon Hall experiment he attributed to my teachings, without the least justification.

At No. 1 Major Street these three families undertook this method of living, with the usual results of disappointment and failure. Mrs. Stevens had a daughter by a former marriage, Harriet White, and for her I conceived my second devout affection. As with the Talcott child, this expressed itself in giving her what I best loved, my three chiefest treasures, a garnet ring, a gold cross, an old mother-of-pearl cardcase—the only lovely, precious things I had. It now looks to me a little grasping, to take such presents from a child, but these were accepted.

It was a strange group, immersed in the mystic doctrine of "Correspondence," according to which everything in the Bible means something else; floating and wallowing about in endless discussion of proofless themes and theories of their own, with a sort of revelation occasionally added by Mrs. Stevens, the real leader. They would sit around the table long after meals were over, interminably talking on matters of religion and ethics.

My brother and I got from this atmosphere a settled distaste for anything smacking of the esoteric or occult; but it had one advantage, to me at least, that of hearing ideas discussed as the important things of life, instead of gossip and personalities.

Our great-aunts in Hartford died, one of them leaving her half of their tiny property to us children. Mother raised money on Thomas's share and sent us to good private schools.

Mine was kept by Mrs. Fielding and Miss Chase, in the Music Hall building. So behold me at fourteen, earnest and eager, beginning again at school. It was always beginning again my bits of schooling, as I never had time to finish anywhere. Teachers were always impressed, at first, by the natural intelligence manifested, and the unusual array of general information, but later they were disappointed. I never did very well in school studies.

The trouble was that the methods pursued seemed to me wrong, a perception correct enough, as later knowledge showed, but interfering with academic progress. A tendency to versify, giving recitations in history, grammar, once even in arithmetic, in rhyme, was perhaps indicative of future powers, but no help in examinations. There was one instance of what seemed to me an injustice, for which I carried a grudge for twenty years or more. In grammar I was in the infant class, never having studied it before. One of the exercises given was to rewrite from memory a fable of Æsop's previously read to us. This I did in verse, clearly and correctly. The paper was perfect, but I had made three little curly lines under my signature, and for that the teacher took off half a point, and I just missed the only 100 per cent I ever came so near.

In 1897 or so, giving a lecture in Providence in that same Music Hall, my old grammar teacher was present, and when she came up, pleased and proud, to congratulate me, I brought up this incident of 1875 for which she expressed regret. Nice temper to have.

Not particularly good in any study as far as I recall, unless in elocution, in which I delighted. This abstruse art was taught by a slender little gentleman named Wentworth, who trained us in "Curfew Shall Not Ring Tonight" and "The Brides of Enderby."

Poetry was always a delight to me. I learned it by heart, miles of it, from early childhood, and at this time used to keep a book open on my bureau and learn long poems while combing my hair, such as "Horatius at the Bridge," "The Rhyme of the Duchess May," and "The Letter L." That had over two hundred stanzas, quatrains only.

I was not afraid of dramatic expression, exulted in it, and having always liked tongue-twisters, followed the elocutionist's exercises with ease and pleasure. One of these was to give the word "strangledst," leaving off one consonant after another to the last "t" and then building it up again, sounding each one distinctly. "Gldst," pronounced clearly, is quite a task for even a nimble tongue. We were set to whispering, a loud clear whisper, and the little man said to me: "Your whisper could be heard in Music Hall," to my great pride.

Calisthenics, taught by an upright young Dr. Brooks, strongly appealed to me. I became so erect that I fairly leaned backward, and marched with such conscientious precision that he called me out as an object lesson, to march around with him.

Dr. Studley, a woman physician, gave a lecture to the school, on hygiene, which made an indelible impression on my earnest mind. Forthwith I took to "dress reform," fresh air, cold baths, every kind of attainable physical exercise. To that one lecture is to be attributed the beginning of a life-long interest in physical culture. Dress reform was a young movement then, it reached me in what were then called "chemiloons," a wrist-and-ankle reaching garment of red flannel in winter, more merciful cotton in summer.

A little Latin I tried, with a more advanced class, but gave it up later, writing,

Farewell to thee, O Latin Class, no more with sisters dear,
The verbs I cram from *Sum,* I am, to *Audio,* I hear.
Farewell to thee, a long farewell! I shall forget with rapture
That *Moneo ere* meant Advise or *Capio* to capture.

The one real study which did appeal to me, deeply, was Physics, then called Natural Philosophy. Here was Law, at last; not authority, not records of questionable truth or solemn tradition, but laws that could be counted on and *Proved.* That was my delight, to know surely. There were experiments, and to those given I added more. When we were shown how a pen-knife, inserted in a lead pencil, slant-wise, near the point, would make it balance on the end of a finger, precariously leaning forward, I inserted two pen-knives, opposite one another, and made the pencil stand upright.

Adhesion, cohesion, torsion, the law of the screw, and the lever, the pendulum, and that crowning miracle, the law of the hydraulic press, these were meat and drink to me. Presently I made the observation that these laws had parallels in psychology. Friction produces heat, yes, in the bureau drawer that sticks and in the person pulling it. Friction, i.e., hindrance, interference, produces anger as naturally as heat. Action and reaction are equal, yes, and oppression produces rebellion. The law of inertia, both active and passive, operates in mind as well as matter, and from the hydraulic press mystery—that inward pressure of one

pound on one inch of water in a closed vessel results in
outward pressure of one pound on every inch of that
vessel—I derived the commensurate law that strength
developed in the small matters of everyday life will
serve to meet the greatest tests in larger need. One
could practice courage on mice for instance, and find
it ready to use on lions.

Outside of schooling, what? Not much. Mother had
put upon me two more prohibitions, I was to read no
novels and to have no intimate friends.

The very greatest and most rare delight was the
theater. There was given in the Providence Opera
House, about the time we moved in town, a most successful amateur performance called "The Frog
Opera." It was arranged by an early friend of my
mother's and acted in by many of her friends and
relatives; we children were allowed to go. Then and
there I developed a grand passion for the Prince, a
tall, imposing youth whose success in the part resulted
in his becoming a professional actor.

This was a most remote and visionary affair, for I
never met the young man, and, as I heard him spoken
of disparagingly by those who knew him, never much
wanted to. But I was used to living on visions, and
one sight of him on the street or in a theater lobby
thrilled me for a week. All my scanty allowance, whatever gifts I acquired, every cent was saved to buy
theater tickets—for three, mother and Thomas had
to go too. Fortunately the cost was but a dollar then.
Not only did I take rapturous delight in the plays, but
the Prince was sure to be hanging about, there was a
sort of stag-line in the lobby watching the audience
come out.

I chanced to read the life of one of our best actresses, and author of one of the first good American

plays. Of course I wished to be an actress, and later experience has shown that I should have been a good one, but also that such a life would never have satisfied me.

Another pleasure well remembered of those years was a visit to Uncle Edward Hale in Roxbury. Father was, I think, boarding with his sister then, he was at the head of the Boston Public Library, and she wished to keep alive his interest (if any) in his children. Thomas and I went down one Christmas time, and were most affectionately received by a whole flock of cousins, from dear Ellen, the second mother of the family, down to charming little Robert. Here, for the first time, I saw how lovely family life could be. Instead of teasing and ridicule here was courtesy and kindness. Arthur, the eldest, was playing chess with me when little Robert came up and interrupted. I expected the big brother would shove him off, perhaps harshly, but he put his arm around him, tenderly—it was quite a revelation to me. My brother and I "had fun" together, we should have missed each other no doubt, but tenderness—never. Never from any one, and I did want it.

Two proposed inventions I had visualized in my mind before leaving Rehoboth, one a sort of bicycle, with wheels, parallel, the seat and pedaling apparatus between; the other a color concert, such as we have seen approximated in recent years. My theory was that the colors of the spectrum and the notes of the octave could be connected, so that on touching a piano key, a spark was lit behind a jar of tinted water, and the color thrown on a screen. For piano music a rain of falling sparks, but for the organ I wanted it to be in rolling clouds.

The vivid attraction of the "Frog Prince" did not

interfere with my heart's devotion to Miss White. With her I studied shorthand with Mr. Hemperly, the pale and slender young Swedenborgian minister. This art was forgotten later, but proved amusing for several years, as when my cousin Arthur Hale and I played chess, by post-card, in shorthand.

Books of travel I was allowed, and made pleasant acquaintance with Bayard Taylor. Some historical novels were permitted, for I enjoyed the Rev. William Ware's book about *Zenobia,* and one about Egypt. Also, iniquitously, I read the *Wandering Jew.* This had been long forbidden, yet with profound confidence in our obedience we were allowed to look at the pictures, most exciting pictures, by Tony Johannot. I do not doubt that adolescent curiosity was an influence in this signal piece of disobedience—the only one I recall in those years—yes, and the only one I can think of before that was also reading something forbidden. I read the two volumes through, standing before the book-case and promptly looking for another book if mother came near. But I was completely disappointed in finding anything which seemed to me evil. We waste a great deal of anxiety in protecting children from things they do not see at all.

Aside from this misdemeanor I was bent on doing my best, and eager for self-improvement. Being a somewhat hollow-chested little New Englander, probably from much reading, mother was constantly urging me to "hold my shoulders back"—it was many years later when I learned that lifting the sternum is the real need. I strove to comply, holding back those slender shoulders till they fairly ached, but the following reaction left them more drooping than before. Observing this I made my first real discovery in practical psychology, working out a system of self-development which is of genuine value. At the time I could by no means realize the basic truth of the process, save only that I found it worked.

My formula was simple: "Do it whenever you think of it, stop *before* you are tired."

The first difficulty in acquiring any new self-determined habit is to think of it, the second to make it easy and unfailing. Application of nerve force along unaccustomed lines soon exhausts the carrying power, time must pass before we can repeat the effort, and more effort is required to produce the same result. We are tired, discouraged, give it up. But if, in undertaking the process, at every flicker of remembrance the effort is made, strongly, of set purpose, and then deliberately withdrawn while yet unwearied, there is no reaction, the thought recurs at shorter intervals, the effort may be longer maintained, the victory is as good as won. By "rule of thumb" I discovered this, and practised it successfully, from straightening those shoulders to many years of progressive improvement, physical and mental.

And then occurred one of the major events of a lifetime, making an indelible impression, opening an entire new world of action. Scene, the little bedroom I shared with mother. I was sitting up in bed, my hands clasped around my knees. She stood by the bureau, combing her hair, holding it at the crown of her head in one hand while she combed. The kerosene lamp threw moving shadows on the ceiling.

"You must do it," said mother, "or you must leave me." "It" was to apologize to Mrs. Stevens—for a thing I had not done. The alleged offense was this: there was a grape-vine in the back yard. Mrs. S. had eaten a bunch of grapes from it, I, sitting at a window, had observed her. She, being something of a psychic, asserted that I had thought harsh things of her—that as one of a coöperative group she had no right to eat those grapes. I denied having thought anything about it, which was true, but mother, being greatly under this woman's influence, believed her, and insisted that I apologize. This I declined to do. Hence the ultimatum.

"You must leave me" was no threat of being cast off deliberately, it was an expression of her profound belief that the only *modus vivendi* for a child with a parent was absolute obedience. Never before had my own conscience come squarely against hers. To apologize for what I had not done was flatly dishonest, a lie, it was wrong.

So I sat there and made answer, slowly, meaning to say the first part, and the last part saying itself: "I am not going to do it,—and I am not going to leave you—and what are you going to do about it?"

Doubtless she was horrified beyond words at this first absolute rebellion from a hitherto docile child. She came over and struck me. I did not care in the least. She might do what she would, it could not alter my decision. I was realizing with an immense illumination that neither she, nor any one, could *make* me do anything. One could suffer, one could die if it came to that, but one could not be coerced. I was born. . . .

CHAPTER IV

BUILDING A RELIGION

THE incident passed with no visible consequences at the time, but the great discovery remained, and there followed a period of mental turmoil, with large ultimate results. If I was a free agent what was I going to do with my freedom? If I could develop character as I chose, what kind of character was I going to develop? This at fifteen.

The Major Street group broke up in February, 1876. We children were not told why. School was finally ended for me. We spent a month with mother's half-sister, Mrs. Caroline Robbins, on Vernon Street, another with Mrs. Peck, our opposite neighbor in Rehoboth, thereafter settling again in Providence on the second floor of a two-family house on Manning Street, just east of Gano. I think father must have contributed to the support of his children at this time, however irregularly. More than once I saw mother without any money or any definite prospect of any.

The lack of money never impressed me at all. Not only were we used to it, but in the literature we fed on, as Louisa Alcott, Mrs. A. D. T. Whitney, the *Youth's Companion,* etc., the heroes and heroines were almost always poor, and good, while the rich people were generally bad. It was many years before I was wholly assured that rich people could be just as good as poor ones.

We lived in this small flat, four rooms, with two on

the top floor and half-rights in the cellar and yard, for about five years. Thomas presently went to the Massachusett Institute of Technology, father paying.

Out of much consideration I finally came to a definite decision as to my duty. The old condition of compelled obedience was gone forever. I was a free agent, but as such I decided that until I was twenty-one I would still obey. I saw that mother was probably wiser than I, that she had nothing to live for but us two children and would probably suffer much if we were rebellious, and that, furthermore, she had a right to her methods of education, while we were minors. So I told her that I would obey her until I was of age, and then stop. Dismissing this matter, I then marked out a line of work.

In my seventeenth year I wrote to my father, saying that I wished to help humanity, that I realized I must understand history, and where should I begin. He was always effective in book advice, none better, and sent me a fine list of reliable works. I have the little scrap of paper yet, in his handwriting—

Rawlinson's	Five Great Empires
" "	Sixth Great Empire
" "	Seventh " "
Dawkins,	Cave Hunting
Fergusson,	Rude Stone Monuments
Lubbock,	Prehistoric Times and Origins of Civilization
Tylor,	Early History of Mankind
"	Primitive Culture

Also he sent a large number of *Popular Science Monthlies,* a valuable magazine then, in the hands of the Youmans, carrying the still fresh discussion of evolution, such works as Andrew White's *Warfare of*

Religion and Science, the general new urge in studies of natural law.

This was the beginning of a real education, always allowing for the excellent foundation laid by mother in early years. I now read connectedly, learning the things I most wanted to know, in due order and sequence, none of them exhaustively but all in due relation; enough of astronomy to get a clear idea of the whirling wonder of the earth's formation, enough of geology to grasp the visible age of this small world and the fossil evidence of evolution.

Humanity was always the major interest, the sciences held useful as they showed our origin, our lines of development, the hope and method of further progress. Here the path was clear; biology, anthropology, ethnology, sociology. History soon showed itself as an amusingly limited and partial account of what had happened; Lecky was helpful here. I presently joined "The Society for the Encouragement of Studies at Home," headed by Miss Tichnor of Boston. My courses were in Ancient History, a year with the Ancient Hebrews, one on Egypt, another with several early peoples, all intensely interesting. At one of our annual meetings, in the house still standing on the corner of Park and Beacon streets, Boston, we were addressed by Oliver Wendell Holmes, a small, delightful man.

In none of these studies could I have passed a college examination, I suppose, but the result of studying from a strong desire to know, and in orderly sequence and relation, was to give me a clear, connected general outline of the story of life on earth, and of our own nature and progress, which has proved lastingly useful.

Soon I realized the importance of religion as a cultural factor, but also the painfully conspicuous absurdities and contradictions of the world's repeated attempts in this line. As I followed the evolution of religion, saw it still dominated by some of its earliest errors, and universally paralyzed by the concept of a fixed revelation, the view was somewhat discouraging. But as clearly I saw the universal need of it, the functional demand of the brain for a basic theory of life, for a conscious and repeated connection with the Central Power, and for "sailing orders," a recognized scale of duties. I perceived that in human character there must be "principles," something to be depended on when immediate conditions did not tend to produce right conduct. James Freeman Clark's *Ten Great Religions* was a long step in this field of study, with much besides, and with wide illustration from both real life and fiction.

One may have a brain specialized in its grasp of ethics, as well as of mechanics, mathematics or music. Even as a child I had noted that the whole trouble and difficulty in a story was almost always due to lying or deceit. "He must never know," she cries, or "She must never know," he insists, and the mischief begins. Also, I observed a strange disproportion in the order of virtues, the peculiar way in which they vary in the order of their importance, by race, class, age, sex.

So I set about the imperative task of building my own religion, based on knowledge. This, to the "believer," is no satisfactory foundation. All religions of the past have rested on some one's say so, have been at one in demanding faith as the foremost virtue. Understanding was never required, nor expected, in fact it was forbidden and declared impossible, quite beyond "the poor human intellect."

"It may be poor," said young Charlotte to herself, "but it is all the intellect there is, I know of none better. At any rate it is all I have, and I'll use it." As this religion of mine underlies all my Living, is the most essential part of my life, and began in these years, it will have to go in.

"Here I am," said I, "in the world, conscious, able to do this or that. What is it all about? How does it work? What is my part in it, my job—what ought I to do?" Then I set to work calmly and cheerfully, sure that the greatest truths were the simplest, to review the story of creation and see what I could see. The first evident fact is action, something doing, this universe is a going concern.

"Power," said I. "Force. Call it God. Now then, is it one, or more?" There are various forces at work before us, as centripetal and centrifugal, inertia and others, but I was trying to get a view of the whole show, to see if there was any dominant underlying power.

Looking rapidly along the story of the world's making and growing, with the development of life upon it, I could soon see that in spite of all local variations and back-sets, the process worked all one way—up. This of course involves deciding on terms, as to what is better or worse, higher or lower, but it seemed to me mere sophistry to deny that vegetable forms and activities are higher than mineral; animal higher than vegetable: and of animal life man the highest form and still going on. This long, irresistible ascent showed a single dominant force. "Good!" said I. "Here's God— One God and it Works!"

The next question was of the character of this Force and its effect on the growing world, was it Good? Or Bad?

Here loomed before me the problem of evil, long baffling so many. But I knew that mighty thinkers had thought for ages without discovering some of the most patent facts; their failure did not prove the facts difficult to discover, it merely showed that they had not thought of them. Also, I was strengthened by an innate incredulity which refused to accept anybody's say-so, even if it 'had been said for a thousand years. If a problem was said to be insoluble, I forthwith set out to solve it. So I sat me down before the problem of evil, thus:

"I will go back to the period of a molten world, where we can call nothing right or wrong, and follow carefully up the ages—see where it comes in." So I followed the process until the earth was cool enough to allow the formation of crystals, each square or pentagonal or whatever was its nature, and then if one was broken or twisted, I pounced upon the fact— "here it is! It is right for this to be a hexagon, wrong for it to be squeezed flat." Following this thought in vegetable and animal growth, I was soon able to make my first ethical generalization: "That is right for a given organism which leads to its best development."

It is told that Buddha, going out to look on life, was greatly daunted by death. "They all eat one another!" he cried, and called it evil. This process I examined, changed the verb, said, "They all feed one another," and called it good. Death? Why this fuss about death? Use your imagination, try to visualize a world *without* death! The first form of life would be here yet, miles deep by this time, and nothing else; a static world. If birth is allowed, without death, the resulting mass would leave death as a blessed alternative. Death is the essential condition of life, not an evil.

As to pain—? I observed that the most important continuous functions of living are unconsciously carried on within us; that the most external ones, involving a changing activity on our part, as in obtaining food, and mating, are made desirable by pleasure; that just being alive is a pleasure; that pain does not come in unless something goes wrong. "Fine!" said I. "An admirable world. God is good."

As to the enormous suffering of our humankind, that we make, ourselves, by erroneous action—and can stop it when we choose.

Having got thus far, there remained to study the two main processes of religion, the Intake and the Output. (The phrasing of all this is of more recent years, but the working out of it was done in those years of early girlhood from sixteen to twenty.)

The Intake; the relation of the soul to God. All manner of religions have wandered around this point, and in spite of wide difference in terminology, the fact is established that the individual can derive renewed strength, peace and power from inner contact with this Central Force. They *do it*, Christian, Hebrew, Moslem, Buddhist. It is evident that this Force does not care what you call it, but flows in, as if we had tapped the reservoir of the universe.

However, one cannot put a quart in a pint cup. Sucking away on this vast power and not doing anything with it, results in nothing, unless it may be a distention of the mind, unfitting it for any practical contacts. So we sometimes see the most profoundly religious persons accomplishing the least good, while more is done by some who spend less time in prayer.

Seeking to clarify my mind on this point I deliberately put myself in God's place, so to speak, tried to imagine how I should feel toward my creatures, what I should expect of them. If that Power is conscious we may assume it to be rational, surely, and in no way *less* than we! If not conscious, we must simply find out how it works. What does God want of the earth? To whirl and spin and keep its times and seasons. What of the vegetable world? To blossom and bear fruit. Of the animals? The same fulfilment of function. Of us? The same and more. We, with all life, are under the great law, Evolution.

I figured it out that the business of mankind was to carry out the evolution of the human race, according to the laws of nature, adding the conscious direction, the telic force, proper to our kind—we are the only creatures that can assist evolution; that we could replenish our individual powers by application to the reservoir; and the best way to get more power was to use what one had.

Social evolution I easily saw to be in human work, in the crafts, trades, arts and sciences through which we are related, maintained and developed. Therefore the first law of human life was clear, and I made my second ethical generalization: "The first duty of a human being is to assume right functional relation to society"—more briefly, to find your real job, and do it. This is the first duty, others accompany and follow it, but not all of them together are enough without this.

This I found perfectly expressed in a story read in later years, of a noted English engineer, whose personal life was open to much criticism, and who was about to die of heart disease. His nurse, a redoubtable Nova Scotian, annoyed him by concern about his soul, his approaching Judgment and probable damnation.

"My good woman," said he, "when I die, if I come to judgment, I believe that I shall be judged by the bridges I have built."

Life, duty, purpose, these were clear to me. God was Real, under and in and around everything, lifting, lifting. We, conscious of that limitless power, were to find our places, our special work in the world, and when found, do it, do it at all costs.

There was one text on which I built strongly: "Whoso doeth the will shall know of the doctrine." "Good," said I. "That's *provable;* I'll try it." And I set to work, with my reliable system of development, to "do the will" as far as I could see it.

CHAPTER V

GIRLHOOD—IF ANY

SIXTEEN, with a life to build. My mother's profound religious tendency and implacable sense of duty; my father's intellectual appetite; a will power, well developed, from both; a passion of my own for scientific knowledge, for real laws of life; an insatiable demand for perfection in everything, and that proven process of mine for acquiring habits—instead of "Standing with reluctant feet where the brook and river meet," I plunged in and swam.

I am giving the girlhood which I remember, the dominant feelings, the most earnest efforts. As I look over the diaries of the time, the first one is for 1876, the records are trivial enough, hardly anything is shown of the desperately serious "living" which was going on. It was my definite aim that there should be nothing in my diary which might not be read by any one; I find in these faintly scribbled pages most superficial accounts of small current events, an unbaked girlishness of no special promise.

Very occasionally some indication of the inner difference appears, as once while seventeen: "Am going to try hard this winter to see if I cannot enjoy myself like other people." This shows the growing stoicism which was partly forced on me by repeated deprivations, then consciously acquired. The local life in which we moved seemed to me petty in the extreme. The small routine of our housekeeping, the goings and comings of friends

44

and relatives, and the rare opportunities for small entertainment, have left almost no impression.

What I do remember, indelibly, is the cumulative effort toward a stronger, nobler character. At the end of the eighteen-year-old diary is written: "Goodby old Year! It has been one of much progress and considerable improvement. My greatest fault now is inordinate egotism." A persistent characteristic, this.

Our living was of the simplest, mother and I doing the little housework, washing and all. There were coal stoves to care for, and I, "in the vicious pride of my youth," could take a hod of anthracite coal in both hands and run up two flights of stairs with it, singing all the way. Also, I could lift a full water-pail in one hand up to the level of my ear.

I improved in painting my little water-color portraits of flowers, and began to get small orders for them. Mrs. C. C. Smith, a friend of both my parents, a Boston woman, high in educational circles, visited us, and was not pleased to see a girl of my age so untrained. She suggested that I attend The School of Design, about to be opened in Providence. Mother objected to this on the ground that it would take me out of her influence and management; she held that a girl should, as she put it, "remain in her mother's sphere until she entered her husband's." This was somehow derived from her Swedenborgianism. My natural query, "Does a girl never have a sphere of her own?" was ignored. But the good lady from Boston was a friend of father's as well as mother's; she doubtless represented to him that I had talent, he was willing to pay the fees, and the matter seemed to me so important that I decided to stretch my determined obedience for once.

We sat at our little dining-table, mother and Aunt

Caroline and I. Calmly I stated the advantages offered, improvement in my work, means of earning a living, a chance to make friends and connections, ending: "If you command me not to go I shall obey you, but do you dare refuse such an opportunity?" She didn't. So I went to the Rhode Island School of Design, and learned much.

The school was on the top floor of a five-story building on Westminster Street, about a mile from our house. There was an elevator, but I was always looking for additional exercise, and walked up. At first slowly and sedately, then I ran one flight and walked three, then ran two and presently all, then began again with two steps at a time, and in a month or so I was running up the whole four flights two steps at a time and beating the elevator, to my immense satisfaction.

I was no artist, but a skilled craftsman. My flower-portraiture was perfect of its kind, but not "art." The study in free-hand drawing I liked, the charcoal work, even the beginnings in oil, but chiefly delightful was perspective, which just fitted some corner of my mind. When the exercises were given I had the example done before the description was hardly finished, and then it was hung on the wall as a specimen of class-work.

Which calls to mind a story about another specimen and a discomfited young man. We were taught modeling, and I had a medallion to copy, a head of Couture by William M. Hunt. The copy was a good one and was kept among the school exhibits. Years later another principal of the school, a young man and cocky, passed it around at an artist's club supper as Hunt's own, expatiating dictatorially on its merits. But a friend of mine present saw my monogram on it, and pointed out that it was done by C. A. Perkins while a student, to the chagrin of the exhibitor.

One odd result of the art school experience was temporary employment in a monument shop. They wanted some student to assist in their drawing work, and I got the job. All I remember of that effort is how to put on a "flat wash"—to tint evenly a large surface, and the shape of an "ogee curve."

Another was to teach drawing in a small private school. There I encountered the only child I ever saw who really could not draw. She was "form blind," could not distinguish between a square and a circle, as it were.

One amusing source of income was the painting of advertising cards for Kendall's Soap Company. Cousin Robert Brown was in that business, and the fashion of distributing small lithographed cards to attract customers had just begun. Robert had a fertile imagination, he devised the pictures he wanted and I drew and colored them. I did not know how, did not do them well, but neither of us minded that. One of their established figures was "The Soapine Whale," this animal I labored with repeatedly. Another of his involved a big gray-dappled horse which used to lead in pulling freight-cars through the city, and with much effort I drew him, my first horse.

Little by little I added to my earning capacity, selling the little cardboard panels with groups of flowers on them, and giving lessons both in school and privately. This flower-painting developed to a sort of limited perfection. I was told later by a competent judge that if I would give myself to it I could paint still life as well as any one on earth. But this seemed to me a poor ambition, not conducive to my object— the improvement of the human race.

Some lasting friendships were contracted during these years, one, somewhat unique in its character, with

a gentle, lovely, intellectual girl, Martha Luther by
name. She was sixteen, I seventeen. We liked each other
immensely. Said I to her: "We seem to be on the
brink of what they call 'A schoolgirl friendship,' which
so often breaks up in foolish quarrel or misunderstanding. Let's make ours safe and permanent."

So we undertook to be always utterly frank with
each other in word and deed, never to pretend anything we did not fully feel. I explained, furthermore,
that I was irregular in fervor, that for a time I should
want to see her continually, and that there would be
spaces when affection seemed to wane, but if she would
understand and be patient it would well up warmly
again. We earnestly entered into this compact of mutual understanding, kept its agreements, enjoyed years
of perfect companionship, and as grandmothers are
still friends. This was my first deep personal happiness.

The Hazards, one of the "noble families" of Rhode
Island, were extremely kind to me in these years of
girlhood. There was the grandfather, Rowland Hazard
I, the son, Rowland Hazard II, the grandson, Rowland Hazard III, later came a fourth, and there may
be a fifth of the dynasty by now.

Mrs. Rowland II was like some beneficent duchess.
There chanced to be a strong resemblance between me
and her sister, Mrs. Blake, who was dead; also to her
daughter, Ada Blake, and to Mrs. Hazard's daughter
Helen. There was no connection between our families,
but the resemblance was so marked that I was repeatedly taken for one or the other of the girls even in her
own house.

Mrs. Hazard engaged me to give lessons to her
youngest daughter, which never struck me at the time
as pure benevolence. She invited me occasionally to
parties, and to visit them at their lovely home in Peace-

dale, Rhode Island. I recall now with the keenest appreciation how wisely kind they were to me, all of them, trying to help this obstinate young stoic, to ameliorate somewhat the hard conditions in which I lived.

My mother was anxious as to my conduct in all this grandeur. "Does Charlotte know how to behave?" she asked, and gracious Mrs. Hazard answered: "If she does not know what to do, she does something of her own that is just as good."

I had no suitable clothes for such society, which distressed me not a whit. On my way home from giving lessons I would stop at their splendid home for an afternoon tea or something, wearing what was practically my only dress, hanging up what was practically my only hat in the hall, perfectly unconcerned in the matter of clothes. If, hatless, I was taken for one of the family, why that was a compliment.

More formative and valuable was friendship with the family of Dr. William F. Channing, son of William Ellery Channing, the great Unitarian divine. Here I found broad free-thinking, scientific talk, earnest promotion of great causes—life. There were two beautiful daughters, lifelong friends, one closer than a sister to this day.

The handsomest girls of all I knew were Helen Hazard, Nellie Sharpe, and Jessie Luther, the last two still alive and lovely; the most utterly charming was May Diman, cut off by an accident in her rich youth. Another kind and helpful friend of my youth, somewhat older than I and appreciative of my strenuous efforts at well doing, was Miss Kate Bucklin, who used to take me to the theater and buy me books. Dear woman! she is still sending me presents.

Among other benefactions she took me to Ogunquit,

Maine, for vacation visits, with other friends. We stayed at the Cliff House, successor to which still stands on that sheer cliff, about which is a turmoil of rock delightful to geologists. One deep, narrow chasm they named Charlotte Perkins's Leap, because I jumped across it. It was not really very wide, but looked dangerous enough if one was not clear-headed and sure-footed.

One year there was a handsome Harvard boy in the party, who invited me out to sit on the rocks in the moonlight. Thus romantically placed, he confided to me that he had kissed more than one girl for what he was sure was the first time. Replying, I soberly inquired if he did not expect to marry some day, which he admitted. "When you first kiss the girl you mean to marry, don't you wish that to be her 'first time'?" Yes, he did. "Then don't you see that every time you kiss these other girls first you are robbing some other man of that dear pleasure?" He saw. Our conversation continued on a most friendly and confidential basis, but I noticed that next night he took one of the pretty waitresses out on the rocks—they were nice neighborhood girls.

Some months after, that fine young fellow shot himself. His parents were sternly pious people and thought he would be damned, for committing suicide, and I was most happily able to lift that load from their hearts by repeating to them what he had told me of black misery of mind, of how he often thought of suicide, but intended not to use the pistol his father gave him, lest such a use of it hurt his feelings! The indication of growing melancholia was so clear that the agonized parents felt sure he was insane, and even the kind of God they believed in would hardly damn a lunatic.

One frequent pleasure of my youth was whist. I liked all games, as far as I knew them, save cribbage and backgammon, but whist and chess best of all. There were several cousins of mother's who used to play whist with us, and two serious-minded young Brown students who called often, but solemnly inquired for Aunt Caroline instead of me.

Aside from such safe and limited companionship, mother was rigorous in refusing all manner of invitations for me. I was denied so often that I found it saved emotion to "fight fire with fire," to deny myself beforehand, and, strengthened by Emerson, Socrates, Epictetus and Marcus Aurelius, I became a genuine stoic.

This process was promoted by one experience so drastic as to render later deprivations of small account. During my seventeenth year one of mother's cousins, ten years older than I, invited me to a students' concert at Brown. Mother declined for me. She, in her lovely girlhood, had known many college boys—she had some obscure objection to my "getting in with the students." I made no complaint, being already inured to denial. But that same day another of those cousins, twenty years older than I, asked me to go with him and his sisters to sit in a box, and see Edwin Booth in *Hamlet*.

Booth! *Hamlet!* A box! Nothing in all the world could have meant so much to me at the time. And mother refused. Why? She afterwards explained that having refused Robert, she feared that if she accepted Edward's invitation it would hurt Robert's feelings. How about mine?... The unparalleled glory offered and the pitiful inadequacy of the reason for its denial made a ghastly impression on my mind. Something broke. Perhaps it was like what is called "a broken heart." At any rate I have never since that day felt the sharp sting of disappointment, only a numb feeling. So deep was the effect of continuous denials and my own drastic training in endurance, that it was many years later before I learned to accept an offered pleasure naturally.

There is strong contrast between my clear memories of the earnest "living" which was going on inside during these years, and the trivial entries in these juvenile diaries of mine. Externally it was a meager, poverty-stricken, repressed life. There was the housework—"Rose at four. Ironing done by six" (This was for two only). There was the sewing and mending and dressmaking: a new hat—"first in three years, $3.75." There was, while sixteen, the record of that unattainable Prince, "Saw him! Oh joy!" and "didn't see him! Oh dear!" and then mention of various minor hims now quite forgotten, some of whom seem from this distance to show a forthcoming disposition, but whom I note only with the remark, "Poor little snipe!" or "Nice little fellow!"

One I do remember who brought his guitar, and essayed a compliment as to the clear luster of the white of my eyes, to which I encouragingly replied, "What color should they be?" By the local youth I was set down as too smart, what would now be called a "highbrow." My theory was that a girl should meet a boy with the same straightforward friendliness she would show another girl; that it was ignominious and wrong to flaunt one's femininity so to speak. It was far too late for popularity before I learned that this was precisely what men wanted, ordinary men, that is.

It was different when I visited in Boston and Cambridge, with our good friend Mrs. Smith and her son Walter, with the Hales, and with the dear Hedges in

Cambridge. Walter Smith and Arthur Hale were in Harvard, I met the kind of people I liked, young and old, and was far more popular than in Providence. Here is a day which seems to be high-watermark. I was nineteen:

CAMBRIDGE. 11 P.M., Thurs., Jan. 1st, 1880. Pen of gold and pearl [This must have been a Christmas present, the adored hope of childhood at last—only it wasn't pink.] and book of stainless paper are none too good for such a day as this. Rose late. Conversed with the charming Walter. Wrote note to mother asking to stay til Monday. Made New Year's call on May Diman and Retta Clark. Then on Aunt Emily Hale. Saw Arthur. Edward goes down to the Clark's with me, departing with George, while May, Retta and I go to Nellie's Studio. See my portrait there. Home to Mrs. S's to lunch. More Walter. Much Walter. Goes out with me and my bag when I start for here at 3:30. On arriving here whom do I find but Mr. Dodge! My first New Year's call. Is very. Very. *Very*. Scurry and dress. Very pretty, lace and flowers. Go to party at Mrs. Wells' in carriage with Mrs. Holland and Henry Holland. Quite a crowd. 1st, talk quite a lot with Ivan Panin. 2nd, long and interesting "One Word" with Henry Holland. 3rd, Mr. Greeley at supper time. 4th, Ben Wells. 5th, "Criticism" Am criticized. Good fun. 6th, "Blow out the candle." Beastly game. Come home at eleven or near it, regretting not having said good-by to Greeley, and, can I believe my senses, find that identical youth artlessly happening by as we get out of the hack!!! Am going to a museum with him to-morrow!—I never was so courted and entertained and done for in all my little life. It seems as if the memory of to-day would last me in solid comfort through all the ills that flesh is heir to. I thought noth —(it is Jan. 2nd.)ing was needful to my happiness when I rode home, and then to find Lewis Greeley actually loitering about to see *Me!* I cannot understand it. Not that I mean him especially, but the attention.—The—the—why to think of its being *me!*

My facility in verse crops out even in the diary, as:

Jan. 23rd: Refrained like a fool from going to school as
Mama with a headache appeared, but was grieved to remain
for she suffered no pain the moment the weather had cleared.
6 cents did I spend for three pinks to the end of enhancing
L. G.'s valentine, and the day spent in painting the spray, with
effect most uncommonly fine. Went round to see Ray, at 2 P.M.
to-day, to get means for our next month's survival; had a letter
from T. full of pleasure and glee announcing his box's arrival.
Left the dishes to Belle, who delighteth full well on some pre-
text to come in and stay, and by Bolan the gifted our ashes were
sifted and the cellar cleaned up on small pay. i.e., 60cts.

There was plenty more of the kind, verse was as easy
as prose.

A special blank book has a large collection of valen-
tines, which I wrote with joyous abandon. One year I
sent fifteen to charming May Diman, a few carefully
arranged so that she would attribute them to me, the
others written to seem as if from different men she
knew, and had them copied by various friends and
mailed to her from afar.

The best worth quoting is one with an answer. In
Cambridge, at a little party with the Hedges, we
played some game with forfeits. I was a victim, and
Miss Hedge being arbiter, said, "You must propose
to Fred Almy." ... The Almy twins were two delightful Harvard boys, most gifted and entertaining were
they. I thought it well to get this over with at once,
so I kneeled to him before them all and begged, "Wilt
thou be mine?" The youth was somewhat flustered,
murmured something about delay, suggested that I
wait a year. After which, next Valentine's Day, I sent
him this:

O rock and ice! I offered you my hand,
    I owned I loved you, dear,
You only smiled with heartless self-command
    And bade me wait a year.

And I have waited, with an aching breast,
    While spring to summer turned;
Waited while darkly in the distant west
    The autumn sunsets burned.

Waited until the winter came at last
    With whirling snow and rain,
Waited until the weary year was passed
    And I might ask again.

Will you be mine? The true love on my part
    I think you well can guess,
I listen with a horror in my heart
    Lest you should answer "Yes!"

Before night I got an answer, *by telegraph*—

Can ice resist the sun?
    Do icebergs melt and live?
An answer, ruthless paragon,
    I prithee give.

Death be my happy fate,
    Gladly for thee I die
Yet hold—what words of cunning hate
    Appall mine eye!

Does horror fill your heart?
    O woful words to me!
I now consent, a harder part
    To live for thee.

Aside from such very occasional divertissements, my real "living" became increasingly strenuous. Childish dreams of being the best of everything turned to a determination to become the best I could in all lines possible to me. This pious ambition was stiffened by a practical philosophy and made easy in execution by that excellent process of mine.

Up to sixteen or seventeen there was no character to be specially proud of; impressionable, vacillating, sensitive, uncontrolled, often loafing and lazy—only a few years earlier good Mrs. Smith had said to mother that I seemed "all froth and foam." Mother told me this, for my good, knowing how much I respected that lady, and I laid up the saying most solemnly. Five or six years from the time of her dictum I asked her if she still thought so, and she reversed her opinion completely, said I was the most determined and firmly based young woman she knew, to my immense satisfaction. Perhaps that relentless memory and determination to make her "eat her words" shows some inner force of character, if only contradictoriness.

The flaccidity of will which had impressed that kind critic I saw to be a weakness to be outgrown, and set about it. The first step was to establish prompt and easy execution of decisions, to connect cerebral action with the motor nerves. Short of idiocy we all have this power, but most of us neglect it. "You couldn't do it if you hadn't inherited the capacity!" says the fatalist. Of course we inherit it. If you inherit a fortune does it prove that you haven't any? We do have the capacity, and can develop it, like any other power, by use.

My advantage was the Yankee inventiveness which devised means for doing easily what is usually found difficult. I deliberately set about a course of exercises in which small and purely arbitrary decisions were sharply carried out: "In ten minutes I will take another chair." "At five-thirty-eight I will walk around the block." "I will get out of bed at thirteen minutes to seven." The essence of this method is in its complete detachment. There is no temptation to be overcome, no difficulty to be met, nothing but a simple expression of will. Such exercises, carried on thoroughly, do develop the habit of executing one's decisions, and make it easy when there is something serious to be done.

With each trait to be acquired the Process was used; determination, self-suggestion, "making up the mind" —"I *will* think before I speak!" This was one of my most needed ones. The determination is forgotten, the thoughtless words go on, but after a while the memory revives—then welcome it, waste no moment in regret, say, "Ah, here you are!," and jam it in again, harder than before, "I *will* think before I speak!" You will remember it sooner next time, smile and jam it in again. At last the thought comes before the word, you catch yourself in the act and check the unkind or unwise speech—but only once that day. Twice the next day, then three times, and so slowly, not straining the new connection, until you have established the habit you desire.

One of my worst characteristics was bitterly bewailed by mother. "Shall I never teach you to think of other people! You *are* so thoughtless." She was right. I was not thoughtful of others, I could see that the characters I admired and strove to imitate were so, and I set to work to acquire this virtue. Evidently a large order, a year, perhaps two, required for its acquisition. First the firm determination, repeated as it recurred. When at last I thought of it in time, I'd gaze at some caller of mother's and consider what, if anything, I could do for that person; get a foot-stool, a glass of water, change a window-shade, any definitely conceived benefit. So with other people in other places, laboriously seeking to think of them. With this I undertook a course of minor self-denials, for the sole purpose of reversing the current, turning my mind from what I wanted to what other people wanted. This from no delusion of virtue; what I was after was the reversal of tendency, the turning of consciousness from self to others.

But this was too slow, too restricted, and I devised a larger scheme. There was a certain crippled girl, with a poor little mother, maker of lace caps for old ladies. Among the benevolent church members who cared for them were some of mother's cousins, and it was easy to be introduced to the poor invalid. Half-blind she was, wearing a shade over her eyes, lying curled up on her couch, a most unhappy object. Of this damsel I inquired, "Will you do me a service?"

She laughed with some bitterness at the idea that she could do anything for me, but I explained that I was quite in earnest, that she could help me most practically. "You see," I pursued seriously, "I don't think about other people, and I'm trying to learn. Now I don't care anything about you, yet, but I'd like to. Will you let me come and practise on you?"

This she thought to be merely a concealment of benevolent feelings, but it wasn't. I didn't care in the least about her, but I knew that I should if I did things for her; love grows by service. So I visited that unhappy creature, and studied what I could do to benefit her, beyond being amusing.

Her limitations were many and painful. I read to her, that was easy. Her eating was restricted, but she could smell, and I brought her flowers. Then, with a long, careful saving from my most narrow and uncertain resources, I bought her a small musicbox, for $3.00—a huge sum for me; it was a mere toy, but proved a great comfort to her. And sure enough, after a while I became quite fond of the girl.

In about two years I heard through a kind cousin that some old lady had said that she did like Charlotte Perkins—she was so thoughtful of other people. "Hurrah!" said I, "another game won!"

Each year I would lay out one, or perhaps two, desirable traits to acquire, and in a leisurely manner acquire them. We are told to hitch our wagons to a star, but why pick on Betelgeuse? I selected more modestly, more gradually, carefully choosing for imitation some admired character in history or fiction, not too far beyond me, and then catching up; followed by the selection of another more difficult. At the time when this long effort calamitously ended I had got as far as Socrates. . . .

One New Year's prayer heard during these years provoked me almost to interrupt. The minister was droning along in the "Thou knowest" style—(if it was plain "you know" how inelegant it would be!) "Thou knowest how a year ago we made good resolutions and have broken them. Thou knowest how we undertook to develop a better character and have failed." . . . I wanted to speak out and tell him that there was one person present who had undertaken to develop better character and succeeded, who had made good resolutions and kept them every one. But I was careful not to make too many at once.

One of the later and more difficult was the establishing a habit of absolute truthfulness. Not that I had ever been a liar, but that now I meant to practise the most meticulous accurary, to become so reliable that people would declare, "If Charlotte Perkins says so, it's so." There came a day when I was sorely tried in the acquirement of this stern reputation. A young acquaintance, well known for the exact opposite, called on me with solemn purpose.

"Charlotte, I have heard that you said that I lied! You didn't, did you?" This was not easy. We are more carefully trained in not hurting people's feelings than stark truth. But I hung on to my principles, and the arms of my chair. "Yes, I did."

She was thunder-struck, had never dreamed that I would own it, protested, "But you don't believe it do you?" Another effort, harder than the last. "Yes, I do."

That was a real test. Being successfully met it enabled me to meet others with less strain. And as to consequences—I lost a "friend," but she gained what should have been a salutary lesson.

Self-righteous? Tremendously so. For eight years I did not do anything I thought wrong, and did, at any cost, what I thought right—which is not saying that all my decisions were correct.

CHAPTER VI

POWER AND GLORY

AMONG our immediate associates I heard nothing of the larger movements of the time, but with the Channing family and their friends was a larger outlook, while in my steady reading I lived in the world as a whole. This world seemed to be suffering from many needless evils, evils for which some remedies seemed clear to me even then. I was deeply impressed with the injustices under which women suffered, and still more with the ill effects upon all mankind of this injustice; but was not in close touch with the suffrage movement. Once I went to a meeting of some earnest young temperance workers, but was not at all at home in that atmosphere of orthodox religion and strong emotion. My method was to approach a difficulty as if it was a problem in physics, trying to invent the best solution.

It was a period of large beginnings in many lines. "Strong-minded" girls were going to college under criticism and ridicule, the usual curriculum in those days was held quite beyond "the feminine mind." Some thirty years later, an editor, sadly impressed by the majority of prize-takers being girls, protested that these same curricula were "evidently too feminine." I recall part of a bit of newspaper wit at the time, about 1880:

She'd a great and varied knowledge she'd picked up at a woman's college,
Of quadratics, hydrostatics and pneumatics very vast;

She'd discuss, the learned charmer, the theology of Brahma,
All the 'ologies of the colleges and the knowledges of the past.

She knew all the forms and features of the prehistoric creatures,
Icththyosaurus, megliosaurus, plestosaurus, and many more,
She could talk about the Tuscans and the Greeks and the
    Etruscans,
All the scandals of the Vandals and the sandals that they wore.

But she couldn't get up a dinner for a gaunt and starving sinner,
Or concoct a simple supper for her poor old hungry Poppa,
For she never was constructed on the old domestic plan.

The "charmer" before marriage and the cook afterward were the prevailing ideas at the time, as indeed
they still are in some places. But things began to
change, women appeared in stores and offices—I once
met a man from Maine who told me how he was
severely criticized for employing saleswomen—so un-
womanly! such a public occupation! Doubtless our
Civil War, like this last one, drove women to do what
men had done before. Clothing changed, there appeared the "tailored suit," even made by men! made
for street wear, plain and serviceable. Ideas began
to change. Mona Caird in England produced that then
much talked of book, *Is Marriage a Failure?*
Education was advancing, the kindergarten making
slow but sure impression. Far-seeing mothers were beginning to give their children information about sex.
There was a start toward an equal standard in chastity,
equal *up,* not down as at present. A little paper called
The Alpha was brought out in Washington to urge this
ideal. The first poem I had published was in this tiny
paper. It was called "One Girl of Many," a defense of
what was then termed the "fallen" woman.
In the present-day lowering of standards of behavior

one exhibition of ignorance and meanness of spirit is the charge, "You did the same in your day, only you were secretive about it." Any one whose memory covers fifty years knows better. There were plenty of young men who were "fast," and some girls who were called "pretty gay," but even at that the words had different meanings.

For instance there was just one damsel in all my acquaintance who was certainly "gay." She was so proud of the "wasp-waist" admired at the time, that she tied her corset-laces to the bedpost and pulled, to draw them tight enough. Her behavior with young men was so much discussed that I determined to learn something of her.

"You know I am not 'in society,' " I told her. "I am interested as a student, and I wish you would tell me just what the game is—what it is that you are trying to do." She recognized my honest interest, and was quite willing to explain. Considering thoughtfully she presently replied, "It is to get a fellow so he cannot keep his hands off you—and then not let him touch you."

This was bad enough in all conscience, but she was the only one out of scores. Among the more daring girls there was some discussion of whether, when a fellow came home with you, he might also claim a kiss. But there was also discussion, quite popular, of this question of Emerson's, "Does the soul underlie a condition of infinite remoteness?" I remember coming to the conclusion that it did.

On sleighing-parties and "straw-rides" there was a good deal of holding hands and some kissing, all in cheerful, giggling groups; and I do not doubt that going to ride with what livery-stable men called a "courtin' horse" involved a good deal of hugging.

But the standards and general behavior of "nice girls" —and most of them were nice—are shown clearly in the books of Louisa M. Alcott and Mrs. A. D. T. Whitney.

Among the many splendid movements of the late nineteenth century was one dear to my heart, that toward a higher physical culture. In Europe and then here the impulse was felt, building gymnasiums, practice of calisthenics even for girls, and the rapid development of college athletics. In this line of improvement I was highly ambitious. With right early training I could easily have been an acrobat, having good nervous coördination, strength, courage, and excellent balancing power.

High places never daunted me. As a child in Rehoboth I used to parade the ridge-pole of the barn and stand on the very end of it, to alarm people driving by—mischievous wretch! In the simple task of walking rails, railroad rails, I have kept on steadily over a hundred of them. Dancing would have been a passion, but dancing was one of the many forbiddings of my youth.

What I did determine on and largely secure was the devleopment of a fine physique. Blaikie's *How To Get Strong and How To Stay So* was a great help. Early country life gave a good start, and housework kept some muscles in use, the best of it is scrubbing the floor. That is good back and arm work, and not dusty or steamy like sweeping and washing.

Going to the art school gave me two miles' walk a day. In the coldest weather I'd start off so briskly that before long I'd have my mittens off and coat unbuttoned, smiling triumphantly at chillier people. All manner of "stunts" I delighted to practise, that were within my range. There was one favorite, which I will

now try to describe—and a more difficult literary task
I never undertook!

Hold a yard-stick horizontally behind you, arms
hanging at your sides, palms front. Without changing
this grip, raise it behind and bring forward over your
head until it is horizontal in front of you. Raise and
somewhat advance the left-hand end, lowering and
drawing back the right to within a foot of the floor
directly before you. Raise the right foot and put it
outside the hand and inside the stick, while you balance
on the left foot. Then move your left hand forward and
toward the right, never changing that grip, passing the
stick behind your head and downward, until you can
lift your right foot over it again and stand as you
began. Repeat with the other foot first. I used to do
this with each foot three times before going to bed.
It is easy enough for slender, pliable girls, but strong
men, somewhat muscle-bound, cannot do it.

Needless to say that I never wore corsets, that my
shoes were "common sense" (and more people seemed
to have common sense at the time), that all my clothing "hung from the shoulder"—the custom being to
drag all those heavy skirts from the waist. I devised
a sort of side-garter suspender, to which skirts were
buttoned, and, not a flat bandage to make a woman
look like a boy, but after many trials evolved a
species of brassière which supported the breasts without constriction anywhere. It had elastic over the
shoulder and under the arm, allowing perfect freedom
for breathing and arm-motion, while snug and efficient
as a support.

Textile construction always delighted me, inventing,
composing, making suitable and if possible lovely garments. There has been plenty of it to do. During all
my youth I had to wear other people's clothes, gifts

from friends and relatives. Mother bought my first new dress when I was thirteen or fourteen. Later I had some pretty frocks for those Boston visits, and enjoyed them like any girl.

Never in my life have I been able to dress as I would like to. That requires one or more of three things I never had enough of, time, strength, or money. And since I would not wear what others did if against my principles of hygiene, truth, beauty, comfort or humanity—as for instance the use of feathers for trimming, or unnecessary furs—the result has left much to be desired. Real beauty I cared for intensely, fashion I despised.

In the fall of 1891 I wanted a gymnasium for women. There was none in Providence. I went to Dr. Brooks, who had taught calisthenics in my last school, and who had a man's gymnasium, and asked him why he did not have one for women. He said not enough women wanted it. "How many would you need?" He said about thirty. Then I set forth, visited every girl I knew and many that I didn't, and got up a class, not thirty indeed, but enough to encourage him to begin. He opened a high-grade woman's gymnasium, beautifully fitted, and let me design a stencil for the wall-border! Thanks to Mrs. Hazard's patronage some of the "first families" were represented among the pupils, which ensured success.

For three years I had the use of this well-appointed place, free, and found it a joy indeed. Aside from its initial purpose it provided social pleasure. There were a lot of nice girls, and I even learned some dancing, for we had polka-races, the witchy "slide and kick, slide and kick, slide and slide and slide and kick" of the racquet, and long lines of high-swinging legs in the "Patience step," from the then new opera.

My special efforts were not toward anything spectacular, but directed to the building up of a sound physique. Going twice a week, each day I ran a mile, not for speed but wind, and can still run better than many a younger woman. I could vault and jump, go up a knotted rope, walk on my hands under a ladder, kick as high as my head, and revel in the flying rings. But best of all were the traveling rings, those wide-spaced single ones, stirrup-handled, that dangle in a line the length of the hall.

To mount a table with one of those in one hand, well drawn back, launch forth in a long swing and catch the next with the other, pull strongly on the first to get a long swing back, carefully letting go when it hung vertically so that it should be ready for the return, and go swinging on to the next, down the whole five and back again—that is as near flying as one gets, outside of a circus. I could do it four times in those days.

Life does not offer many opportunities for this exercise, but I had a chance at it when about thirty-six, again when somewhat over fifty, and last, lecturing in Oklahoma University, I did it once, the whole row and back, at sixty-five. Whereby it is apparent that a careful early training in physical culture lasts a lifetime. I never was vain of my looks, nor of any professional achievements, but am absurdly vain of my physical strength and agility.

Five little rules of health I devised: "Good air and plenty of it, good exercise and plenty of it, good food and plenty of it, good sleep and plenty of it, good clothing and as little as possible." How I should have delighted in the short, light garments of to-day! But I would have made mine wide enough to walk in, this pinched pillow-case effect is far from freedom. The re-

sult of all this training was to establish a cheerful vigor
that enjoyed walking about five miles a day, with working hours from six A.M. to ten P.M. except for meals.

We moved, April, 1881, to a better house, on the
north-west corner of Manning and Ives Streets. Ours
was the ground floor, Aunt Caroline took the second,
and I had a little room on the third, where the little
landlady kept three for herself. That little chamber of
mine, with its one arched window facing south, was
hot in summer and cold in winter, but I enjoyed it
hugely—thus celebrating its prospect:

My View

From my high window the outlooker sees
　　The whole wide southern sky;
Fort Hill is in the distance, always green,
With ordinary houses thick between,
　　And scanty passers by.

Our street is flat, ungraded, little used,
　　The sidewalks grown with grass;
And, just across, a fenceless open lot,
Covered with ash-heaps, where the sun shines hot
　　On bits of broken glass.

It's hard on Nature, blotting her fair face
　　With such discourteous deeds;
But one short season gives her time enough
To softly cover all the outlines rough
　　With merciful thick weeds.

Then numerous most limited back-yards,
　　One thick with fruit trees, overgrown with vines,
But most of them are rather bare and small,
With board and picket fences, running all
　　In parallel straight lines.

Hardly a brilliant prospect, you will think,
　　The common houses, scanty passers by,

Bare lot thick strewn with cinder-heaps and shards,
And small monotonous township of backyards—
Ah! You forget the sky!

The window I promptly took out of the casing, it
stayed out for the three years we lived there. In very
stormy weather I used to stand one of the spare leaves
from the dining-table against it; that and closed blinds
kept out most of the snow. There was no bathroom in
this house, that luxury I never possessed till living in
Oakland in 1891, but I took my daily cold bath from
the wash-bowl until the ice in the water-pail was so
thick I could not break it with my heel. A rough face-
cloth, a triple scrub—it used to leave me steaming.

"Oct. 5th, 1881. Ice! Up at six, cold as I ever want
to be. Warm up with bath and do chores as usual."
Rising hours were early, "6:10," "6:50," "5:55," "6,"
"6:5" they run. The day began with three coal-stoves
to attend to, in winter; get breakfast, do chamberwork,
be ready for pupils at nine. These were two girls who
came to the house for tutoring; in the afternoons there
were others in different parts of the city to whom I
went, teaching drawing, painting, gymnastics, and
ordinary branches with cheerful enthusiasm.

I gave drawing lessons to a boy and girl, the girl
died, and the lonely little brother begged to have me
come and stay with him. So I tried governessing, for
ten weeks, and learned more about the servant question in that time than most of us ever find out.

No long-tutored heir to a kingdom ever came to the
throne with a more triumphant sense of freedom and
power than mine when I reached my twenty-first birthday. I had lived six steady years of self-enforced obedience to management I heartily disapproved of, and
which was in some ways lastingly injurious; submission

to a tutelage so exacting that even the letters I wrote were read, as well as those I received; an account was always demanded of where I had been, whom I had seen, and what they had said—there was no unhandled life for me.

Afterward mother used to grieve because I did not give her my confidence. One does not readily give what was so long a compelled tribute. Naturally a confiding child, it required many years of misunderstanding and enforced exhibition to teach me complete reserve. For instance, at sixteen, I wrote the first bit of verse that seemed to me real poetry, a trifling thing about white violets. I went with it at once to mother. She listened with no apparent interest, and as soon as I had finished said, "Go and put on the tea-kettle." As a matter of fact she thought the verses beautiful, and kept them carefully, but at the time the tea-kettle was vividly in mind and the sensitiveness of a budding poetess was not. A trifling incident, but it hurt so that it was never forgotten, and I did not go to her so readily with later verses.

Twenty-one. My own mistress at last. No one on earth had a right to ask obedience of me. I was self-supporting of course, a necessary base for freedom which the young revolters of to-day often overlook. This freedom never meant self-indulgence. From sixteen I had not wavered from that desire to help humanity which underlay all my studies. Here was the world, visibly unhappy and as visibly unnecessarily so; surely it called for the best efforts of all who could in the least understand what was the matter, and had any rational improvements to propose.

It is the fashion to-day for our alien critics and their imitators to ridicule the American urge toward improvement, personal or social. Why it should seem absurd for human beings to try to improve their conditions, physical, mental, moral, mechanical, industrial, economic, ethical or social, I cannot see. There certainly is room for it.

The nature of the work which loomed so large in my mind was by no means definite at that time. Painting, drawing, teaching, these were but means of support; though I did look forward to being a cartoonist as one form of influence. Writing was expected to be mainly didactic and gratuitous, and lecturing never came into my range 'til ten years later. But there was a tremendous sense of power, clean glorious power, of ability to do whatever I decided to undertake.

I contemplated much further study, meaning to spend time in various countries and learn each language like a native; much more in the sciences, a wide outline knowledge of history, economics, politics, there was no field of knowledge applicable to human need which was outside my purpose. Astronomy I never cared for; it seemed so definitely apart from social progress.

My health was splendid, I never tired, with a steady cheerfulness which external discomforts or mishaps could not dim. When asked, "How do you do?" it was my custom to reply, "as well as a fish, as busy as a bee, as strong as a horse, as proud as a peacock, as happy as a clam."

As to looks, if I had been sex-conscious and dressed the part I think I should have been called beautiful. But one does not call a philosophic steam-engine beautiful. My dress was not designed to allure. When from Lily Langtry came the lovely and sensible "Jersey" I seized upon it with delight, and wore it, with a plain, and for those days, markedly short skirt, and a neckerchief, continuously. Clothes were still given me, to make over. I spent little. In one eleven months my total outlay was $5.11—including shoes! But a pair of "button boots," kid, cost only three dollars then.

This tremendous surge of free energy at twenty-one had no result in misbehavior. It found expression mainly in locking my door, actually and metaphorically. Once I sat up all night, just to see how it felt after having been sent to bed so inexorably from infancy; no revelry, just reading and working. Once I slept on the floor; once with a friend, on her roof—an unforgettable experience to me, to look up at the stars—to wake in the night with a soft breath of pure air on one's face and look straight up into that deep, glittering sky—if ever I build a house of my own (which becomes increasingly doubtful), it shall have a habitable roof.

One new indulgence was to go out evenings alone. This I worked out carefully in my mind, as not only a right but a duty. Why should a woman be deprived of her only free time, the time allotted to recreation? Why must she be dependent on some man, and thus forced to please him if she wished to go anywhere at night?

A stalwart man once sharply contested my claim to this freedom to go alone. "Any true man," he said with fervor, "is always ready to go with a woman at night. He is her natural protector." "Against what?" I inquired. As a matter of fact, the thing a woman is most afraid to meet on a dark street is her natural protector. Singular.

Personally I have never known fear, except in dreams, that paralyzing terror born of indigestion. But if the streets were not safe for women they should be made so. In the meantime, if there is real danger, let them carry a pistol. So far, in forty-five years of free movement at night, from San Francisco to London, I have never met danger, and almost never the slightest impertinence.

As mother could no longer forbid my going, she tried to prevent me by saying that it made her feel badly. This I considered carefully. What I had decided was right she thought wrong. I was not afraid but she was. There did not seem to be any real danger, her fear was not based on present facts but on the way she had been brought up, for which I was not in the least responsible. Mothers and other relatives would always feel badly about it until it became habitual, a custom. Customs have to be made. I was sorry that mother should worry, but the reason lay in earlier standards, not in my conduct. So out I went.

Ever since the beginning of the character-building, I had established the inflexible habit of doing what I had decided to be right, unmoved by any further consideration. This inflexibility of youthful judgment becomes more malleable with passing years. One is not so certain of ethical values. With all my stern devotion to duty as I saw it, I was still painfully sensitive to the opinion of others. An old friend of mother's came to visit us, and was shocked at my independence. She strove to rebuke and improve my conduct, and I cried like a child being scolded—but did not change.

So far there was a good record of health, strength, cheerfulness and patience, and constant industry. Within, the splendid sense of power, the high though indefinite purpose, the absolute consecration to coming service. Regarding consequences I had no illusions. No one who sets out to make the world better should expect people to enjoy it, all history shows what happens to would-be improvers.

In ancient times such persons were promptly killed,

I noticed; later they were persecuted, ostracized. What I had to expect was mostly misunderstanding, and the ceaseless opposition of that old enemy, General Apathy. Emerson's remark, "Misunderstood! It is a right fool's word!" pleased me much. So I looked ahead to a steady lifetime of social study and service, with no reward whatever, on the theory that one should face life giving all and asking nothing.

One day in the gymnasium during a rest period, the girls were discussing what age they would rather be, for life. Most of them agreed on eighteen, which many of them were at the time. When they asked me I said fifty. They didn't believe it. *"Why?"* they demanded. "Because," I explained, "when I'm fifty, people will respect my opinions if they are ever going to, and I shall not be too old to work."

This I remembered when starting the *Forerunner* at fifty.

My philosophy was efficacious to a degree. One very hot night in the boarding-house at Ogunquit, sleeping was difficult. The mattress was stuffed with corn-leaves, but some of the cobs or stalks seemed to be included, and stuck out determinedly. There were mosquitoes many and persistent, and I was freshly sunburned—the real burn that smarts.

These conditions I calmly considered one by one. "Heat? Cannot be helped, window and door both open. Mosquitoes? Can't avoid them, nothing to shut them out, nothing to use as a deterrent. Sunburn? Nothing to put on that either, at present. The bed? It's pretty bad, but there's no choice except the floor, and that would be worse." So, having dismissed each difficulty as irremediable at the time, I went to sleep.

A far better test of my boasted powers of ratiocination came one night, in my lonely room on the top floor.

Mrs. Springer was away. Aunt Caroline had become a boarder and the second floor was vacant. I was wakened suddenly, with that sharp sense of something wrong which is so unmistakable. I made sure I was awake, and listened carefully—yes, there was something moving under the bed. It was winter. I had no desire to get up, unnecessarily, in that utterly cold room.

Here, thought I, is a good chance to use my mind, to find out what is under my bed by ratiocination. It is not wind, there is no wind. It stirs, pushes about stealthily, therefore it is alive. Being alive it is either human or some other animal. If human it is either man, woman or child. Women and children do not conceal themselves under beds in strange houses, nor do men without reason, such as robbery, murder or worse. There is nothing in this house to tempt robbers, no reason for murder—and besides, I listened carefully, if it were a man he would either keep still or come out. That quite satisfied me, it was inconceivable that any man should lie there nosing about those bundles and do nothing else.

So I dismissed human beings and began on the others. If an animal it is either wild or tame. There are no wild animals in Providence, and no circuses in winter. Of tame animals the only ones capable of climbing to the third story to fuss around under my bed are dogs, cats, or rats. If it was a dog I should hear him scratch, snuffle, thump, breathe—no, it's not a dog. It's either a cat or a rat, and I don't care which. So I went to sleep again calmly, as sure as if I had seen the beast, and sure enough in the morning I found a stray cat in the vacant rooms below.

The only physical pain I knew in my youth was once an infected finger, and dentistry. When that hurt, hurt

horribly, I would think all round it, say to myself:
"Well, it hurts; that is a pain in my tooth, what of it?"
and sit quite still, fanning the dentist while he drove
the buzzer in.

In physical pain I am a partial anesthetic, things do
not hurt me as much as other people. Up to recent
years I could truly say that I had never had a headache, backache, earache or toothache—except in the
dentist chair. That hurt. But this physical insensitive-
ness was counterbalanced by a pitiful susceptibility to
mental pain, and of that I had plenty.

Young people are commonly unhappy at being "misunderstood," and alone, but this usual condition was
added to in my case by the wide range of my studies,
hopes and purposes, and the complete lack of understanding or sympathy in those about me. No one that
I knew had any interest in "the human race," their
interests were all for individuals, and as for plans for
improving social conditions—such ideas seemed utterly
absurd.

Long since I have learned to come down from my
high horse and take solid comfort with good folks
who ride different steeds, and do it better than I, but
in those days my horse was so tremendously high, and
I had struggled so hard to mount him, that I could
not easily get down. These verses, intensely felt,
give an accurate picture of "home comfort" in those
years:

In Duty Bound

In duty bound, a life hemmed in,
　　Whichever way the spirit turns to look;
No chance of breaking out, except by sin;
　　Not even room to shirk—
　　Simply to live, and work.

An obligation preimposed, unsought,
  Yet binding with the force of natural law;
The pressure of antagonistic thought;
    Aching within, each hour,
    A sense of wasting power.

A house with roof so darkly low
  The heavy rafters shut the sunlight out;
One cannot stand erect without a blow;
    Until the soul inside
    Cries for a grave—more wide.

A consciousness that if this thing endure,
  The common joys of life will dull the pain;
The high ideals of the grand and pure
    Die, as of course they must,
    Of long disuse and rust.

That is the worst. It takes supernal strength
  To hold the attitude that brings the pain;
And there are few indeed but stoop at length
    To something less than best,
    To find, in stooping, rest.

Nevertheless, good health, great hopes, and constant industry kept me content. For happiness I had my close friend Martha; that was perfect. I was used to bearing things, so tremendously upheld inside by the sense of power, of purpose, of big work before me, and by the triple-plated defense of my strong philosophy, that I used honestly to say I could not imagine the combination of circumstances that would *make* me unhappy.

CHAPTER VII

LOVE AND MARRIAGE

LOOKING back on my uncuddled childhood it seems to me a sad mistake of my heroic mother to withhold from me the petting I so craved, the sufficing comfort of maternal caresses. Denied that natural expression, my first memory of loving any one—not to mention the Polite Boy—was the pale and pious child in Hartford; the next was Hattie White, the next, and immeasurably the dearest, was Martha. Martha stayed. We were closely together, increasingly happy together, for four of those long years of girlhood. She was nearer and dearer than any one up to that time. This was love, but not sex.

That experience was in the Frog Prince affair, intense though remote, and never coming to anything at all. But while it lasted there was an unforgettable thrill in the mere sight of the "beloved object." Sex but not love.

With Martha I knew perfect happiness. We used to say to each other that we should never have to reproach ourselves with not realizing this joy while we had it; we did, thoroughly. We were not only extremely fond of each other, but we had fun together, deliciously. One summer while she was away we agreed to write letters describing not only things that happened, but things which didn't—and see if we could discriminate. Those were amazing letters. We wrote nonsense verses together in alternate lines, long ballads of adventure.

78

I have one yet, written on a roll of three-inch ribbon paper.

Our best-loved sport was The One Word Game. This is not only such a delicious amusement, but such an unfailing rest and restorative for a weary and worried mind, that it is worth describing. The whole procedure is for each in turn to contribute one word (only one, save for proper names which may be given in full), to an unfolding story which no one composes, but which is most astonishingly produced by the successive additions. Any word which follows in grammatical sequence will do, no matter how sharply it disagrees with what the previous speaker had in mind.

The game was taught me with no rules whatever, but I have made these three, from experience. First, you must not try to make the story go your way, with, "Now you must say" this, or "Why didn't you say" that; it must be allowed to unfold from the successive words, the whole charm is in the total unexpectedness. Second, it must be about persons. "Once there was a pig," or the like, does not interest. Third, it should be a simple descriptive tale, like a child's fairy story, about persons and what they wore, said and did. As a sample—

"Mr. Aminadab Hugus—entered—his—uncle's—church—for—fish." (A player may put a period to the sentence if he chooses and if his word ends it.) "Unfortunately—Mrs. Hugus—did— Now here the person who said 'did' had in mind 'did not like fish,' " but the next player says "washing." (period)

For hilarious young persons this is simply a means of amusement, but for a lifetime I have found it an unfailing source of relaxation, a complete and refreshing change of mind. It touches combinations impossible to any single thought-process, it is like massage to the brain, it is a "sure fire laugh" that does not cost three dollars a seat. Never could any individual mind conceive of the exquisite absurdities which occur from the interplay. Two intimate minds are best, but any number who can similarly relax will do.

Four years of satisfying happiness with Martha, then she married and moved away. In our perfect concord there was no Freudian taint, but peace of mind, understanding, comfort, deep affection—and I had no one else.

My Mother and her half-sister, with whom I lived, were unutterably remote—alien—and out of hearing. So were the other people I knew. "Why she's still your friend, isn't she?" they said. Of course she was—but she was gone. It was the keenest, the hardest, the most lasting pain I had yet known. There was no appreciation or sympathy anywhere.

I strove with it. "I wrote it out"—always a relief. I wrote "Grief is an emotion, it may be used as a spur to action—like anger, or love."

Also this, one of those I used to keep stuck in the edge of my looking-glass to see every day and gather strength from:

For Loneliness and Grief

If I live, (as live I do,) for others—if all my high desires for self-improvement are solely with a view to the elevation of the race—if my mission is to lead a self-sacrificing life and "give to him that asketh" as I go—to teach and guide, to love, protect and care for—then it behooves me to crush all personal sorrow and drop the whole ground of self-interest forever. Neither is this Quixotic or impossible. If I keep every physical law as far as I know, feed the mental life as I learn to more and more, and love every one as far as I can reach—why, it stands to reason that such a one will be cared for and made happy by mere reaction. It is and must be so. I thoroughly believe it. Strength will come, courage will come, yes, and peace and joy will follow, inevitably. Though my heart swell mountain-high it is only so much the higher thing to stand on. Strength! and Courage!

So I pushed on, working every minute of the day except for meals, and three hours in the evening mostly, and carrying this, to me so grievous pain, as best I could, finishing that year's diary thus:

A year of steady work. A quiet year and a hard one. A year of surprising growth. A year internally dedicated to discoveries and improvements. A year in which I knew the sweetness of a perfect friendship and have lost it forever. A year of marked advance in many ways, and with nothing conspicuous to regret. I am stronger, wiser and better than last year, and am fairly satisfied with the year's work. I have learned much of self-control and consideration for others; often think before I speak and can keep still on occasions. My memory begins to show the training it has had, I can get back what I want when I want it, pretty generally. Most of all I have learned what pain is, have learned the need of human sympathy by the unfilled want of it, and have gained the power to *give* it, which is worth while. This year I attained my majority—may I never lose it.

As to men: That unattainable Prince had lasted me for two years or so. Then I was very fond of the cousin who was so devotedly polite to me at first, and so rude afterward, so suddenly and unaccountably rude that I always felt he had been reasoned with by his family and sought to choke off my young affection by this sharp method. As I had not been in the least "in love" with him as with my tall actor, but was generally fond of him, this was something of a blow, though nothing compared to losing Martha later.

Meanwhile there were various youths in Providence who came and went harmlessly, only one being con-

spicuously attentive—and he was far from bright!
Those I met in Cambridge were vastly more attractive,
yet left small impression, and in my "home town" I
am puzzled by the diary's frequent mention of young
men. "Most devoted," "Walks home with me," and
so on—and by my utter forgetfulness of any of them.

Then, in January, 1882, I met Charles Walter Stetson, the painter.

He was quite the greatest man, near my own age,
that I had ever known. He stood alone, true to his
art, in that prosaic mercantile town, handicapped with
poverty, indifference and misunderstanding. His genius
was marked; although largely self-taught, his work
was already so remarkable for its jeweled color that a
dishonest dealer tried to suborn him to paint Diazes
for him—in vain.

In a very minor way I had been painting, drawing
and teaching the same for years, and was able in some
small degree to appreciate his splendid work, and
wholly to sympathize with his gallant determination.
In courage, in aspiration, in ideals, in bitter loneliness,
we were enough alike to be drawn together.

Very promptly he asked me to marry him. Very
promptly I declined. Then, reviewing the occurrence
with that cold philosophy of mine, I asked myself, "Is
it right so lightly to refuse what after all may be
the right thing to do?" This is a vivid commentary on
my strenuous youth. Between deprivation and denial
from outside, and intensive self-denial from within,
there was no natural response of inclination or desire,
no question of, "Do I love him?" only, "Is it right?"

So I took up the matter again, said that I had no
present wish to marry him, but that it was possible
that I might in time, and that if he so desired he might

come to see me for a year and we would find out—
which he was very willing to do.

Followed a time of what earlier novelists used to
call "conflicting emotions." There was the pleasure of
association with a noble soul, with one who read and
studied and cared for real things, of sharing high
thought and purpose, of sympathy in many common
deprivations and endurances. There was the natural
force of sex-attraction between two lonely young
people, the influence of propinquity.

Then, on my part, periods of bitter revulsion, of
desperate efforts to regain the dispassionate poise, the
balanced judgment I was used to. My mind was not
fully clear as to whether I should or should not marry.
On the one hand I knew it was normal and right in
general, and held that a woman should be able to have
marriage and motherhood, and do her work in the
world also. On the other, I felt strongly that for me
it was not right, that the nature of the life before me
forbade it, that I ought to forego the more intimate
personal happiness for complete devotion to my work.

Having lived so long on clear convictions, on
definite well-reasoned decisions, there was something
ignominious in feeling myself slip and waver in uncertainty. Once I demanded a year's complete separation, to recover clear judgment, but could not secure
it. It was a terrible two years for me, and must have
been wearing for him, but he held on. Then, at one
time when he had met a keen personal disappointment,
I agreed to marry him. After that, in spite of reactions
and misgivings, I kept my word, but the period of
courtship was by no means a happy one.

There are poems of this time which show deep affection, and high hopes, also doubt and uncertainty.

On the opening of the year of my wedding appears this cheerful inscription:

1883—1884. Midnight—Morning. With no pride, with little hope, with uncertain occasional happiness, with no glad energy and living power, with no faith or nearly none, but still, thank God! with firm belief in what is right and wrong, I begin the new year. Let me recognize fully that I do not look forward to happiness, that I have no decided hope of success. So long must I live. One does not die young who so desires it. Perhaps it was not meant for me to work as I intended. Perhaps I am not to be of use to others. I am weak. I anticipate a future of failure and suffering. Children sick and unhappy. Husband miserable because of my distress, and I—

I think sometimes that it may be the other way, bright and happy—but this comes oftenest, holds longest. But this life is marked for me. I will not withdraw, and let me at least learn to be uncomplaining and unselfish. Let me do my work and not fling my pain on others. Let me keep at least this ambition, to be good and a pleasure to *some* one, to some others, no matter what I feel myself.

More of this, and then:

And let me not forget to be grateful for what I have, some strength, some purpose, some design, some progress, some esteem, respect and affection. And some Love. Which I can neither see, feel nor believe in when the darkness comes. I mean this year to try hard for somewhat of my former force and courage. As I remember it was got by practice.

This was evidently a very black hour. Succeeding days show more cheer and vigor, as March 24th, "Then gym. enjoying it *intensely* and doing more than usual. Carried a girl on *one arm* and hip—easily!"

We were married in May, 1884. . . .

Mr. Stetson's father, a Baptist minister, married us, in the house on the corner of Manning and Ives Streets, and then, with some last things to carry, we walked down to Wayland Avenue, where our three rooms awaited us. We had the whole second floor, big corner rooms every one, and the young artist had made it beautiful.

"Do it just as you choose," I told him. "I have no tastes and no desires. I shall like whatever you do."

The house stood on a high bank, looking southward over the chimneys of a few small buildings below to the broad basin of the Seekonk, ringed at night with golden lights. White ducks drifted like magnolia petals along the still margins. Opposite us was a grove of tall pines—a pleasant place to walk and sit.

The housework for two in this tiny place was nothing to me, then some time I definitely devoted to deliberately breaking the regular habits of doing things on set days and hours in which I had been trained, repudiating the rigid New England schedule. Orderly habits of working are good, and later I established my own, but the immutable submission of the dutiful housewives I know, bred rebellion in me.

I determined to learn to cook. "I won't have a cook-book in the house," quoth I. "I'm going to learn how." Knowing already the ordinary needful dishes, I began to alter the relative amount of ingredients, in small degree, and note the results, as of a little more sugar or less flour. Soon I learned the reaction of the different materials, and then was able to compose. The common method of merely following recipes is like studying music by learning a collection of tunes.

One of the most pleasing compliments of later years was that of a New York club man who told me I could command a high salary as chef in his club. During the period of experimentation no harm was done, I had enough practical knowledge to keep things edible, they merely varied from time to time, as indeed "home-cooking" frequently does.

Two instances were funny, however. Our first pair of chickens were in the oven. Walter went out to see how they were getting along. He sat down on the floor in front of the stove and laughed loud and long. I presently joined him in the position and the laughter. There lay the poor dears, their legs sticking out at casual angles, simply wreathed in stiff ringlets of slowly exuding stuffing, crisping as it oozed. I had made that stuffing too soft, the stitches wherewith it was sewed in too wide, the oven was too slow, and I had not tied their legs. But they tasted just as good.

The other experiment we gave to the neighbor's children; it was harmless but peculiar. Mother used to make a plain cake flavored with almond, of which I was fond. I made one, and in the course of my researches I put in more flour than was usual. The result was a meritorious cake, a solid cake of sterling character, a cake which would have gone well among lumbermen in winter, or lost in the woods with no other food. It lingered, that cake, growing no softer.

Then said I, "I will make 'trifle' of this cake." One might as well have undertaken to make a ballet dancer of a Swedish servant girl. "First it must be soaked in wine," I mused. I had no wine, and was a total abstainer at that. "Wine is a fruit juice," quoth I, and having no fruit at hand but apples and lemons, I made a thin apple-sauce, seasoned as usual with nutmeg, and vivified with a little lemon juice. In this I soaked the slices of cake, and up to that time the dish was good. I ate a piece and enjoyed it. Then came the soft custard, and never did I make a smoother one, flavoring it as I liked best, with cinnamon.

This in a tall glass dish, the piled slices of softened and enriched cake, the perfect custard flowing over all. My husband gazed upon it with a happy smile, and put some of the almond-apple-lemon-nutmeg-cinnamon mixture into his mouth. As many expressions chased across his countenance as were the tastes encountered, and with amazing discernment he unraveled the combination and named them all. It was a noble confection, but too composite, and served as a wholly sufficient lesson in the art of flavoring.

We were really very happy together. There was nothing to prevent it but that increasing depression of mine. My diary is full of thankfulness for happiness and prayers for deserving it, full of Walter's constant kindness and helpfulness in the work when I was not well—the not-wellness coming oftener and oftener.

The record dwells on delectable meals in full enumeration, as if I was a school-boy. As a note on current prices this: "Dinner vilely expensive, chops, six little chops, .50 cts.!" "Walter home about five. Brings me flowers. Dear boy!" "Walter gets most of the breakfast." "Amuse ourselves in the evenings with funny drawings." These were works of art of an unusual nature, a head and body to the waist being drawn by one of us and the paper folded back at the waistline leaving the sides indicated; and then the other finished the legs, not knowing in the least what the other part was like. The results are surprising.

I think Walter was happy. A most successful exhibition in Boston had established him more favorably and enabled him to meet domestic expenses; and an order for a set of large etchings was added.

A lover more tender, a husband more devoted,

woman could not ask. He helped in the housework more and more as my strength began to fail, for something was going wrong from the first. The steady cheerfulness, the strong, tireless spirit sank away. A sort of gray fog drifted across my mind, a cloud that grew and darkened.

"Feel sick and remain so all day." "Walter stays home and does everything for me." "Walter gets breakfast." October 10th: "I have coffee in bed mornings while Walter briskly makes fires and gets breakfast." "O dear! That I should come to this!" By October 13th the diary stops altogether, until January 1, 1885. "My journal has been long neglected by reason of ill-health. This day has not been a successful one as I was sicker than for some weeks. Walter also was not very well, and stayed at home, principally on my account. He has worked for me and for us both, waited on me in every tenderest way, played to me, read to me, done all for me as he always does. God be thanked for my husband."

February 16th: "A well-nigh sleepless night. Hot, cold, hot, restless, nervous, hysterical. Walter is love and patience personified, gets up over and over, gets me warm wintergreen, bromide, hot foot-bath, more bromide—all to no purpose."

Then, with impressive inscription: "March 23rd, 1885. This day, at about five minutes to nine in the morning, was born my child, Katharine."

> Brief ecstasy. Long pain.
> Then years of joy again.

Motherhood means giving. . . .

We had attributed all my increasing weakness and depression to pregnancy, and looked forward to prompt recovery now. All was normal and ordinary enough, but I was already plunged into an extreme of nervous exhaustion which no one observed or understood in the least. Of all angelic babies that darling was the best, a heavenly baby. My nurse, Maria Pease of Boston, was a joy while she lasted, and remained a lifelong friend. But after her month was up and I was left alone with the child I broke so fast that we sent for my mother, who had been visiting Thomas in Utah, and that baby-worshiping grandmother came to take care of the darling, I being incapable of doing that—or anything else, a mental wreck.

Presently we moved to a better house, on Humboldt Avenue near by, and a German servant girl of unparalleled virtues was installed. Here was a charming home; a loving and devoted husband; an exquisite baby, healthy, intelligent and good; a highly competent mother to run things; a wholly satisfactory servant— and I lay all day on the lounge and cried.

CHAPTER VIII

THE BREAKDOWN

In those days a new disease had dawned on the medical horizon. It was called "nervous prostration." No one knew much about it, and there were many who openly scoffed, saying it was only a new name for laziness. To be recognizably ill one must be confined to one's bed, and preferably in pain.

That a heretofore markedly vigorous young woman, with every comfort about her, should collapse in this lamentable manner was inexplicable. "You should use your will," said earnest friends. I had used it, hard and long, perhaps too hard and too long; at any rate it wouldn't work now.

"Force some happiness into your life," said one sympathizer. "Take an agreeable book to bed with you, occupy your mind with pleasant things." She did not realize that I was unable to read, and that my mind was exclusively occupied with unpleasant things. This disorder involved a growing melancholia, and that, as those know who have tasted it, consists of every painful mental sensation, shame, fear, remorse, a blind oppressive confusion, utter weakness, a steady brainache that fills the conscious mind with crowding images of distress.

The misery is doubtless as physical as a toothache, but a brain, of its own nature, gropes for reasons for its misery. Feeling the sensation fear, the mind suggests every possible calamity; the sensation shame—

remorse—and one remembers every mistake and misdeeds of a lifetime, and grovels to the earth in abasement.

"If you would get up and do something you would feel better," said my mother. I rose drearily, and essayed to brush up the floor a little, with a dustpan and small whiskbroom, but soon dropped those implements exhausted, and wept again in helpless shame.

I, the ceaselessly industrious, could do no work of any kind. I was so weak that the knife and fork sank from my hands—too tired to eat. I could not read nor write nor paint nor sew nor talk nor listen to talking, nor anything. I lay on that lounge and wept all day. The tears ran down into my ears on either side. I went to bed crying, woke in the night crying, sat on the edge of the bed in the morning and cried—from sheer continuous pain. Not physical, the doctors examined me and found nothing the matter.

The only physical pain I ever knew, besides dentistry and one sore finger, was having the baby, and I would rather have had a baby every week than suffer as I suffered in my mind. A constant dragging weariness miles below zero. Absolute incapacity. Absolute misery. To the spirit it was as if one were an armless, legless, eyeless voiceless cripple. Prominent among the tumbling suggestions of a suffering brain was the thought, "You did it yourself! You did it yourself! You had health and strength and hope and glorious work before you—and you threw it all away. You were called to serve humanity, and you cannot serve yourself. No good as a wife, no good as a mother, no good at anything. And you did it yourself!" . . .

The baby? I nursed her for five months. I would hold her close—that lovely child!—and instead of love and happiness, feel only pain. The tears ran down on my breast....Nothing was more utterly bitter than this, that even motherhood brought no joy.

The doctor said I must wean her, and go away, for a change. So she was duly weaned and throve finely on Mellins' Food, drinking eagerly from the cup—no bottle needed. With mother there and the excellent maid I was free to go.

Those always kind friends, the Channings, had gone to Pasadena to live, and invited me to spend the winter with them. Feeble and hopeless I set forth, armed with tonics and sedatives, to cross the continent. From the moment the wheels began to turn, the train to move, I felt better. A visit to my brother in Utah broke the journey.

He had gone west as a boy of nineteen, working as a surveyor in Nevada, and later, finding Utah quite a heaven after Nevada, had settled in Ogden and married there. At one time he was City Engineer. His wife knew of my coming, but it was to be a surprise to my brother, and succeeded.

He came to the door in his shirt-sleeves, as was the local custom, holding a lamp in his hand. There stood the sister he had not seen in eight years, calmly smiling.

"Good evening," said I with equanimity. This he repeated, nodding his head fatuously, "Good evening! Good evening! Good evening!" It was a complete success.

As I still bore a grudge for the teasing which had embittered my childish years, I enjoyed this little joke, already feeling so much better that I could enjoy. There was another little joke, too. He took me to ride in that vast, shining, mile-high valley, and pointing to some sharply defined little hills which looked about five or ten miles away, asked me how far I thought they were. But I had read stories of that dry, deceiving air, and solemnly replied, "Three hundred miles." They were forty, but that didn't sound like much.

Society in Ogden at that time was not exacting; the leading lady, I was told, was the wife of a railroad conductor. We went to a species of ball in a hotel. The bedrooms were all occupied by sleeping babies, as described in *The Virginian.* Among the dancers there was pointed out to me a man who had killed somebody— no one seemed to hold it against him; and another who had been scalped three times—the white patches were visible among the hair. I had thought scalping a more exhaustive process. At that rate a disingenuous savage could make three triumphant exhibits from one victim. As I did not dance we had a game of whist, and I was somewhat less than pleased to see each of the gentlemen playing bring a large cuspidor and set it by his side. They needed them.

From Utah to San Francisco—on which trip I first met the San Francisco flea. Long since he has been largely overcome, but then was what the newspapers call "a force to be reckoned with"—not California newspapers, of course.

My father was then at the head of the San Francisco Public Library. He met me on the Oakland side, and took me across to a room he had engaged for me for a day or two. Here he solemnly called on me, as would any acquaintance, and went with me across the ferry again when I started south.

"If you ever come to Providence again I hope you will come to see me," said I politely, as we parted, to which he courteously replied, "Thank you. I will bear your invitation in mind."

So down the great inland plain of California, over the Mojave Desert, and to heaven.

Pasadena was then but little changed from the sheep-ranch it used to be. The Channings had bought a beautiful place by the little reservoir at the corner of Walnut Street and Orange Avenue. Already their year-old trees were shooting up unbelievably, their flowers a glory.

The Arroyo Seco was then wild and clean, its steep banks a tangle of loveliness. About opposite us a point ran out where stood a huge twin live oak, still to be seen, but not to be reached by strangers. There was no house by them then, callas bloomed by the hydrant, and sweet alyssum ran wild in the grass.

Never before had my passion for beauty been satisfied. This place did not seem like earth, it was paradise. Kind and congenial friends, pleasant society, amusement, out-door sports, the blessed mountains, the long, unbroken sweep of the valley, with snow-peaks at the far eastern end—with such surroundings I recovered so fast, to outward appearance at least, that I was taken for a vigorous young girl. Hope came back, love came back, I was eager to get home to husband and child, life was bright again.

The return trip was made a little sooner than I had intended because of a railroad war of unparalleled violence which drove prices down unbelievably. It seemed foolish not to take advantage of it, and I bought my ticket from Los Angeles to Chicago, standard, for $5.00. If I had waited for a few days more it could have been bought for $1. The eastern end was unchanged, twenty dollars from Chicago to Boston, but that cut-throat competition was all over the western roads, the sleepers had every berth filled, often two in each. So many traveled that it was said the roads made quite as much money as usual.

Leaving California in March, in the warm rush of

its rich spring, I found snow in Denver, and from then on hardly saw the sun for a fortnight. I reached home with a heavy bronchial cold, which hung on long, the dark fog rose again in my mind, the miserable weakness—within a month I was as low as before leaving. . . .

This was a worse horror than before, for now I saw the stark fact—that I was well while away and sick while at home—a heartening prospect! Soon ensued the same utter prostration, the unbearable inner misery, the ceaseless tears. A new tonic had been invented, Essence of Oats, which was given me, and did some good for a time. I pulled up enough to do a little painting that fall, but soon slipped down again and stayed down. An old friend of my mother's, dear Mrs. Diman, was so grieved at this condition that she gave me a hundred dollars and urged me to go away somewhere and get cured.

At that time the greatest nerve specialist in the country was Dr. S. W. Mitchell of Philadelphia. Through the kindness of a friend of Mr. Stetson's living in that city, I went to him and took "the rest cure"; went with the utmost confidence, prefacing the visit with a long letter giving "the history of the case" in a way a modern psychologist would have appreciated. Dr. Mitchell only thought it proved self-conceit. He had a prejudice against the Beechers. "I've had two women of your blood here already," he told me scornfully. This eminent physician was well versed in two kinds of nervous prostration; that of the business man exhausted from too much work, and the society woman exhausted from too much play. The kind I had was evidently beyond him. But he did reassure me on one point—there was no dementia, he said, only hysteria.

I was put to bed and kept there. I was fed, bathed, rubbed, and responded with the vigorous body of twenty-six. As far as he could see there was nothing the matter with me, so after a month of this agreeable treatment he sent me home, with this prescription:

"Live as domestic a life as possible. Have your child with you all the time." (Be it remarked that if I did but dress the baby it left me shaking and crying—certainly far from a healthy companionship for her, to say nothing of the effect on me.) "Lie down an hour after each meal. Have but two hours' intellectual life a day. And never touch pen, brush or pencil as long as you live."

I went home, followed those directions rigidly for months, and came perilously near to losing my mind. The mental agony grew so unbearable that I would sit blankly moving my head from side to side—to get out from under the pain. Not physical pain, not the least "headache" even, just mental torment, and so heavy in its nightmare gloom that it seemed real enough to dodge.

I made a rag baby, hung it on a doorknob and played with it. I would crawl into remote closets and under beds—to hide from the grinding pressure of that profound distress. . . .

Finally, in the fall of '87, in a moment of clear vision, we agreed to separate, to get a divorce. There was no quarrel, no blame for either one, never an unkind word between us, unbroken mutual affection—but it seemed plain that if I went crazy it would do my husband no good, and be a deadly injury to my child.

What this meant to the young artist, the devoted husband, the loving father, was so bitter a grief and loss that nothing would have justified breaking the marriage save this worse loss which threatened. It was not a choice between going and staying, but between going, sane, and staying, insane. If I had been of the slightest use to him or to the child, I would have "stuck it," as the English say. But this progressive weakening of the mind made a horror unnecessary to face; better for that dear child to have separated parents than a lunatic mother.

We had been married four years and more. This miserable condition of mind, this darkness, feebleness and gloom, had begun in those difficult years of courtship, had grown rapidly worse after marriage, and was now threatening utter loss; whereas I had repeated proof that the moment I left home I began to recover. It seemed right to give up a mistaken marriage.

Our mistake was mutual. If I had been stronger and wiser I should never have been persuaded into it. Our suffering was mutual too, his unbroken devotion, his manifold cares and labors in tending a sick wife, his adoring pride in the best of babies, all coming to naught, ending in utter failure—we sympathized with each other but faced a bitter necessity. The separation must come as soon as possible, the divorce must wait for conditions.

If this decision could have been reached sooner it would have been much better for me, the lasting mental injury would have been less. Such recovery as I have made in forty years, and the work accomplished, seem to show that the fear of insanity was not fulfilled, but the effects of nerve bankruptcy remain to this day. So much of my many failures, of misplay and misunderstanding and "queerness" is due to this lasting weakness, and kind friends so unfailingly refuse to allow for it, to believe it, that I am now going to some length in stating the case.

That part of the ruin was due to the conditions of

childhood I do not doubt, and part to the rigid stoicism and constant effort in character-building of my youth; I was "over-trained," had wasted my substance in riotous—virtues. But that the immediate and continuing cause was mismarriage is proved by the instant rebound when I left home and as instant relapse on returning.

After I was finally free, in 1890, wreck though I was, there was a surprising output of work, some of my best. I think that if I could have had a period of care and rest then, I might have made full recovery. But the ensuing four years in California were the hardest of my life. The result has been a lasting loss of power, total in some directions, partial in others; the necessity for a laboriously acquired laziness foreign to both temperament and conviction, a crippled life.

But since my public activities do not show weakness, nor my writings, and since brain and nerve disorder is not visible, short of lunacy or literal "prostration," this lifetime of limitation and wretchedness, when I mention it, is flatly disbelieved. When I am forced to refuse invitations, to back out of work that seems easy, to own that I cannot read a heavy book, apologetically alleging this weakness of mind, friends gibber amiably, "I wish I had your mind!" I wish they had, for a while, as a punishment for doubting my word. What confuses them is the visible work I have been able to accomplish. They see activity, achievement, they do not see blank months of idleness; nor can they see what the work would have been if the powerful mind I had to begin with had not broken at twenty-four.

A brain may lose some faculties and keep others; it may be potent for a little while and impotent the rest of the time. Moreover, the work I have done has never been "work" in the sense of consciously applied effort. To write was always as easy to me as to talk.

Even my verse, such as it is, flows as smoothly as a letter, is easier in fact. Perhaps the difficulty of answering letters will serve as an illustration of the weakness of mind so jocosely denied by would-be complimenters.

Here are a handful of letters—I dread to read them, especially if they are long—I pass them over to my husband—ask him to give me only those I must answer personally. These pile up and accumulate while I wait for a day when I feel able to attack them. A secretary does not help in the least, it is not the manual labor of writing which exhausts me, it is the effort to understand the letter, and make intelligent reply. I answer one, two, the next is harder, three—increasingly foggy, four—it's no use, I read it in vain, *I don't know what it says.* Literally, I can no longer understand what I read, and have to stop, with my mind like a piece of boiled spinach.

Reading is a simple art, common to most of us. As a child I read eagerly, greedily; as a girl I read steadily, with warm interest, in connected scientific study. No book seemed difficult. One of my Harvard boy friends told me no girl could read Clifford and understand him. Of course I got Clifford at once—and found him clear and easy enough.

After the débâcle I could read nothing—instant exhaustion preventing. As years passed there was some gain in this line; if a story was short and interesting and I was feeling pretty well I could read a little while. Once when well over forty I made a test, taking a simple book on a subject I was interested in—Lucy Salmon on the servant question. I read for half an hour with ease; the next half-hour was harder, but I kept on. At the end of the third I could not understand a word of it.

That surely is a plain instance of what I mean when

I say my mind is weak. It is precisely that, weak. It cannot hold attention, cannot study, cannot listen long to anything, is always backing out of things because it is tired. A library, which was once to me as a confectioner's shop to a child, became an appalling weariness just to look at.

This does not involve loss of clear perception, lack of logic, failure to think straight when able to think at all. The natural faculties are there, as my books and lectures show. But there remains this humiliating weakness, and if I try to drive, to compel effort, the resulting exhaustion is pitiful.

To step so suddenly from proud strength to contemptible feebleness, from cheerful stoicism to a whimpering avoidance of any strain or irritation for fear of the collapse ensuing, is not pleasant, at twenty-four. To spend forty years and more in the patient effort of learning how to carry such infirmity so as to accomplish something in spite of it is a wearing process, full of mortification and deprivation. To lose books out of one's life, certainly more than ninety per cent of one's normal reading capacity, is no light misfortune.

"But you write books!" Yes, I have written enough to make a set of twenty-five, including volumes of stories, plays, verse, and miscellany; besides no end of stuff not good enough to keep. But this was all the natural expression of thought, except in the stories, which called for composition and were more difficult—especially the novels, which are poor. The power of expression remained, fortunately for me, and the faculty of inner perception, of seeing the relation of facts and their consequences.

I am not skilled in mental disorders, and cannot say what it was which paralyzed previous capacities so extensively, while leaving some in working order. Perhaps another instance will be indicative. For nearly all these broken years I could not look down an index. To do this one must form the matrix of a thought or word and look down the list until it fits. I could not hold that matrix at all, could not remember what I was looking for. To this day I'd rather turn the pages than look at the index.

Worst of all was the rapid collapse of my so laboriously built-up hand-made character. Eight years of honest conscientious nobly-purposed effort lost, with the will power that made it. The bitterness of that shame will not bear reviving even now.

All progress in definite study stopped completely. Even so light a subject as a language I have tried in vain—and I meant to learn so many! Lucky for me that the foundation laid in those years of selected study was broad and sound; and lucky again that with such a background, what I have been able to gather since has fitted in reliably.

In periods of special exhaustion, and those first years which should have meant recovery were such as to involve endless exhaustion, this feeble-mindedness often meant an almost infantile irresponsibility in what I said. At one of those times, in 1891, when I was so far below zero that I should have been in a sanitarium, but instead was obliged to meet people, there bustled up a brisk young woman to greet me. She told me her name, and added, perhaps noticing my empty eyes, "You don't remember me, do you!"

I looked at her and groped slowly about in that flaccid vacant brain of mine for some association. One memory arose, one picture of where I had seen her and with whom, but no saving grace of politeness, of common decency, of any consideration for her feelings. I spoke like a four-year-old child, because I thought of it and thought of nothing else—"Why yes, I remember you. I don't like your mother." It was true enough, but never in the world would I have said such a thing if I had been "all there."

There have been other offenses. My forgetfulness of people, so cruel a return for kindness; an absent-mindedness often working harm; many a broken engagement; unanswered letters and neglected invitations; much, very much of repeated failure of many kinds is due wholly to that continuing weakness of mind.

The word "exhaustion" is a loose term, carrying to most minds merely the idea of being tired, of which we all know something. There is a physical weariness when it "feels good to sit down"; the first two weeks of gymnasium work used to bring that lovely feeling.

Exhaustion of wilted nerves is quite another matter. There is no "appetite" in the mind, no interest in anything. To see, to hear, to think, to remember, to do anything, is incredible effort, as if trying to rise and walk under a prostrate circus tent, or wade in glue. It brings a heavy darkness, every idea presenting itself as a misfortune; an irritable unease which finds no rest, and an incapacity of decision which is fairly laughable.

For all the years in which I have had to pack a suit-case and start on a trip, that packing is dreaded; and often finds me at midnight, after several hours' attempt, holding up some article and looking at it in despair, utterly unable to make up my mind whether to take it or not. In one of the worst times, in 1896, I stood on a street corner for fifteen minutes, trying in vain to decide whether or not to take the car home.

As to the work accomplished in spite of all this. The lecturing is a perfectly natural expression of as natural clear thinking. It never has been felt as an effort, save when the audience was dull or combative. Yet at that I can only do so much of it; in regular Chautauqua work, for instance, I'm a failure.

The writing similarly is easy and swift expression, running at the rate of about a thousand words an hour for three hours—then it stops, no use trying to squeeze out any more. Any attempt at forced work stops everything for days. At that ordinary output the work I have accomplished would have required far less time, had I kept the natural power of my mind. All the writing, in easy five-day weeks, between four and five years; all the lectures, a thousand or more, with necessary traveling, another five years. All other work, as organizing, helping in club-work, every possible activity I can remember, including dressmaking and cooking and gardening, might be stretched to fill another five. There are fifteen years accounted for, out of, to date, forty-two.

That leaves twenty-seven years, a little lifetime in itself, taken out, between twenty-four and sixty-six, which I have lost. Twenty-seven adult years, in which, with my original strength of mind, the output of work could have been almost trebled. Moreover, this lifetime lost has not been spent in resting. It was always a time of extreme distress, shame, discouragement, misery.

Is a loss like this, suffering like this, to be met with light laughter and compliments? To be waved aside as if I were imagining it? It is true that the persistence of a well-trained physique is confusing to the average observer. A sympathetic lady once remarked, "Yes, it is a sad thing to see a strong mind in a weak body." Whereat I promptly picked her up and carried her around the room. "Please understand," said I, "that what ails me is a weak mind in a strong body."

But she didn't understand, they never do. Only those near enough to watch the long, blank months of idleness, the endless hours of driveling solitaire, the black empty days and staring nights, know.

An orthodox visible disease that sends one to bed, as scarlet fever or mumps, is met by prompt sympathy. A broken arm, a sprained ankle, any physical mutilation, is a recognized misfortune. But the humiliating loss of a large part of one's brain power, of more than half one's working life, accompanied with deep misery and anguish of mind—this when complained of is met with amiable laughter and flat disbelief.

What is the psychology of it? Do these friends think it is more polite to doubt my word than to admit any discredit to my brain? Do they think I have been under some delusion as to all those years of weakness and suffering, or that I am pretending something in order to elicit undeserved commiseration? Or do they not think at all?

I try to describe this long limitation, hoping that with such power as is now mine, and such use of language as is within that power, this will convince any one who cares about it that this "Living" of mine had been done under a heavy handicap....

That summer of 1887 was so dreadful, as I have said, that it drove me to the final decision that our marriage must end. Once the decision was made I breathed a little easier, there was a remote glimmer of hope. But we must wait till arrangements could be made, proper provision for the child, and so on.

All that winter Grace Channing kept my spirits up with her letters, with talk and plans for work, and in the summer of '88 she came east, and we spent some months together in Bristol, Rhode Island. There we wrote a play, in collaboration, and there gathered background for later work; and I revived with such companionship and interest. We came back to the city September 1st. She was to return to Pasadena on October 8th, and I planned to go with her.

For possible assets, there was my quarter interest in the old place in Hartford, still undivided, and half of which must be returned to my brother, who had earlier borrowed on his quarter for family use. With this for my one resource and a month to work in I promptly engaged carpenters to make the crates and boxes for such furniture as I meant to take.

"How can you engage them when you have no money?" asked Walter.

"I shall get the money by selling my property."

"How do you know you can?"

"I shall have to, to pay the carpenters."

And I did. Good Rowland Hazard II bought it for two thousand dollars, and I'm sure he got fully that when the place was sold, later. There were debts to pay, clothes to be made, the men to pay—all the work of breaking up housekeeping and packing for the journey.

Our pretty little home was dismantled. Mother was to go back to my brother in Utah. Mr. Stetson went to live in his studio. There was an elderly dressmaker well known to us, who had a desire to see California. She undertook to go with me, help with little Katharine and otherwise, and pay her own way back, if I furnished her fare going.

So I set forth on October 8th, with Katharine, Grace, this inadequate dressmaker, a large lunch-basket, my tickets, and all my remaining money in my pocket—ten dollars.

"What will you do when you get there?" asked anxious friends.

"I shall earn my own living."

"How do you know you can?"

"I shall have to when I get there."

CHAPTER IX

PASADENA

WITH Pasadena begins my professional "living." Before that there was no assurance of serious work. To California, in its natural features, I owe much. Its calm sublimity of contour, richness of color, profusion of flowers, fruit and foliage, and the steady peace of its climate were meat and drink to me.

Dr. Channing, always kind, had engaged for my coming a small cottage near his place, on the corner of Orange Grove Avenue and Arroyo Drive, right opposite "Carmelita," then the home of Dr. and Mrs. Carr, now a park. To-day that corner lot is worth a fortune. In 1888 I rented that little wood-and-paper four-room house for $10.00 a month.

It stood in a neglected grove of orange trees rich with fragrant blossoms, roses ran over the roof, tall oleanders stood pink against the sky. There was a lemon verbena in the border by the front path; one day I broke off a new shoot to give a visitor from the east—it was six feet long. When the Channings gave roses to tourist friends, they brought them in a trunk tray.

Everywhere there was beauty, and the nerve-rest of steady windless weather. Living was cheap in all local supplies. A man came to the door one day, selling white grapes from a wagon-load. These seemed to me a luxury, but I said I'd take ten cents' worth if he'd give me that. He did, about a peck. The "vegetable

Chinaman" came often, with his dainty bundles of green things tied with long grass. For ten cents I could buy a rambling collop they called a mutton chop, big enough to make two meals for an invalid woman and a small child.

Long, long hours in a hammock under the roses. Occasional times when I could write. I felt like a drowned thing, drifting along under water and sometimes bobbing to the surface.

At first my tiny house was encumbered and my nerves wrung by the incubus I brought from Providence as "mother's helper." She had been a fairly capable dressmaker, in a dull, slow way, taking a week to make a dress. That was not so extreme a time as it looks now, one day for cutting out—the skirt with its lining and facing; the overskirt, to be elaborately draped; the "five-seamed-basque" with its careful fitting, and all the binding and boning, buttons and buttonholes which went to make a dress in those days. But now she proved in all ways useless.

With the child—and a more amenable darling never was, with intelligent treatment—she failed utterly. She could not cook, she would not sweep nor dust nor wash dishes—said it coarsened her hands! Her density was such that any direction had to be given with a slow explicitness suitable to the under-witted. When unpacking crates and arranging furniture I asked this unpromising Irish woman, picking my words with care, "Have you seen a long wooden shelf with iron brackets?" She answered, "Do you mean a small marble slab?" This she could not have seen, as I did not own such a thing.

Summing up the wide variety of things she would not do, I finally told her I would ask but one service— that she mend and put away the clean clothes. And that moron would roll up and put in the drawer un-mended hose! She stayed on, in the face of clearest suggestions of departure, until one day when these became direct and urgent requests with directions about trains, she burst into tears and quaveringly protested: "I do believe you are trying to get rid of me!" I was.

Then I had a boarder for a while, an anachronism. She was the daughter of a country clergyman of the old school, brought up on Addison and Dr. Johnson. Her ideal of social ecstasy was Conversation with the largest of C's. . . . She had it too, at the Channings.

By Christmas Mr. Stetson joined me, hoping that the change might have so bettered my condition that we might even yet reconsider; but it was no use, a dragging year followed, and in January, 1890, he finally left me, called suddenly to the bedside of his dying mother. This was the definite open separation, following the decision of the fall of 1887.

As the mutual agreement of two rational adults who have found by experience that they cannot live together is not "ground for divorce" as it should be, but is termed "collusion" and prevents it; as my wrecked health could not be traced to any fault of a devoted husband; and as neither of us would lie; it was neces-sary to conform to some legal requirement as a "cause." Desertion and non-support was agreed upon, and after a year of this I brought suit.

The lawyer I went to was a courteous gentleman, and made his inquiries with every consideration for my feelings. I found that "failure to provide" was nugated by the California law of community property; whatever either party earned belonged to both, so if I lived on my own earnings half the sum was still con-tributed by the absent one. As to desertion—"Does your husband write to you?" "Yes." "About how often?" "Two or three times a week." And the case was off.

The more immediate problem was how to provide, even in that land of low prices, for self and child. I had to start with a present of a hundred dollars, highly appreciated. For the rest I depended on teaching and writing, with the preliminary necessity of getting strong enough to do any steady work.

The utter failure and loss of my marriage was bitter enough, but compensated by the blessed child; the loss of health was worse, the weakness, the dark, feeble mind. But my religion remained, and my social philosophy, that perception of the organic unity of the group which so dwarfs all individual pain. When able to think clearly I faced the situation thus:

"Thirty years old. Made a wrong marriage—lots of people do. Am heavily damaged, but not dead. May live a long time. It is intellectually conceivable that I may recover strength enough to do some part of my work. I will assume this to be true, and act on it." And I did.

One of the Grand Old Women of California, Mrs. Caroline B. Severance, was so impressed by my sad case, that she wrote a pathetic letter about my lack of any special capacity to earn my bread, to my great-aunt, Isabella Beecher Hooker, who forwarded it to Uncle Edward Everett Hale, who referred it to Mr. Stetson, who sent it to me.

This letter I never mentioned to the dear old lady, who was afterward deeply impressed by my achievements and remained a warm friend as long as she lived, which was to be well over ninety. I went with her once, when she was ninety-three, to call on Mrs.

Rebecca Spring, who was ninety-nine—a memorable experience.

Shriveled and shrunken was the almost centenarian, her eyes mere buttonholes. I felt as helpless before her as a man with a baby. "What do you do with your time?" I ventured. In a high, thin, squeaky voice she replied, "I read nov-els. When I was young they would not let me read them, and now I read them all the time."

In that first year of freedom I wrote some thirty-three short articles, and twenty-three poems, besides ten more child-verses. Almost all the poems were given to various progressive papers, the one or two sold brought but two or three dollars. The same with the articles, though I did sell more of them, at prices like ten dollars or six dollars and seventy-five cents.

Except for two or three bits published before marriage, I had written in six years only a half-dozen or so, as "Nature's Answer," and "The Ship" while at home, and two good ones while away, "A Nevada Desert," and "The Rock and the Sea." That one was begun on Bass Rock, Narragansett Pier, and finished on the floor after I was at home again. Almost all of my descriptive poetry is about California. To this day, when in that lovely country, the verses come of themselves. The little "Nevada Desert" is good of its kind, though T. B. Aldrich sent it back from the *Atlantic,* with the remark that it needed the spot of color without which no picture was perfect. He had not seen Nevada.

With Grace I wrote plays. Our collaboration was fluently happy. One day, entering perfectly into the characters, we simply talked the dialogue, writing it down as fast as spoken. Not only did we write plays, we acted in them, most successfully. There was an admirable group of amateur actors in Pasadena. Some-what to my surprise I was usually cast in comic parts—being always willing to make a fool of myself.

One of the oddest jobs ever offered me was during Pasadena days. A new Opera House, fruit of a "boom" time, awaited final decoration, the selection of seat-coverings, curtains, etc. Grace and I went to see it, I said it was a pity Mr. Stetson was not there to finish the decoration, and lo! they asked me to do it. Never in my life had I done anything of the sort, but on that established precept of mine—"Always accept an op-portunity unless it's wrong"—I undertook this. It was fun too, selecting materials, winding ropes and cover-ing large wooden balls with plush like the hangings, and ornamenting the curtains to the box-entrances with impressive Turkish characters copied from a scarf I had—perhaps some Oriental visitor may have been astonished by what he read.

In this theater we gave plays for the benefit of local needs, and in one of them I was a too-affectionate old maid, dressed in a costume of elaborate absurdity. To this day I remember the ripple of laughter which greeted my entrance, as I tipped up the huge hoop-skirt to get through, and how that laughter continued all the time I was on. It is a fascinating art, acting. Once I was Lady Teazle and had to wear a corset—the only time in my life; and I almost fainted.

One of our plays was afterward almost accepted by Mr. Frohman; he meant to bring out in it young Mrs. Blaine, and had it all cast, with penciled names of Georgia Cayvan, Herbert Kelsey and other notables of the period. But, not knowing this we asked for it, and he sent it back.

The first real success, in that first year, was my poem

"Similar Cases," concerning which I received this unforgettable letter from William Dean Howells:

BOSTON, June 9th., 1890.

DEAR MADAM,

I have been wishing ever since I first read it—and I've read it many times with unfailing joy—to thank you for your poem in the April *Nationalist*. We have nothing since the Biglow Papers half so good for a good cause as "Similar Cases."

And just now I've read in *The Woman's Journal* your "Women of To-day." It is as good almost as the other, and dreadfully true.

Yours sincerely,

WM. DEAN HOWELLS.

That was a joy indeed. I rushed over to show Grace and the others. There was no man in the country whose good opinion I would rather have had. I felt like a real "author" at last.

There were classes of some kind among friendly ladies, there were pupils of sorts; I remember one group of small children to whom I taught drawing. Children draw by nature, as do savages, but these had had their powers paralyzed in school. They declared they could not draw, "Can't you draw *anything?*" "No, Ma'am." "Can't you draw a horse?" "No, Ma'am."

Then I proceeded to develop a system which works well. "Oh, come on, let's draw something. Can you draw a cow?" "No, Ma'am," "Do you know the difference between a horse and a cow?" They emphatically did and could mention some of the distinctions.

"Now we'll draw the horse, anyway, we'll make his body first, a horse's body is three-cornered isn't it?" Loud denial. "Well, it's square then—no? Is it kind of long like a barrel?" To this they agreed, and we all made a longish roundish body on our various pieces of brown paper. I used wrapping paper and very soft pencils, and we threw away our sketches—"You're not making pictures to take home," I told them, "you are just drawing, like dancing or singing."

Then the horse's head: "It's round like an apple, isn't it?" It wasn't, not at all, nor was it, as I further suggested, stuck tight to his body; nor did he have a neck like a swan, not in the least. Those youngsters knew perfectly well what a horse looked like, that his ears stood up and his tail hung down, and presently they all had a shaky sort of a sketch which any one could instantly tell was a horse.

Then came the triumphant sense of power, of achievement, they could draw! Pursuing this triumph, I continually set them amusing copies, as of hopping hobgoblins, or something of like appeal to the child mind, with such glaring peculiarities of outline and proportion as it was impossible to miss; and they drew them, recognizably. With enough practice of such easy and entertaining sort, their powers of perception and execution quickly developed and the road was open to better work.

In the scrappy little two-by-four diary I tried to keep that first year, I find but very occasional notes, as "Class, rained, no one came but Mrs. Mitchel." "Did two cards for Mr. Taylor, charged $3.00." "Rose Rowley, paid for two lessons, this and next." "Mrs. Crank calls about giving her son lessons." "Lessons to Mary Wood, Paint on Mrs. K's cards. Get extremely tired over them."

"Tired" always means that ghastly below-zero weariness, and it was a frequent item, as—"Jan. 26. Tired." "Mon. 27. Very tired." "Tues. 28. Tired." "Wed. 29. Very tired." "Thurs. 30. Awfully tired." "Fri. 31. Still tired, weak and sad." And so on. Again

Feb. 22nd, "Am pretty miserable just along here."
"23. Am really miserable." Then gradually, "25. Sad
enough." "27. Feel better. Arrange ms. to send off."
"March 5. Work with Grace on new play." "8th. A
fine busy day. Am feeling better. Write by myself in
the evening." A comment on lack of strength—"Sweep
parlor, proud."

There are plenty of blanks in this diary, and mistakes, two weeks with nothing down but two days' lessons, eight weeks absolutely blank, more with only one
lesson set down. The blanks were the drowned time,
not even sense to make those scanty notes.

Yet there was much of pleasantness all along—the
dear Channings always good to me—Mrs. Channing
had me give her lessons in painting and did well at it;
other kind friends, games of whist, and entertainments
of various sorts. The Channings had a masquerade,
and I made for Harold, Grace's brother, a zany's
costume, for which I had no pattern. It was the kind
having a hood fitting around face and head, neck and
shoulders, and with two horns. All this in alternate
red and green, tunic, hose and pointed long-toed shoes.
I remember my pride in this difficult piece of construction, but do not at all remember what I wore.

Fortunately for my poor efforts it cost but little to
live, I think twenty-five dollars a month would have
covered it all for little Katharine and myself. Our small
housework I managed except washing, and an occasional day's cleaning. The little house stood on an
exposed corner, Mexicans lived in tiny shacks down in
the Arroyo, more than once things were stolen from me
if left outside, a rug from the porch, a step-ladder that
stood against the house.

But I refused to worry. "There is little to steal and
I am quite willing to be killed," was my attitude.

When tramps came for food I devised a special reception, giving them, not charity but hospitality. "Could you give me something to eat, Ma'am?" "Certainly, I can, come in," and I set a place at the table with us. When, as was often the case, the man was a decent person, honestly looking for work, this was welcome and appreciated; if he was a hobo he didn't like it as well. But no one ever presumed on it. Only once did a man come back for more, and he apologetically explained, "You know I chopped wood for you before."

On one of those long useless afternoons during the first months in that cottage there came an opportunity for the execution of a long-cherished scheme of revenge, an amusing instance of impersonal resentment and enduring vindictiveness. As a child I had read stories of the shameless persistent intrusion of book-agents, how they refused to take no for an answer, but continued to press their wares regardless of protest, wasting their victim's time. It had always seemed to me that something might be done in retaliation, now after many years, here was the opportunity.

Two pests were continuous in California, flies and agents—there was no way of freezing them out. The agents usually came in vehicles, this one did. He dismounted, tied his horse, and approached. It was about two o'clock, the afternoon stretched before me, empty and useless, mine enemy was delivered into my hand.

First I told him definitely that I should not buy his book. These people are trained to pay no attention to a "prospect's" refusal, which disregard is an insult to begin with; however, I cleared my skirts before starting. Down he sat and began on his task.

I let him talk and he talked a long time, the invalid in the hammock making a good listener. More than once I told him I should not buy, which did not daunt him in the least. If, after some time, he paused for a bit, seemed a trifle discouraged, then a question would set him going again. If, upon long effort to no purpose, he really seemed to think of departure, I asked to look at his volume, or made some further inquiry. When he finally seemed to weary of his monologue and gathered up his things to go, then I began to talk—and I was a good entertainer in those days.

In this particular case the "prospect" could afford to waste an afternoon, it was wasted anyway. But the agent's time was probably of some value to him, and he spent three hours of it, entirely in vain. "I told you I should not buy the book," I gently reminded him, on his departure about five o'clock.

There is another tale of that time more amusing, and, in intention at least, more creditable. The place was owned by two poor old people—it was their only remaining bit of property. They sold the orange crop on the trees to another shabby old party, who came one morning with horse and wagon, to gather it. He worked all day, but could not quite finish, so he came to me and asked, "Could I put my horse in your barn, Ma'am, and sleep on the porch—I hate to go nine miles home and back just for that little jag?"

This was something of a poser. I was alone there with my small daughter, and already quite open to gossip and criticism. But principles were strong. "This is a Christian duty," I decided. "It is in no way wrong." So I told him the barn was not mine but I had no doubt my neighbor would allow him to stable his horse there, and he might sleep on my porch or in the little lean-to kitchen, as he preferred.

That kitchen by the way was a sort of joke, built from the big boxes and crates my furniture came in, with windows supplied by some large pieces of glass found on the place. It cost me only some nails and carpenter work, about thirteen dollars as I remember.

The old fellow washed his hands at the hydrant and came in to supper with us. Then I sought to get rid of him, as Grace was coming as usual to work with me on a play. No proposed place of entertainment attracted him however, not even the Y. M. C. A. So he sat around while I read to Katharine, and then I helped him move my hard little lounge out into the kitchen.

"If you should git skeered in the night don't be afraid to call on me," he gallantly urged, and I said nothing of the risk I was taking. Grace came, we worked as usual, and the night passed without event. In the morning my undesired guest again made his toilet at the hydrant, and came to breakfast. While eating a thought struck him, a misgiving, possibly.

"Where is your husband, Ma'am?" he asked.

"In Providence, Rhode Island," I told him.

He thumped down both fists on the table, knife and fork upheld. "If I'd 'a known that," quoth he with decision, "nothin' would have induced me to stay here!"

So that's what I got by facing scandal to do a kindness, and it paid richly in amusement.

Another incident of that year was that I was driven to consult a physician, an excellent woman, Dr. Follansbee of Los Angeles, and found that there were now certain internal difficulties of a purely physical nature added to my mental ones with ensuing complications and need for prolonged treatment.

Besides "Similar Cases" the most outstanding piece of work of 1890 was "The Yellow Wallpaper." It is a description of a case of nervous breakdown beginning something as mine did, and treated as Dr. S. Weir Mitchell treated me with what I considered the inevitable result, progressive insanity.

This I sent to Mr. Howells, and he tried to have the *Atlantic Monthly* print it, but Mr. Scudder, then the editor, sent it back with this brief card:

DEAR MADAM,
Mr. Howells has handed me this story.
I could not forgive myself if I made others as miserable as I have made myself!
Sincerely yours,
H. E. SCUDDER.

This was funny. The story was meant to be dreadful, and succeeded. I suppose he would have sent back one of Poe's on the same ground. Later I put it in the hands of an agent who had written me, one Henry Austin, and he placed it with the *New England Magazine*. Time passed, much time, and at length I wrote to the editor of that periodical to this effect:

DEAR SIR,
A story of mine, "The Yellow Wallpaper," was printed in your issue of May, 1891. Since you do not pay on receipt of ms. nor on publication, nor within six months of publication, may I ask if you pay at all, and if so at what rates?

They replied with some heat that they had paid the agent, Mr. Austin. He, being taxed with it, denied having got the money. It was only forty dollars anyway! As a matter of fact I never got a cent for it till later publishers brought it out in book form, and very little then. But it made a tremendous impression.

A protest was sent to the Boston *Transcript,* headed "Perilous Stuff"—

To the Editor of the Transcript:

In a well-known magazine has recently appeared a story entitled "The Yellow Wallpaper." It is a sad story of a young wife passing the gradations from slight mental derangement to raving lunacy. It is graphically told, in a somewhat sensational style, which makes it difficult to lay aside, after the first glance, til it is finished, holding the reader in morbid fascination to the end. It certainly seems open to serious question if such literature should be permitted in print.

The story can hardly, it would seem, give pleasure to any reader, and to many whose lives have been touched through the dearest ties by this dread disease, it must bring the keenest pain. To others, whose lives have become a struggle against an heredity of mental derangement, such literature contains deadly peril. Should such stories be allowed to pass without severest censure?

M.D.

Another doctor, one Brummel Jones, of Kansas City, Missouri, wrote me in 1892 concerning this story, saying: "When I read 'The Yellow Wallpaper' I was very much pleased with it; when I read it again I was delighted with it, and now that I have read it again I am overwhelmed with the delicacy of your touch and the correctness of portrayal. From a doctor's standpoint, and I am a doctor, you have made a success. So far as I know, and I am fairly well up in literature, there has been no detailed account of incipient insanity." Then he tells of an opium addict who refused to be treated on the ground that physicians had no real knowledge of the disease, but who returned to Dr. Jones, bringing a paper of his on the opium habit, shook it in his face and said, "Doctor, you've been there!" To which my correspondent added, "Have you ever been—er——; but of course you haven't." I replied that I had been as far as one could go and get back.

One of the *New England Magazine's* editors wrote to me asking if the story was founded on fact, and I gave him all I decently could of my case as a foundation for the tale. Later he explained that he had a friend who was in similar trouble, even to hallucinations about her wallpaper, and whose family were treating her as in the tale, that he had not dared show them my story till he knew that it was true, in part at least, and that when he did they were so frightened by it, so impressed by the clear implication of what ought to have been done, that they changed her wallpaper and the treatment of the case—and she recovered! This was triumph indeed.

But the real purpose of the story was to reach Dr. S. Weir Mitchell, and convince him of the error of his ways. I sent him a copy as soon as it came out, but got no response. However, many years later, I met some one who knew close friends of Dr. Mitchell's who said he had told them that he had changed his treatment of nervous prostration since reading "The Yellow Wallpaper." If that is a fact, I have not lived in vain.

A few years ago Mr. Howells asked leave to include this story in a collection he was arranging—*Masterpieces of American Fiction*. I was more than willing, but assured him that it was no more "literature" than my other stuff, being definitely written "with a purpose." In my judgment it is a pretty poor thing to write, to talk, without a purpose.

All these literary efforts providing but little, it was well indeed that another avenue of work opened to me at this time.

California is a state peculiarly addicted to swift enthusiasms. It is a seed-bed of all manner of cults and theories, taken up, and dropped, with equal speed. In 1890 the countryside was deeply stirred by Bellamy's *Looking Backward*. Everywhere was new interest in economics, in the labor question. The *Nationalist,* in which "Similar Cases" appeared, was the chief organ of the Bellamy doctrines, and Nationalist clubs sprang up over the land; California, always fertile, blossomed with them.

One day, while riding in the bus, a lady spoke to me, a stranger, and asked me to speak for the Nationalist Club of Pasadena. This was an entirely new proposition. I had never given a public address nor expected to. But here was an opportunity, not wrong, and I accepted it. All I knew of the art of oratory was something I had read in a newspaper when a child—that a public speaker should address the farthest person in the room, then every one could hear. That had struck me as good sense, and I had laid it up, to prove most useful now.

I wrote the lecture, on the main topic of all my work —Human Nature—I have it yet. The meeting was held in a vacant store, the small audience sitting on benches, chairs, whatever they could find, one big fellow on a barrel over against the wall. He was the farthest one, and when he came up, among others to shake hands and make complimentary remarks, I asked him if he could hear me. "You bet I could hear you," he cheerfully replied, "If I couldn't I'd 'a come nearer."

The lecture was warmly received, others followed, soon I was speaking on alternate Sundays in Los Angeles and Pasadena, and in neighboring towns occasionally. It was pleasant work—I had plenty to say and the Beecher faculty for saying it. My hearers were

for the most part rather ignorant, at any rate un-
critical, knowing which, I was saved from undue pride
in their approval.

Their method of financing these lectures was simple.
A collection was taken, out of which they paid for the
hall and whatever expenses there were, and they gave
me the rest. "$3.50" I find in that scrappy little diary
of mine, and again, "Collection $3.00." Once a big,
black-bearded working man, shaking hands after the
lecture, cordially urged, "You come and talk to us—
we'll give you a nickel every time!"

One poor woman was extremely anxious that I
should come to dinner with her, after the lecture in
Los Angeles, and I went. Her husband was a day
laborer, her daughter in service, and she herself worked
out by the day. They lived in a henhouse, literally, one
of those longish, slant-roofed affairs, divided into three
compartments, bedroom, living-room, kitchen. I rested
on a sagging couch in the middle room and thought,
"Why this isn't so bad—it's small and shabby, but
here are the necessities—" and then I thought, "Suppose I could never get out of this henhouse!" and it
looked less possible.

All those early lectures are written. I have them
yet, a goodly number of them, for the two or three
years before I took to notes, and then embarked
on the purely extemporaneous. Opening the larger and
fuller diary of 1891 I find on Jan. 3rd, Sat. "Begin
lecture on Nationalism and Religion," 4th, "Write 24
double pages on Nationalism and Religion." Deliver
same in afternoon. Mrs. Carr there, Dr. Channing and
Miss Knight. Very successful. Got $4.30—Mrs. Carr
put in a whole dollar! Awfully tired with the day's
work."

On the twenty-first was another good one, of which

I made entry: "It was a great success. Some of the women cried, and they actually clapped at times! Then an attempt at organizing, lots of enthusiasm and introductions without number. Also an engagement there for next Wednesday fortnight, and one in Rosedale to be arranged. Also $6.20 in cash! That is worth while. And money more fairly earned I never saw—free gift for well appreciated honest work. It does me good."

There were many great plans made by our own earnest little group. While Mr. Stetson was still there we all became hotly interested in a proposed new magazine which was to be a credit to the coast. Mr. Stetson made beautiful designs for the cover and department heads. Professor Holder was to be the principal editor. I wrote to Uncle Edward Hale, Charles Dudley Warner and other literary lights I knew, to bespeak contributions; we had our letter-paper printed; all looked very promising. But at the last moment, Professor Holder wisely shrank from the financial risk, and the whole thing dropped out of sight. Yet for a while I was almost an editor, and received some manuscripts in that capacity. Of these I have preserved a gem, from an ambitious German-American girl about fifteen years old, so delightfully funny that it is good enough to insert:

A WINTER IN CALIFORNIA

"Well, father have you desided"? asked a prurient young lady who had been sitting or standing for the last half hour, waiting for this question answered. She had been pacing the room like an excited child, and when she heard the well-known foot-steps she had quickly seated herself, to appear in a composed manner; as she knew how her father hated her "hilarious" or "puerile" ways. The gentleman apparently did not notice the anxious tone of the speaker, or else he was an obdurate old man who liked to keep people in suspense. Anyhow he was comfortably seated in an easy chair; arranged his necktie and put on his glasses before he spoke. "I think we will go to the west," those were all the words he said, but they sent a glad thrill through the girl; losing all composure she cried; "Oh how good of you pa. Wont we have a fine time," and clasping her arms around his neck she laught for joy. "Come, come this is enough," said the curator to his charge. "I've told you, and now you must help me to get ready." "When will we start?" "That is just what I was going to say," replied the father impatiently. "It depends on ourselves," so saying he left the room. Verbena stood by the vacant chair a long while seemingly in a impeccable hallucination. She heard the hurrying foot-steps in the hall. She heeded them not. Far off her thoughts had carried her. She was already in the west. It would be her first winter in society. Wasn't she eighteen last week? She must then throw off her child's guise, and wear a woman's. A gentle hand touched her at this junction "Verbena must dress for supper" said her maid, and she found herself suddenly in her own room staring at a vacant chair. A month or so, after this found her and her father whirling out of New York bound for California. It was the month of November, and the snow was falling fast, covering all the landscape with a white coating. In the warm cars the passengers were amusing them-selfs in various ways. Some were reading, while others in an loquacious mood, were chiping away like woodpeckers. Verbena with the help of her maid was arranging her baggage in their several places. In the farther end of the car stood a young man gazing listlessly around, when his eyes fell on Verbena. "A pretty girl and a good housekeeper, from the looks I admit. I wonder who she is; looks like a sensible girl." He had not long to wonder; as down the aisle of the car strode a man of middle age. "Who is this now," he asked himself, his attention attracted by this new object. "Well if this isn't old Merrit." They both recognized each other, and were surprised to meet in such an unexpected place. "So you are for the west also," conjugated the old man, after the brief greeting was over. "Yes, for a season, the winters here are to hard on me. I suppose

you are along?" asked the younger man. "No, not so, that puts
me in mind of my daughter" the other elated. "Come I will
give you an introduction." He lead the young man towards the
seat where Verbena was. "This is my daughter, Mr. Aster,"
proudly he spoke, presenting her to him. Mr. Aster with his
frank, courteous ways; put her in a comfortable situation, and
they were soon engaged, with a cosmorama of their unseen
winter resort; each seeing it with the minds eye, by the others
vastless reflux on the subject. They were both on high terms
before they parted, and many afternoons were spent likewise.
The days rolled rapidly away amidst friends and newfound
acquaintances. The eastern states had long been past, and now
or then an endless chapparral opened before them. The scenery
was grand in some parts. The days of their journey was nearly
ended, and one more day will bring them to their destination.
One morning the passengers are awakened with the sudden
cessation of the train, a snort, a slamming of doors, and the
voice of the conductor shouting—"Raymond." This produced
what was desired, baggage was grappled, out went the pullmen
people, and what a picture meet their eager eyes. On a green
declivity stood the large Raymond Hotel resting peacefully
under a clear, blue canopy. The surrounding grounds laid in
various shaped parterres; covered with the morning dew, the
rare flowers looked fresh, and their odor fill the air. In the
distance rested a town, its painted roofs and walls looked like
a painting engraved on a green back-ground, "green walled"
by the neighboring hills. To the north were part of the Coast
Range, whose high peaks were covered with snow, including
Mount Old Baldy, who reared his white head in the north-
east. It seem to them a new summer was there, a glorious one
to the frozen easterners. Verbena was not considered handsome,
but this morn as she stept from the car, draped in her citrine
dress, she looked real pretty, at least to her father, who watched
her pleased face. There were weeks of enjoyment for the guests,
the walks, drives and excursions were made delightful, by the
warm sunshine, and the jaunts along the green hills spread over
by a coverlet of countless colored flowers. But through all these
social engagements, Verbena found time for her charitable work.

The great boom was over, leaving property in a terrible depreciation. They had their land, certainly they did, but this would not pay for bread. Then did the lazy real-estate men take their legs from the desks and follow the plow: Some said they were glad it had come to this. Mr. Aster was her true chaperon in these rounds of charity. One afternoon as she was putting on her driving gloves, when Mr. Aster stopped her in the hall. "I have just heard of a young man without money," he said looking anxiously at her. "Come, we can go now," she answered, leading the way, to the carriage. They were on the way, arriving in front of a pretty cottage, clustering in a grove of orange trees "A cosy place," thought Verbena as she stepped from the phateon. A handsome girl came to admit them. Being told their errand, she lead them into a sunny room. Near the window on a sofa laid a young man. He attempted to rise, but fell back wearily on a plead of weakness. The young girl quickly gave him something from a glass which gave him relieve. Verbena looked on with symatizing feelings. His eyes meet hers, and there came a look of pleasure in them. Seeing that the patient could not talk much, they left the room followed by the girl. She ushered them into a finely furnished parlor where they learned the brief story and life of sister and brother. They had came to California with their father, who had died lately. He had been a speculator in the boom, losing almost all. He had left his children penniless. He had then entered on a course of study for the bar, being a sedulous scholar, he had overtaxed his brain. Everything they had, except money. She did not acknowledge that, but you could see it was the only thing wanted. Edwin Aster thought of that handsome girl, and Verbena said to herself, what a pretty girl she was. He must be a fine looking man when he was in health. Every day some new dainty was sent to the cottage; every day its invalid was growing stronger, till one day, when Verbena called, she found him sitting on the veranda looking for her. (She always came Mondays.) "You look much better, Mr. Carreth," she said, looking smilingly up at him. "I feel much better every time I see you," he retorted, as he rose to meet her. "This is a beautiful country; no one ought to be sick," was her sentence.

The conversation grew very interesting to the two. The exquisite Knowledge of Verbena put her in a light where she shone brilliant to her hearer. The vivacious, natural tendency in which he spoke, and the polite attention he showed, spoke for him as a gentleman of culture. They were closer friends, and know more of each other from that starting point. The merry girl, said, as she dropped a scented envelope in his hands; "Don't disappoint us next week, but try and do what this message requires." After she was gone he opened it, and there fell out an invitation to a soiree for next Wednesday at the Raymond. When the evening came it found Carreth and his sister Margot on their to the Hotel, as they entered the large, cool drawing rooms Verbena and her father came to meet them. She was attired in a dark magenta dress giving a bewitching hue to the brunette. After supper the rooms seemed hot, and couples went out for a stroll, among them Verbena and Carreth, The garden was light with electric lamps, shading their fulgency over the flowers, the gentle zephers lifting their perfume from them. It seemed like fairyland to the two. They were walking silently towards a bench. Carreth stopped her. "Verbena I have some—something to tell you." He did not sit down, but stood by the seat. "Go on please let me hear it," she laughted un-easily. "I am poor Miss Merrit you know, and—and—people will say if—if—." And there he told his first love story, and the girl listened to one the first time.

*　　*　　*　　*　　*　　*　　*

Mr. Aster tried to shun her all during the next day, in fact he had fell in love with Margot. He thought Verbena had been after him, and Verbena had thought the same, So there they were, but the truth came out at last. "What a fool I was, could not I have seen it?" Aster had said when being told. Verbena had tried to appear very much surprised when she heard of it. At the supper table they seemed embarrassed, but soon it was of the past, and they were on as good terms as before. The last Raymond excursion took two happy couples and an old gentleman for the east. What did he say? The rich inauspicious man said, "It was all right."

Always there were things afoot for some local benefit in Pasadena. In the interest of establishing a public library, a prolonged fair or kirmess was held, wherein there were loan exhibits, shows, sales and booths of all sorts, for a week. I had a small booth with signs upon it such as, "Poetry made while you wait." "Rondeaux ready in a moment." "Try a triolet." "Verses to order on any subject." From this I anticipated considerable quick work, some fun and some money, but it met with absolutely no recognition from those Pasadenians —and I had but one order, from a transient visitor, a boy from Harvard.

One local undertaking I sought to promote was a sort of residence shop where women out of work— there were ever so many stranded women there, who had come with tuberculous relatives—too late—could fill the frequent need of other tourists for sewing and mending. This was good business and a double benefit, but it was too much for the residents to visualize, and fell through. I remember this well, because it, and the proposed magazine, came to a premature end on the same day. With my numb immunity to disappointments I took both blows with stoical indifference.

On February 21, 1891, Uncle Edward Everett Hale and Cousin Nellie arrived in Pasadena. It was a great joy to me to see some of "mine own people" again. He was most kind; I find in the diary, "Uncle Edward says, 'You are getting to be a famous woman, my dear.' Says 'Similar Cases' is 'a great campaign document.'" He was kind enough to listen to one of my lectures, as a critic, and told me that I put too many ideas into it; that a sermon should have but one, and a lecture but two or three.

He was a friend of Edward Bellamy, and a Nationalist, said it was true Americanism. At my request he gave the Los Angeles group an address on the new faith, crowds attending, which was an immense pleasure to me.

Meanwhile, a call had come from San Francisco, where a brilliant and farseeing woman, Mrs. Emily Parkhurst, was organizing the Pacific Coast Woman's Press Association. I was asked to join, railroad transportation was furnished to all delegates, Mrs. Parkhurst asked me to visit her, and on March 14th I went, with Katharine, to the city by the Golden Gate.

Uncle Edward was there also, and I received some reflected glory from his relationship. My paper read at the P.C.W.P.A. Convention made an impression, other engagements opened, both to write and speak.

Mrs. Parkhurst was more than kind. Her mother, Mrs. Swett, most thoughtfully invited little Katharine to stay with her in the country while I was so crowdingly occupied in town. The dear child went, and won golden opinions for her sweet reasonableness, at six. She was a very nice person, that child—and is yet.

When I returned from a few days with her there, I was amazed to find my picture in the windows, and that I had a "manager." This young man had just arrived from Australia, with a theatrical troupe, was stranded, and as my name was prominent at the time, he thought he saw an opportunity. Mrs. Parkhurst thought so too, and I found myself booked for several lectures, at $50.00 each. I gave one or two, but as he did not give the money promised I refused to go on unless he paid up, and we parted without affection. He expressed himself with some virulence to the effect that I might be a writer, but that I should never make a lecturer.

CHAPTER X

OAKLAND

In two years of work in Pasadena something had been accomplished. Verses widely quoted, not "poetry" in exalted sense, but living words; and enough in story and article to have already won some small market. The lecturing was a valuable asset, though fees were almost negligible still, as $5.00 for a paper at the Friday Morning Club of Los Angeles, $9.50 from the W.C.T.U. in San Francisco, and the little driblets from my Nationalist groups. But it was free expression of a growing philosophy, and a power of delivery which increased with use.

My Socialism was of the early humanitarian kind, based on the first exponents, French and English, with the American enthusiasm of Bellamy. The narrow and rigid "economic determinism" of Marx, with its "class consciousness" and "class struggle" I never accepted, nor the political methods pursued by Marxians. My main interest then was in the position of women, and the need for more scientific care for young children. As to women, the basic need of economic independence seemed to me of far more importance than the ballot; though that of course was a belated and legitimate claim, for which I always worked as opportunity offered. The first visit to San Francisco made a favorable impression, and some friends, even receiving some pleasant press comment. Colonel Irish, a prominent newspaper man, with the personal peculiarity of eschewing neck-ties, wrote something on California Literary Genius in which he said, "It seems to us that a genius has arisen here that may deserve the honor of compelling the definite beginning of a distinct character for California. Mrs. Stetson, to whom many have listened with raised spirits, and who has been read by more with emotions entirely new, is in our judgment the distinct product of the physical individuality of California." (sic!) "It is quite impossible to foresee the further effects of environment upon this evident genius, and all that one can ask is the respect and kindliness of California to the promise that is in it." (This is amusing in view of what California did give me.) Then he foretold the appearance of a distinct literary group like that of Boston, "all wrought out under the inspiration of this young priestess who has caught the spark and lighted the waiting lamp."

Altogether, I felt that there was a better opening for my work than in the south. One other necessity drove me. My brother in Utah, with whom mother had been living, wrote that he could no longer keep her—it was my turn. This was something that had to be met. I borrowed the money to send for her, and she arrived in Oakland the same day I did.

At first we boarded, at 673 Grove Street, with a very pleasant woman, Mrs. Barrows. It was cheap enough. I find in the diary, "Board for month (this was for the three of us) $62.50," and again, $63.00." Debts I brought with me, owing my former landlord $35.00, and various people $20.00, $50.00 and $100.00. It was many a long year before there was no load of debt to carry.

On September 26th I faced the position: It was always my custom to put things on paper, hopes, purposes, difficulties—I could meet them better.

On Friday, Sept. 18th, I came here to live with Dora [I will call this new friend Dora, which is not her name.] Mother is with me also, and Katharine, of course. The pleasure in the new relation is that I now have some one to love me, and whom I love [This meant Dora]. It is a Home. The duties of the position are these; First as always to live higher daily, to be loving, tender, thoughtful, courteous, wise, dignified, true, gracious. To do right by mother and by Katharine, to help Dora. To maintain the position it is necessary that I should earn twenty dollars a week. Let me now consider ways and means.

To follow fairly the adventures and misadventures of these years it should be borne in mind that, although thirty-one years old, I was green; young in the sense of lack of social experience. I had always lived among friends, where mannerisms were understood, and intentions respected. My outside work, so far had been among simple people who were warmly appreciative, and groups of women of interests somewhat similar to mine. I had not yet stood alone in what we call "the world"—as if we had previously lived elsewhere!

Moreover, all my early impressions had been of life in New England, among people of clean and dignified traditions. Now I was to live and teach among an entirely different sort. At first the impression made in the earlier visit, with my distinguished Uncle as a strong assistance, remained; but as time passed and the nature of my teaching became clearer, I was not so popular.

I tried every kind of work that opened, even to a brief attempt at reporting: "Oct. 12th. Call at *Tribune* office and am detailed to work up Mary Gilson case—Christian science and a bullet wound. Do it successfully." But this avenue soon closed, instead of bringing in facts, I would persist in offering opinions!

There was a class formed for me in San Francisco;

"Oct. 27th. Meet at Mrs. Lansing's. Eleven ladies present. Coffee and cakes. Very pleasant and encouraging, $25.00 paid in (that was for the course). Came home hilarious." The opening paper was on "What we Were, Are and Might Be." Next day, "Go to *Times* office and get pay for Woman's Papers, $3.75." This day ends, "Came home exhausted," which I hope was not due solely to the difference in income. On the twenty-ninth, visiting my doctor: "She says I put myself back three weeks by my exhaustion of yesterday." "Nov. 7th, Nationalists send up whole collection— $3.40."

On November 25th a very special entry: "I am called to the ministry!" More particularly: "Mr. and Mrs. Salzer (Nationalists), come and invite me to preach, Sunday evenings, a little group guaranteeing $5.00, and the Gilsons willing to let Hamilton Hall for half that." Next day being Thanksgiving I find: "I am exceedingly thankful. For Dora, mother here, Katharine, improved health, outlook on work—and last night's honor."

I had a class in Oakland also, and one in Alameda, close by. There were but few interested, and fewer who came regularly, the fees were small, but it kept me busy writing papers for them and developing ideas. Always the personal work kept on, people coming to me for advice, help, encouragement; as "Dec. 23rd. Mr. —— comes for me in great distress to go with him, help him, try to see his wife—she has left him. I go to court with him, he had got her there on a writ of *habeas corpus,* but he could not prove she was detained against her will. Ride a little with him and try to cheer him up." I haven't the faintest memory of this sad husband, nor for that matter of most of the names in the diary, but the record shows the kind of calls I had, from all kinds of people.

Health remained poor. "Dr. Kellog in. She doubts
if I can stand the strain of our present family arrangement much longer. Write some of sermon on 'Pain.'"
Next day: "Still pretty weak. Write entire new sermon
on 'The Human Will.' Give it in the evening. Dora
nurses me all day." The "strain" was with mother, my
friend was still a deep comfort, and Katharine always
an unfailing joy, never a care or trouble. December
31st: "I am by no means well. Two fits of wretchedness in a week is bad. Still the year shows some gain.
It is the anxiety about mother that is wearing me now.
That must be borne. May next year help more!"

In "Memoranda" at the back of the book I find the
following characteristic bit: "N. Y. Dec. 15th, 1890.
Scurrilous attack on Walter's exhibition of pictures at
Amer. Art Assn. galleries. Find out author and punish
him." But he went unpunished, so far as I know.

Comes the next year's diary. As usual I begin with
recorded aspiration, finishing December 31st with:

> For this new year unknown whose steady wing
> Joy, Peace or Pain may bring, I plan one thing.
>
> In this new year which finds me still so weak
> From loss the past can speak, one thing I seek.
> For one thing shall my soul's hands lift and reach,
> Praying the year may teach more perfect speech.
>
> Clean, honest, wise, correct, strong, gentle too—
> Courteous as angels, set in order due, perfectly true.

Then, watching the old year out, this, near twelve
o'clock:

> I wait the coming year too sad for fear,
> Too old for hope, too wise for real despair,
> Wait it in patient prayer.

It matters little about me if so I be
Able to make the effort of one soul
Help on the whole.

Only not too much pain! Oh not again
That anguish of dead years—
Terror and tears!

Jan. 1st. The year is born. As far as I have power I'll try
To make this year when past nobler than was the last.

January 16th marks a change in method: "The first time I have spoken, not read. Do not make a success of it, nor enjoy it, but shall try again."

On that day, by request of Dr. McLean, a leading Congregational clergyman of Oakland, I spoke in his prayer-meeting: "Read and pray earnestly, Dr. McLean very kind—people interested—a real success." There was soon more of this, reading and speaking in various churches.

On the eighteenth I met some interesting people. A reception was given by our P.C.W.P.A. to visiting delegates from the International League. I went with Susan Hale, Uncle Edward's sister, who had been in San Francisco for some time. Kate Field was there, "very nice to me"; but most impressive was Mrs. Frank Leslie Wilde and her husband, brother to Oscar Wilde. He was a huge person with large ox-like eyes, and in a vast bewilderment at his utterly strange surroundings. She was painted and decorated like a new house, her charms further enhanced by a rubber—shall we say chest-protector? It was finished above by a jeweled "dog-collar," and disappeared below where her dress began, appropriately tinted, and undulating freely as she moved her head. She was a woman of real intelligence and ability, but she did not look it.

On February 6th we moved (Dora, Katharine and I) to 1258 Webster Street, taking three furnished rooms. Good Dr. Kellog, now married to a Mr. Lane, took mother to board for a while. On the eighth: "I take Katharine to her first school, Miss Wyman, on Alice Street a lovely girl, the teacher, just a pleasant little home school, Kate likes it."

An Ethical Society was formed by a group of working people which I was asked to lead, opening February 14th: "About 18 join. Object, The Study of Human Conduct with a view to its Improvement by Scientific Methods." We had most interesting times at these meetings, somewhat marred by a convinced fatalist, who was always on his feet to explain that we had no responsibility. As this doctrine greatly interfered with what I was trying to teach, I sought to counteract it, as thus:

"Do I understand you correctly?—That a bad man is not to be blamed for his acts, that he only sins from the effects of heredity and environment, that he cannot help it; and similarly that a good man is not to be praised for his virtues, since he so behaves because he cannot help it?"

He agreed that this was precisely what he meant. Then said I to the group: "Hereafter when this brother speaks, remember that he is not trying to help you or hurt you, he only talks because he cannot help it." His words lacked weight after that.

Our house was a large and pleasant one, on a nice street, with a good yard behind it, an excellent place for Katharine. The lady who kept it, a Mrs. Palmer, had to leave suddenly to join a sick brother, I think, and I decided to take it as it stood, and keep boarders as she had done. As to furniture, that was to stay till she needed it. "If you won't charge rent I won't charge storage," I told her. There were several boarders, and what we had been paying for our three furnished rooms went a long way on the entire rent, which was $50.00. The house was owned by an aged man who kept one room for himself and took off ten dollars a month for it, so I had to pay but forty. On February 29th— "Nine people in the house. Eight to cook for. I can't have mother yet." I do not remember who it was who did not eat!

Then came a new invitation. "Rev. Mr. Good-enough calls and asks me to take his pulpit next Sunday." Here was something of a facer. I had addressed prayer-meetings as such, but this was to carry the entire service alone. However it was not wrong, he asked me—I did not ask him—and I said I would. As we discussed the service he inquired: "Have you been regularly ordained?" I said "No"—and he made no further remark on that point. It must have been due to pure heredity that I felt as perfectly at home in that pulpit as if I had grown up in it. The congregation were pleased and wanted me to come again, and ever since, in every kind of church which has invited me, I have enjoyed real preaching better even than lecturing, which is mostly preaching too—my kind. I have preached for Unitarians and Universalists of course, for Congregationalists, Methodists, Baptists, once for some reluctant Presbyterians, I think, for "Christians," Spiritualists, and Mormons.

My small daughter had the measles. The record says: "Write to-day and to-morrow's lecture for Unity Club. Long, good. Measles galore. No sleep, no regular meals, housework allee samee." Across two days presently—"Just work and measles." That angel child bore her affliction philosophically, but one day I heard her swearing softly after the fashion of her

beloved Arabian Nights—as she rubbed her poor eyes
—"O Moses! O Aaron! O Ezra's Ass!"

On April 2nd mother came to us. She had a
cancer. . . .

Blanks in the diary now, vacant from April 13th
to May 12th, when it says: "I think this is the date of
my note to Mrs. E. E. Howard for $25.00 falling due
on Nov. 1st, let me say, with Int. at 7%. Mrs. Cohen
the same, with a year's time." The reason for this
heavy financial undertaking was that Mrs. Palmer had
to take away her furniture, and I had to get mine from
Pasadena, just *had to*. There was the house with the
boarders, a going concern. There were mother and
Katharine—I had no better way to care for them, I
must go on. So I had to borrow, had unhappily often
to borrow during these hard years, with more hard
years before I could pay.

Blank in the diary to May 27th, then: "Signed con-
tract with Mrs. Palmer for stoves and carpets. Have
paid up to May 15th. $70.00 in full to date. Am to
pay her the rest before Dec. 31st, 1892 or forfeit
all." Very few more entries, though one on Labor Day
tells of reading a prize essay on Labor, and getting a
gold medal for it. I always suspected that this essay
and medal business was arranged for my benefit by
Eugene Hough, a man influential in the Unions and
one of my strong friends to this day.

It was a hard year. Most of my boarders were in-
valids. There were six sick women in that house at one
time, and they used to come and tell me their troubles,
mostly in the middle of the night. Old Miss Sherman
had what they called "old-fashioned consumption";
it was a slow affair. There was mother, steadily worse,
Dora was unwell a large part of the time. Another
nervous invalid was Mrs. Howe of Los Angeles, a

warmly devoted friend, who came to live with me. She
had a delicate genius in writing, and would have gone
far if her health had been good. Mrs. Ober, a friend
of Dora's, was one more, a nurse of mother's was
another—I was the sixth.

I did all the housework and nursed mother till I
broke down; then I hired a cook and did the nursing
till I broke down; then I hired a nurse and did the
cooking till I broke down. Dr. Kellog Lane said I
must send mother to a hospital. This I could not bear
to do. "If you say definitely as a physician that I shall
die, or go crazy," I told her, "I'll do as you say. But
if I can possibly stand it I want to go on, I do not wish
to have it said that I have failed in every relation in
life."

She said that judging from what I had stood already,
I could pull through. September 13th: "She concludes
to do nothing for me at present. Says I had better
break down honestly than be bolstered up and collapse
more extensively later. A wise physician."

September 30th: "Mother's last day downstairs—I
think."

October 25th a better note: "Am feeling first rate
these days—full of plans to write, sew, build, etc. The
creative instinct rising and promising well for work
when the strain is off." Here's a funny one—November
15th: "Mrs. Haydon, the cook, goes, praise the Lord!
Mrs. Moore and small daughter appear in her stead—
praise the Lord again! Might as well do it always."

Mr. Worcester, a Swedenborgian minister in San
Francisco, came to see mother, December 9th: "Says I
must have help—goes for a nurse." And next day,
with my usual thankfulness: "Mrs. Moore and
daughter depart, praise the Lord again! She was either
drugged or a lunatic. I have now secured a nurse for

Monday, and am to do the housework for awhile."
The nurse, a Miss Bennet arrived: "I experience a
great sense of relief and go out to ride on a cable car."

But alas! on the eleventh: "Miss Bennet proves
totally inadequate, and has a sick headache, which in-
duces her to sit in the kitchen all day." She was followed by Mrs. Alban, who "Proves a delight—kind,
willing, helpful, pleasant, we all like her." She was later
succeeded by her sister, Mrs. Wright, and I remarked,
"These women are the first I have had who were
wholly helpful."

The year runs out sadly. "It appears that I am
sicker than I thought." "I am very weak." "Gave out
in the morning. Sick—sicker." And December 31st:
"It has been a year of great and constantly increasing
trouble. Poverty, illness, heartache, household irritation amounting to agony, care, anxiety, grief and shame
for many many failures. My last love proves even as
others" (That was Dora). "Out of it all I ought surely
to learn final detachment from all personal concerns.
The divorce is pending, undeclared, mother still lives.
There is only to go on. . . ."

There were many kind friends. All my life I have
been blessed with good friends, new and old, in this
country and others, always some one was being kind
to me. My Socialist comrades were most sympathetic.
They even sent a committee of one who said, with
careful search for the least offensive way of putting it,
that they had heard that I was—indigent—and wished
to offer assistance! I explained that I was no worse off
than many another woman keeping boarders, but I was
grateful for their sympathy and kindness. They presently arranged a "pay" lecture for me, $25.00, which
was welcome.

There were some interesting times, too. The

P.C.W.P.A. had a convention, with speakers from afar, and among them was Helen Campbell. As "Helen C. Weeks" her writings in *Our Young Folks* had delighted me when I was six. We became the closest friends, she was one of my adopted "mothers."

Ina Coolbrith, the beloved poet of California, lived opposite to me. She introduced me to Joaquin Miller, who had a spectacular castle-cottage up in the hills back of Berkeley, and he came to see me. So did Edwin Markham, then teaching in an Oakland school, before "The Man with a Hoe" was born; and one Edmund Russell, an æsthete from New York, wearing "romeos" for shoes, and a belt studded with large carnelians, and leaning against a mantel-piece or reclining on the rug in preference to chairs. Hamlin Garland I met also, and with James Whitcomb Riley and others visited Joaquin in castle-ette. There was a trick shower in the garden, which he sprung on us, delighted to surprise and wet his visitors. A daughter of his, part Indian, was in service with Miss Coolbrith at the time.

Meanwhile, Mr. Stetson had filed a divorce suit in Rhode Island, for desertion. This was more honest than my getting it, for I was the one to break off. The Boston *Globe* made a most unpleasant note of this, and the San Francisco *Chronicle* took it up, with interest.

Then the *Examiner*, Hearst's paper, sent a reporter to get an interview with me. Up to this time I had accepted reporters as men and women like the rest of us, governed by similar instincts of decency and kindness. So I saw him, told him the simple facts, that there was no "story," simply a case of broken health and mutual understanding, and that I was doing my best to keep it from my mother who was dying upstairs—

to save her worry; and would he please not spread it about. Foolish woman!

The result was a full page in the *Examiner*, with interviews from various members of the P.C.W.P.A. on the topic "Should Literary Women Marry." I imagine that the reporter was decent about it, but that those higher up would by no means relinquish their opportunity. If there was nothing in the case for them to make game of, they would soon make something. And they did. My name became a football for all the papers on the coast. The worst of it was some singularly discerning friend sent clippings to mother, so that her last days were further saddened by anxiety about my future. . . .

Harder than everything else to me was the utter loss of the friend with whom I had sincerely hoped to live continually. She certainly did love me, at first anyway, and had been most generously kind with money. My return was mainly in service, not only in making a home for her, but in furnishing material for her work. She was a clever writer, and later I learned that she was one of those literary vampires who fasten themselves on one author or another with ardent devotion, and for the time being write like them. The kindest thing I can say of her character is that she had had an abscess at the base of the brain, and perhaps it had affected her moral sense. I do not mean to describe her as "immoral" in its usual meaning; she was malevolent. She lied so freely as to contradict herself in the course of a conversation, apparently not knowing it. She drank—I saw her drunk at my table. She swore freely, at me as well as others. She lifted her hand to strike me in one of her tempers, but that was a small matter. What did matter was the subtle spreading of slanders about me, which I cannot legally prove to have come from her, but which were of such a nature that only one so close could have asserted such knowledge. Also, I do know of similar mischief-making from her in regard to others. At any rate that solace ended not only in pain but in shame—that I should have been so gullible, so ignorant, as to love her dearly.

So the New Year's inscription for 1893 is a doleful one: May this year's misery be less, and new strength through me flow. More power to see and to express the blessed truths I know. And a little less pain if you please! I can do more work if I suffer less."

By January 31st I record: "Have done fifteen pieces of saleable work this month—, three lectures, three poems, nine articles of one sort or another. Received $40.00 so far. Fair work for an over worked invalid." On February 9th: "Unless I learn my desired virtues *now*, I never shall. Difficulties are nothing. The power to live rightly is outside of these difficulties."

Mr. Hearst's *Examiner* was not done with me. Having made my name a by-word, they now wished to take advantage of its unpleasant prominence, and sent a reporter, one Mr. Todd, to interview me on my views on the Marriage Question. "I refuse on the ground of the *Examiner's* reputation—will not write for the paper. He begs, he tries to drag me into conversation, he argues, he offers to pay me, he threatens covertly— I succeed in getting rid of him. Am exhausted by the contest however."

I remember his threat distinctly. He said, "I suppose you know the *Examiner* is a bad paper to get the ill-will of?" I told him I had already tasted it, that they might do as they pleased but they should never have another word from me. Thirteen times before I left the coast I had the pleasure of refusing them, and many times since, in more than one of Mr. Hearst's enlarging list of publications. My refusal was not based on my own experience alone, but on the well-known character of the Hearst papers and methods.

As an instance of those methods, this story: A poor Oakland woman had a drunken, vicious husband. She left him, and took in washing to support her little children. He came to the house, drunk, and pursued her with an ax. She hurried the children out of the house, but he caught her, and had her on the floor with ax uplifted, when she shot him—she had the pistol with her from sheer terror of his coming.

Following her arrest, the San Francisco *Call* sent to one of my boarders, Mrs. Howe, who was a writer, to go to see the woman and get her story. Of course her lawyer had warned her not to say anything to any one, and Mrs. Howe contented herself with doing some small services for the prisoner. The *Examiner*—I think it was Winifred Black, was more successful. She told that poor, frightened, remorseful little woman that she was not a reporter, that she had come because her sister had once been in prison for the same offense; she put her arms about her and the unhappy prisoner cried on her shoulder and told her all about it. It made a good "story"—what else should a reporter care for?

No life and work in California at that time can be fairly described without reference to the Southern Pacific. That great railroad and steamship owner held the state in absolute control by land and sea. It held merciless power in the legislature, in the press, in the courts, even in the churches through wealthy patronage. In the very women's clubs it could not be criticized because some prominent member was sure to be wife to an official of the road.

As to business, there was the famous "pink slip"

scandal, the private rebate arrangements for freight rates. A man, once secretary-of-state, told me how he had offended the Southern Pacific by advocating some bill or some man they found objectionable, and in return they deliberately wrecked his business—he had a store of some sort—by granting large rebates to other dealers and none to him. A whole generation of young men grew up in California who had never seen freedom or honesty in public affairs under the conscienceless tyranny of this powerful Common Carrier. There was no competition.

When a new lawyer of promise arose he was promptly retained by the S. P. If any paper attacked it, it was soon bought up, or ruined. Only the brave little San Francisco *Star*, Single Tax, dared to oppose it—as long as it endured. I was told of a convincing novel written to expose "The Mussel Slough Tragedy," wherein the S. P., with bloodshed and death, had evicted stoutly resisting poor men from their land, which had proved especially desirable to the road, on some well-buttressed claim that it belonged to the Company. This book was promptly bought up and suppressed, and the author similarly disposed of, made editor of an S. P. publication.

Oakland is the natural terminus for transcontinental traffic, but its shore is shallow and the ocean trade comes to San Francisco. The S. P. ran freight boats and ferries across the bay, charging passengers "two bits," twenty-five cents, for the trip. To connect with these boats they needed right of way through the city of Oakland. The city government, struggling to get some return for this invaluable privilege, which involved the ruin of a long street, succeeded only in bargaining for free transit within the city limits. Which, being agreed to by the railroad, and the word-

ing of the agreement carefully arranged by their lawyers, they then put up a sign in each car to this effect
—how often did I read it!—"Whereas, we are forbidden to collect fares within the city limits, we are
not, therefore, compelled to carry passengers free.
All persons found on the train without tickets will be
considered as trespassers, and treated as such."

The long piers which carried those trains to the
boats were the only means of access to the ferries. To
prevent competing lines the S. P. bought up, or otherwise secured the whole water-front of Oakland. An
opposition line was started from Alameda, the neighboring town to the south, but that was purchased, with
its connecting road in Oakland.

While I lived in that city, the railroad had built a
little connecting spur on a street where they had no
right whatever, and the city council, I was told, went
out in person and tore it up. There was repeated effort
to start competing boats, and the S. P. at length built
fences across the ends of streets where they reached
the water. Citizens tore them down at night. The road
built them up again next day. Finally a small bit of
wharfage was found, still belonging to the city, and a
boat line was started by a Mr. Davis, which carried
people across for five cents.

Then there was war. A big S. P. freight boat almost
ran down one of these new ones—accidentally of
course!—but terrifying to passengers. S. P. fares came
down with a rush, to five, to two-and-a-half cents, and
the wharves on the other side were noisy with touters
trying to persuade people to buy tickets at that price.
But the immense crowds that swarmed across the bay
morning and night knew friend from foe, and rode on
the new boats. Furthermore, they delightedly took the

S.P. train in Oakland and rode free till they got off to take the rival boat.

This could not be borne. First, they ran their trains at top speed through the town, without stopping at all, so that citizens could not get on. The city council instantly passed an ordinance forbidding more than a certain speed in city limits, and then they ran so slowly that business men missed their appointments. But still the little boats did a successful business, and the big ones didn't. As a final manœuver the S. P. put gates on the cars, at the foot of the steps, and let no one on without tickets, thus flatly abrogating the agreement by which they bought the right of way. Final? No. They super-capped the climax by driving piles all around the water-front of the city, so that no boats could go in or out. The city government sent out a force and pulled up those piles, stacked them in their yards in the city—I saw heaps of them; but the S. P. merely drove in more. Not until the Atchison, Topeka and Santa Fé broke into California was there any escape from this tyranny.

To show the general attitude of the oppressed citizens, no better instance could be given than that of the Sympathetic Strike of 1894. This began in the town of Pullman, where the makers of Pullman cars struck in their own interests. Their quarrel was taken up by railroad workers all over the country, who refused to run trains having Pullmans on them. The railroad companies promptly put Pullmans on every train, and then accused the strikers of refusing to carry United States mail.

Everywhere the strikers behaved in the most blameless manner, doing no mischief to property, merely seeing that no Pullman cars were moved. In California this meant absolute lack of everything from outside;

we were as if on an island, utterly cut off, we had no letters for a fortnight or so. Yet so deep was the hatred of the people for the Southern Pacific that they sided with the strikers altogether.

In Sacramento a great flourish was made, summoning the militia to start the trains. An eye-witness told me how the officers rode grandly on the engine and the men were sent ahead to clear the track of the immense crowd standing all across the way, men and women, girls in holiday dress; but when the men reached the crowd they promptly joined it, each taking a girl on his arm. No train moved.

It really looked as if the strikers would win, but not so. In a little out-of-the-way country place a small local train, without a Pullman on it, was wrecked, and one or two workmen killed. Upon this the strikers were accused of murder. How likely it was that they, so near to victory, should imperil it all by this useless little wreck and injury to some of their own people!

Several were arrested and were to be tried in a bunch. Be it remembered that all the best lawyers were carefully retained by the S. P., but such legal talent as the strikers could secure claimed that in an accusation of murder each man had a right to a separate trial. The judge gave the other side until next day to produce authorities to the contrary, which they apparently did; at any rate something convinced him, and the trial went on, collectively.

The S. P. had a witness who told not only what he was expected to, but so much more that he was promptly remanded to his place of detention and as promptly escaped that night. The whole public was hotly on the side of the men accused, but no public can keep hot indefinitely, the law's delays were invoked, the trial dragged along till people had about forgotten, and the poor men were convicted.

Such was the S. P.

As for me, as if the fly should try to bite the cartwheel—I record: "Sept. 17. Am roused to new enthusiasm against the S. P. Speak to Ina Coolbrith about a new crusade against it. Go to see Mr. P. and ask him about it. Go to the *Enquirer* (a small Oakland paper), and can have space." And so on and so on—doubtless to no purpose whatever. But since any opponent of that ruthless power was marked for destruction, my later vicissitudes may have been colored by this effort.

My aged landlord was taken very ill, but did not wish his daughter told—wanted me to nurse him! What lay behind I never knew; he got better each night under the nurse I had got for him, and worse each day with the nurse his daughter got him, and presently died.

My various lodgers came and went. One couple with children took three rooms for light housekeeping, for which I had to buy utensils, etc. They left before they had paid enough to cover my outlay, and knew they were going to when they took the rooms. She did try in a half-hearted way to induce me not to spend much on them, but by no means said that they were not staying long enough to make it worth my while. Another couple, who took a big room downstairs, and were to get their meals in my kitchen, brought with them a cat, a dog and a parrot. They quarreled so ferociously I had to get rid of them.

A big noisy man came and wanted my best room. He was one of the old stage-drivers, he said. I did not like him and named a larger price to deter him, but he immediately agreed, and paid in advance. That creature used to lie in bed and spit on the carpet, copiously. I never dreamed, in my New England innocence, that he might have further designs, and when he complained that he was "as lonesome as a wolf," let him remain so. He got drunk, too; came home late, helped upstairs by an obliging friend. I spoke to the friend as he came down (he was drunk too, but not so badly, and I did not know it), and said that he must get him out of my house, that I would not have a drunken man in my house. He went, ultimately.

One night a tramp came, a feeble, exhausted, slender man, who had evidently "seen better days." He said that he had spent his last cent to come to his old Sunday-school teacher who lived next door—and he was away—and could I give him a bed for the night. What he meant was a little ticket, distributed by the Associated Charities, which paid for a bed, but I thought of my empty rooms, and my principles, and said, "Why yes, I can. Come in."

He came in, amazed. I turned him loose in the bathroom, and gave him a little hall-room to sleep in. In a story-book he would have been "a changed man" from that hour, but in fact he merely sat down to stay. I had difficulty in persuading him to leave.

The time dragged on. Outside work, inside work, heartache, anxiety and debt, mother steadily failing. The grocer came to see me one day about my climbing bill, a nice elderly gentleman. I asked him into the parlor, and we sat there while I told him just how I was situated. "You are a brave woman," said he. "You shall have credit at my store as long as you need it." There was nothing brave about it. I went on because there was nothing else to do. Indeed I used to say that

I was willing to "eat crow"—but there was no crow to eat. . . .

March 3rd: "Am hard set by this cold. Sit up till two in the morning with mother—the nurse gets four hours' sleep. Write short powerful paper, 'The Sex Question Answered,' for The Woman's Congress. Nothing seems seriously to affect my power to write. This paper has been done in short laborious efforts during these wretched days, and finished last night by mother's deathbed."

She died early in the morning of March 7th.

As a closing act of wisdom and duty she had arranged to have her body cremated, a courageous step in those days. Afterward the little box of ashes was returned to Providence and buried beside her mother.

CHAPTER XI

MOTHERHOOD

SOMETHING of my mother's passion for children I had inherited, but not especially for babies, as with her. My feeling was a deep sympathy for children of all ages, a reverence for them as the world's best hope; a tenderness for these ever-coming strangers, misunderstood, misjudged, mistreated, even when warmly "loved." In my own childhood and youth I had well learned that "love" by no means ensures understanding or appreciation.

In that eager, youthful effort at self-improvement, I had always as one purpose the handing down of a better character, a better constitution, than I had inherited. Quite early I had formulated the dictum: "The first duty of a mother is to be a mother worth having." The second is to select a father worth having. Upon that follows all that can be given in the way of environment and education.

Always I loved children and children loved me. In the days of my teaching the pupils were happy, enjoying the verses, stories and pictures with which the lessons were accompanied. Even the atrocious little boy upon whom I once wasted ten weeks of governessing, afterward sent me this sad little note, brought by a servant:

Miss Pirkins

  i am very sick and would like to have you make me sum rimes and pictures on squere pieces of paper the way we did when we were down to maine if you please

                                        Yours Truly
                                                        ——

there is a ancer
                  when can I have them

When I looked forward hopefully to marriage I planned to have six children, three of each kind. The coming of my baby was unmeasured joy and hope, with high purposes of wisest, tenderest care.

But the black helplessness into which I fell, with its deadness of heart, its aching emptiness of mind, grievously limited all my usefulness to her. In place of a warm efficient love I could feel nothing but that dull, constant pain. A mother weeping away her days on a lounge is not much good. Yet that lovely child would come "hitching"—she never crept, but sat up and wiggled along—across the room to bring me a handkerchief because she saw my tears.

Nevertheless, there were some things I could do, and some avoid. From Spencer I learned wisdom and applied it. There is much, very much, that can be done in the first few years of a child's life. This one had, not surprisingly, inherited a pronounced disinclination to "mind." A command brought instant opposition. With stern authority and what they used to call "discipline," this would have meant a contest of wills, punishments, bitter unhappiness.

On the other hand she was more than willing to oblige, to do anything and everything to be helpful— if not compelled. Children are of all people most open to suggestion. "Let's" is the magic word with them, from playmate or grown person—if the grown person

is honest! Yet this easy and powerful handle by which
to move them to the conduct we desire, is ignored by
most of us, and we persist in using our superiority to
enforce the behavior demanded, with conflict and resentment. Using the method of suggestion, there was
never any difficulty in these first years of education.

Another piece of forethought I was able to use, of
such marked value to the educator that it is a marvel
so few seem to think of it. I call it "laying pipe." It is
necessary for a child to have confidence in the parent
or teacher, to respect his judgment, to rely on his advice. Every time the parent says, "You'll fall!" or
"You'll catch cold!" and the child does not, his confidence is shaken. I took continuous pains not only to
avoid this mistake, as by saying, "You may fall," but
to take advantage of occasions when I could foretell
consequences with certainty, do so, and point out the
results.

From her earliest years, I always made a steady habit
of mentioning a reason for an action with the act, as
"Please shut the door, I feel the cold air." There is
a reason for every act, and while we cannot always
give a child *the* reason, we can give *a* reason, accus-
toming the young mind automatically to associate cause
and effect. The immeasurable advantage of this training becomes clearer with every year of growth. It soon
becomes enough to mention the cause, and the result
is produced, as "I feel the cold air from that door"—
and the child shuts it.

When we demand, after some piece of foolishness,
"Why did you do that?" a child not accustomed to
associate reasons with actions has nothing to say. He
sees no reason for most of the things we do, or expect
him to do, and has none to produce for his own conduct.

Children are naturally reasonable, and, most of them, well meaning. This one of mine was both, and never gave trouble or caused anxiety by her behavior. An incident when she was between three and four will illustrate this: she had gone down the lane to play with the washerwoman's children, a thing not "forbidden" but advised against. I went after her and led the little sunbonneted figure home.

"Why, Katharine!" I said gravely, "this is the first time I have known you to do a thing I asked you not to." Quoth a calm little voice under the sunbonnet, "All children have to be naughty sometimes." See me condemned out of my own mouth—the *first time*—and I making a fuss about it!

Another instance of the pipe-laying process consists in looking ahead along the years and their inevitable developments, or to coming events, and telling the child beforehand such things as will comfortably prepare the mind. When that transcontinental journey lay before us I talked about it, repeatedly, speaking of the interesting features and of the unavoidable disadvantages.

"It's rather hard on children, being in the cars so many days," I explained, "because they have to keep still. Most of the people are grown up, some are old and some are sick, and they can't bear noisy children. Maybe there will be some children you can play quietly with, maybe not. Anyway, I'll carry some things to amuse you." Then I would dilate on the interesting features of the trip, just casually talking about it as I would to any friend. So when we went there was no shock or disappointment, she was quite prepared to behave as well as anybody, and did—at three and a half.

It is also easy to anticipate some of the questions

children are sure to ask, by telling them beforehand
many things which will make later answers understandable. All the labored profundity people spend on teaching children what we used solemnly to call "the mystery
of life," might be resolved to a pleasant, matter-of-fact
piece of information, in due proportion to the rest of
life, if various simple data as to this chapter of nature's
open book had been made familiar beforehand.

Absolute honesty was another thing I could give her,
sick or well. She never had cause to doubt my word.
If I made a mistake I was quick to acknowledge it, to
apologize if necessary, a custom she easily imitated.
Children are preternaturally quick to recognize pretense in any form. We are too apt to say: "Mama is
angry," or "Mama is hurt," instead of *being* it. Once
when we were playing on the floor together, the child,
not meaning any harm, spit at me.

I got up at once, swiftly, and left her. Nothing was
said, or done to her, but her playmate was gone, and
there was displeasure in the air. Of course she demanded a reason—what was the matter? I replied
coldly, "You have insulted me." My prompt and no-
ticeable reaction showed what an insult was as no
description could have done. She met, not punishment,
but consequence, and did not do it again because she
did not like the consequence.

Childhood is a transient condition; what we are
trying to "raise" is a competent adult. Just "minding"
under compulsion, does not train the mind to govern
conduct by principle or by consequence in later life.
As for the more recent method of not training them at
all—the visible results are not altogether pleasurable,
even to the victims.

Another instance, from that field of conduct in which
children are so incessantly "trained"—table manners.

Katharine and I were living in the Pasadena cottage.
She was four. As a baby in a high chair, her dainty
accuracy in eating had been notable. Now she entered
on a phase of really offensive messing. I used the usual
methods of reasonable appeal, but the misbehavior
seemed a stronger impulse than her reason could mas-
ter. So I set to work to think out the true causation of
the desired conduct, and how to enlist her own desire
in acquiring it:

"What is the real reason I am so anxious she should
have good table manners?" It was not far to seek,
without them she would be cut off from good society
when she was grown. This reason was not one which
could be effectually presented now. A mental image of
what you are told will happen in later years, the pre-
dicted loss of something you do not in the least understand or value, has small weight. Somehow I must
make good table manners the price of desirable society
now.

The next time she joyfully indulged in unpleasant-
ness I said: "Excuse me," rose up quietly, with no emo-
tional stress whatever, took my plate and utensils and
retired into the kitchen, leaving a conspicuous vacancy.
There was no rebuke, no anger, simply a goneness.
"Mama!" "Yes, Dear?" "Where are you?" "In the
kitchen." "Why?" "Well, Dear, I hate to speak of it
again, perhaps I've spoken too often already, but honestly, when you do things like that it makes me a
little sick, and if you don't mind I prefer to eat here."
But she did mind, very much, and to please herself, to
secure something she desired, she mended her manners.

These methods were by no means approved by my
friends and neighbors. Discipline and obedience were
still the ideal then. My ideas looked to them not only
wrong in principle but impracticable. They brought up

instances of danger, need for prompt action— "What do you do when you have to catch a train?" they demanded. "Tell her we have to catch the train," I answered, "with several previous experiences, carefully arranged, wherein she learned how bitterly disappointing it is to be too late."

There arose an occasion for restraint of impulse on her part which called for real strength of character, and found it. Next door lived a friend with small children, nurses, rabbits, a donkey, toys of all kinds, a neighboring heaven for my small lonely one, who played continually and most happily there. Then she had a cough, not a bad one, but Mrs. C. feared it was whooping-cough, which was in town, and of which she had had bitter experience; so she asked me to keep my little girl at home until the cough was gone.

This was a very great loss to her, loss of her principal pleasure, a daily habitual joy. She was five years old. There was no fence or hedge between the places, merely a furrow in the plowed ground of the orange grove. I stated the facts, told her of the undoubted danger of the disease, how one of her little playmates had already suffered from it, how contagious it was, and how she surely did not want to carry danger of injury, perhaps death, to her friends; that Mrs. C. had begged her to stay away until well over her cough.

She stayed. I can see now that small, disconsolate figure, in its blue apron and little sunbonnet, standing with little bare toes touching the dividing line, looking at Paradise and never going in. It was not "obedience," it was understanding and self-control.

Another touching instance; one night she had the earache. I had done all I could for her, but the dull ache went on, and the poor baby naturally cried, a low monotonous dreary cry. We lay in the big bed, by the rose-shaded window, and my wretched nerves broke. One of the results of my ruin, from which I have never recovered, is hyperesthesia of the auditory nerve, noises hurt, even music must be soft and low, a sudden loud sound is worse than a blow, a room full of chattering people is a buzzing torment—so this low, continuous wailing became unbearable anguish. Knowing well the exhaustion which would follow, preventing the work on which we must live, I made the appeal to reason:

"Katharine dear—mother knows you are sick, in pain, and you have a right to cry. I'm not blaming you at all, precious, but you know mother is sick too (poor child, she knew it but too well), and I can't stand some kinds of noises. I've been trying to stand it, but it is beyond me, and if it goes on I'll have to go out and walk about outside. But I think I could stand it a while longer if you could change the sound—cry on a different key."

And that blessed baby did.

The good mamas of Pasadena were extremely critical of my methods. One of them said that she would admit that Katharine was the best child she ever saw, but it was no credit to her mother—she would have ruined any other child by her system! They thought it scandalous that I should so frankly teach her the simple facts of sex, but when one of the piously brought up little boys she played with made proposals which would have been dangerous had they been sixteen instead of six, I felt well repaid by her easy confidence, she did not accede and came at once to tell me about it. I showed no sinister alarm, merely explained again how senseless any such performance was for children, and I was glad she knew better than he did. Self-esteem is an excellent weapon.

I dressed her in little gingham aprons, with bloomers

of the same, carefully made not to show, children being naturally conservative. But she asked, "Why can't I wear boy's clothes *clear?*" Also, she played barefooted in the blessed California sunshine—she grew up with a foot which was the delight of sculptors.

For all this I was harshly blamed, accused of "neglecting my child." It gives me much satisfaction to-day to see the children of equally conservative mamas now "wearing boy's clothes clear" with full approval.

We shared the one bedroom of the tiny house, sleeping close to a south window shaded with white Lady Banksia roses, and with my condition for the only drawback, were very happy together. One of our morning games I put quite literally in verse, and the editor who published it urged that I give myself to the writing of children's verse—said I had a special talent for it. Here is this one:

The Bad Little Coo-bird

In the morning, in the bed,
She hugged her little girl and said,
"You're my little bird and this is our nest,
My little coo-bird that I love the best,
  Now coo! little coo-bird, coo!"
  And what did that bad baby do?
  "Coo," said the mother soft and still,
  And the daughter answered loud and shrill,
    "To-who! To-whit, to-whoo!"

"No, no," said the mother, "no,
I do not like it so,
Such fowls as owls I do not love—
Where is my little cooing dove?
  Now coo, little coo-bird, coo!"
  And what did that bad baby do?
  "Coo!" said the mother, soft and still,

> And the daughter answered loud and shrill,
> "Cock-a-doodle-doo!"
>
> "No, no," said the mother, "no,
> I do not like it so,
> I want no cock-a-biddies in my bed!"
> And she brooded her nestling warm and said,
> "Now coo, little coo-bird, coo!"
> And what did that dear baby do?
> "Coo," said the mother, soft and slow,
> And the daughter answered, sweet and low,
> "Coo-oo, Coo-oo, Coo!"

We had happy years together, nine of them, the last four she was mine alone. In Oakland she had a safe and quiet street, a good yard, a friend of mine opposite with a family of children to play with, and a pleasant little school. When I came home from my work anywhere, toward supper-time, I could see that little red-capped figure on the gate-post, watching for me, and she would come, running. . . .

Some unbelievable brute of a woman told the child that her mother was getting a divorce, that her father would undoubtedly marry again, and then she would have a stepmother! She came to me in tears. "Darling," said I, "if Papa does marry again it will be Grace Channing," and the smiles broke through the tears like April sunshine. Grace she had known and loved since babyhood, loved as another mother.

Then came the end of the Oakland effort. My mother was dead. My friend on whom I had so counted, was gone. I was not able to carry the boarding-house, and there was new work opening for me in San Francisco, but in a place unsuitable for a child. It was arranged that she should go to her father for a while, my father, going East, taking her with him.

Since her second mother was fully as good as the first, better in some ways perhaps; since the father longed for his child and had a right to some of her society; and since the child had a right to know and love her father—I did not mean her to suffer the losses of my youth—this seemed the right thing to do. No one suffered from it but myself. This, however, was entirely overlooked in the furious condemnation which followed. I had "given up my child."

To hear what was said and read what was printed one would think I had handed over a baby in a basket. In the years that followed she divided her time fairly equally between us, but in companionship with her beloved father she grew up to be the artist that she is, with advantages I could never have given her. I lived without her, temporarily, but why did they think I liked it? She was all I had.

While arranging for her journey I never once let her feel that it was pain, a break, anything unusual. It was time to go and see her dear Papa—and she went, happily enough. A pretty little outfit was prepared, a small alligator hand-bag was a special treasure, and full explanation was given about the old gentlemen she was to travel with—there were three of them, taking a state-room.

I took her to the uptown station in Oakland, where the Overland trains stopped for passengers; her grandfather appeared; she climbed gaily aboard. She hurried to the window and looked out, waving to me. She had long shining golden hair. We smiled and waved and threw kisses to each other. The train went out, farther and farther till I couldn't see her any more....

That was thirty years ago. I have to stop typing and cry as I tell about it. There were years, years, when I could never see a mother and child together without crying, or even a picture of them. I used to make friends with any child I could so as to hold it in my arms for a little....

What were those pious condemners thinking of? I had lost home and husband, my mother was dead, my father, never close at all, was now removed across the continent. My recent "best friend" had, as it were, soured on my hands, I had no money at all—I had borrowed again to pay for Katharine's ticket and to move, and left failure behind me, and debt. I explained to the landlady that I would pay her as soon as I could, and moved across the bay.

Some years later, my father was speaking favorably to some one as to my methods in child culture.

"You ought to be able to judge," said I. "You took the child all across the continent, leaving her mother; one nine-year-old girl with three old gentlemen—how did she behave?"

"She behaved," he answered carefully, "as if she was trying to make it as comfortable as possible for every one she was with."

She always did. She always has....

CHAPTER XII

SAN FRANCISCO

OAKLAND and San Francisco are so intermixed during these years, my work taking me back and forth so frequently, that the record overlaps. That "work" was varied and of considerable amount. There were the little classes, the lectures, paid and unpaid, some preaching, much club work, and always the writing. Here is one of those forecasts by which I was always trying to lift myself by my boot-straps:

"May 31st. 1893. Age—near 33. Probably forty years' time before me. Desired to accomplish in that time—the utmost attainable advance of the human race." (Modest purpose!) "Means of accomplishment, the perception and transmission of truth, applicable truth. Most immediate necessity, the maintenance of self and child."

Follows this liberal estimate: "To maintain self alone would require,

Furnished room	$ 5.00
Meals	15.00
Clothes and extras	10.00
per month	$30.00

Ten dollars a week would do me well. One good day's work a week would take care of me, one to rest, five to give." This was before the child left.

Then I figure the cost with Katharine, if I could

keep that nice house, with a few boarders to make it go, and another page with a definite program. All these loose pages, accumulating along the years, mark the incessant effort to drag that shaky mind back to its task, to cheer it, stimulate it, comfort it, through self-suggestion to make it go. So I plan:

June 1st, 1893. Rise at six. Be through housework at nine. Write from nine till twelve. Be through lunch work at two. Nap. Go out till five-thirty. Be through supper work at seven. Free writing must be done evenings. Go to bed by ten if possible. Take a tonic. Eat well. Simply train and work for a year and a half. [I was planning to get all my debts paid by that time.] Will have enough then to take a good rest. Write $5.00 worth a day.

I find this list of undertakings:

I belong to The P.C.W.P.A.
        The Ebell Society.
        The Woman's Alliance.
        The Economic Club.
        The Parents Association.
        The State Council of Women.

For these responsibilities I allow "W. P. A. one afternoon a month, and two days more on an average; Ec. Club two afternoons and one evening; Ebell two evenings and two more to prepare; Pa. Assn. two evenings; St. C. of W. one afternoon. . . ."

As to duties—"W.P.A., I am on Child Labor committee and also on education. I wish to ascertain and present information on these subjects. Try to keep up the general ideal. Ebell; Furnish four more sociological papers. Ec. Club; Write papers, read, discuss, exhort, work. Pa. Assn., Organize and push the general society. Plan for the work at large. Visit local groups as desired. Make it go. St. Council, Help organize. Help push. A large slow thing this. Should be a City council also."

I certainly was a willing worker.

The Rhode Island effort at divorce having failed, I started another, and by some slight improvement in California law, or a better lawyer perhaps, this time succeeded, the decree being granted in April, 1894. I was surprised at the sense of lightness, of ultimate freedom which came with that document. This time, I having the divorce, there was no uproar in the papers about it, no articles on "Should Artistic Men Marry?" no noise at all. Having made the painfully frequent mistake of an untenable marriage, we were at last free from its legal bonds, and before the year was over my conscience was finally relieved of much regret for his sake by Mr. Stetson's happy marriage to my life-long friend, Grace Channing.

That continued friendship was what the pure-minded San Franciscans could not endure. Hatred, jealousy, preliminary misdemeanors, they would have accepted as quite natural. That we three should have remained in friendly correspondence, with mutual understanding, affection and respect, through these hard years, was to them incomprehensible.

They wrote me of the wedding. My sense of gladness, of relief, that some happiness could have been established after so much unhappiness, was intense. I had moved across the bay by that time, and that evening, fresh on the heels of the news, came a San Francisco reporter. I knew at once what he wanted and received him with a high, serene, utterly insensitive demeanor.

He found it difficult to assail that glassy surface, and

got no help from me. Then he produced a clipping and handed it to me, inquiring, "Have you seen this?" I took it calmly, read it through calmly, handed it back calmly. "No," said I, "I had not seen it." It was an account of the wedding, of which fortunately I had already heard by letter. Suppose I had not known. Suppose I had cared, suffered, found it a cruel shock— think of the man's bringing such a notice to a woman and sitting there to "observe her reactions." I made no comment at all, remained as serenely indifferent as before. It was really difficult for him.

"The *Call* sent me to see if you had anything to say on the subject," he essayed, rather feebly.

"Do you think a self-respecting woman *would* have anything to say to a newspaper on such a subject?" I gently inquired. He did not. And since the *Call* was at the time a decent newspaper they said little beyond reprinting the news item.

Returning to Oakland, the most distinctive step of the three years was the publication of my first book of poems, *In This Our World,* 1893. It was a tiny thing, 120 pages, about six and a half by five inches. Seventy-five poems. It was printed by McCombs and Vaughn of Oakland, two of my Socialist friends, on sight of a subscription list covering the cost—some $75.00 I think.

I have the little blank book with the names of those first subscribers. The most important was my friend Harriet Howe, who put up $50.00. The edition was in all 1500 copies. I made the design on the cover, based on Olive Schreiner's *Three Dreams In a Desert.*

These little books I placed in local book-stores, to be sold on commission, and also, in my ignorance, sent them to such stores in the East, asking the dealer to sell them, take out his commission, and send me the remainder. One rather large number I placed with the Humboldt Publishing Company of New York, whose cheap editions of popular science I had enjoyed—not knowing they were pirated. Nothing was heard from them, although I wrote making inquiries. What did a piratical publishing house in the East care about an unknown and visibly impracticable woman in California?

Some years later, being in New York, I wandered into that company's office and mildly asked if I could buy a copy of *In This Our World,* by Charlotte Perkins Stetson. They said they had had some but they were sold. "All sold?" I persisted. Yes, all sold.

"Then," said I, still gently, "suppose you pay me for them. I am Mrs. Stetson," and I showed proof of the same. They were not pleased, but gave me a check. As there were ninety-six copies sold, even at my charge of twenty-five cents there should have been $25.00 total receipts. Wherefore it appears they took out 33 1/3 per cent for the operation of selling. I paid part of my board bill with the check, only to learn later, when far away, that it was not good. Being again in the city I wandered in once more, holding the check, narrated the circumstances, and suggested that they pay cash. They did.

That little book of verse brought small returns in cash but much in reputation. It was warmly reviewed in certain discerning papers. I remember a particularly appreciative notice in *Unity* of Chicago, written by Mr. Frederic Saunders, later a lasting friend. Largely owing to that review it has been widely used by Unitarian ministers, and has also been popular with other kinds, much of the work being richly applicable in sermons.

A strong, liberal-minded woman, Miss Catherine Spence of Scotland, whom I met in San Francisco, took the book home with her, and presently it was brought out in England, printed by a friend of hers, Mr. Maxwell, with T. Fisher Unwin, publisher. This was the first cloth edition, 1895. In England it was taken up with instant recognition by thinking people, with most pleasant consequences, among them this: even before the Unwin edition was out I received an order from the great Chambers Publishing House in Edinburgh, forwarded through the Scribner's Company in New York, from a Mrs. Dowie in Edinburgh, for "one copy, *In This Our World*, $.25."

This struck me as amusing, the long printed order-sheet crossing ocean and continent, for that one small booklet. I took a copy, corrected some of its many mistakes, put in my name and address with some cordial words, and sent it off, without any bill. In answer I got the kindest letter from Mrs. Dowie, saying she should always value this as "an early first," and inviting me to visit her if I came to England.

The second edition, also paper, also the same size but thicker, 184 pages now, was, like the first, brought out by friends in San Francisco, in the office of James Barry, editor of the *Star*. John Marble, a printer, one of the "comrades," remarked that he was out of a job and he might as well put in his time setting up my book. Mr. Barry advanced paper and press work, and so *In This Our World* appeared anew early in 1895, this time selling at fifty cents.

In Oakland my circumstances did not improve, though there were some good friends who stood by me in spite of the newspapers. Mrs. Sarah McChesney was one of these, well loved. When Jane Addams visited the coast, she was impressed by the work I was doing, and asked: "Why is not Mrs. Stetson better thought of? She seems a very able woman." "Yes," they answered, "she is a brainy woman, very, but her views are something dreadful." "Are they?" said Miss Addams. "What are her views?" No one could say.

What the creeping slanders were I never knew. There never were any distinct "charges," never the least hint of anything against my "character," in the usual line. There I was, with my boarders to bear witness, working my head off, doing what I could for mother and child while I had them, wearing clothes that were given me, writing, lecturing and preaching as opportunity offered. I knew well the ordinary risks of a woman in my position among San Francisco-minded people, and took extreme precautions to give no least handle for criticism in behavior. For instance I made it a point to be seen nowhere with any man, to receive no slightest "attention." I remember once Edwin Markham, then a school-teacher in Oakland, not yet known as a poet, asked me to take a soda in a drug-store, and I wouldn't, so absurdly careful was I.

I left Oakland in debt and failure, and moved to San Francisco in the summer of 1894, beginning again, with a great new hope—the *Impress*. This was a small paper which had belonged to the P. C. W. P. A. and which I had run for them, successfully, as the *Bulletin*. It seemed to me, and to Helen Campbell, who was to join forces with me in this enterprise a possible thing to make a good family weekly of this. The P. A. was to retain a double page for its special news. Mrs. C. furnished another department of Household Affairs— she being an expert in those lines, and she brought with her an "adopted son," Mr. Paul Tyner, used to newspaper work, who was to be manager.

Mrs. Campbell had been a speaker at our Woman's Congress, and was my first "adopted mother." I had delighted in her writings when a child. The three of us took half a small house on the corner of Powell Street, and—Jackson or Sacramento—a cable-car crossing. Its parlor was used as the meeting-room of the Executive Committee of the P. C. W. P. A., and they had a piano there—concerning which is an amusing tale.

I was not in the least musical, hardly able to distinguish "Yankee Doodle" from "Old Hundred," or to sing either. But I was fond of good hymn tunes, such as I had been familiar with in church-going days in Providence. Mrs. Campbell had a Unitarian Hymn-book, and there was the piano. I did not know the notes, or the keys, and had no ear, but I had eyes, fingers, and brains. Pointing to the opening note in some well-loved tune, I asked her to show me where it was on the keyboard. This she did, explaining the sharps and flats also. Following the air alone, I slowly counted along, till I could sound the notes in sequence, using one or two fingers, and soon, to my delight, really playing the air, recognizably.

Then I essayed to sing it. Touching a note, I made a sound—alas! there was no faintest resemblance. Poor as my ear was I could at least tell a high note from a low one, so I sang the note first too high and then too low—and then gradually herded them in, as it were, till the note I sang and the note on the piano coincided. Great was my delight. In a few months I was not only able to sing some simple tunes correctly, with the piano, but even to carry some of them without it. "Antioch" is my favorite. When preaching, if allowed to select a hymn, I always ask for that one, it is so creditable to Christianity.

Our little weekly was a clean and handsome paper. Bruce Porter made a beautiful heading for it. Mr. Tyner did the political stuff, theatrical notes, and so

on. I wrote articles, verses, editorials, ethical problems
—a department, and reviews. We needed stories. I
could not write a good story every week, much less
buy one. So I instituted a series of "Studies in Style,"
producing each week a short story, or a chapter from
a long one, in avowed imitation of a well-known author.
The readers were to guess the original, and the first
correct guesser to receive a copy of one of that author's
books. Sad to relate they never did, the *Impress* did not
live long enough.

It was an excellent paper; many years later it was
spoken of by a competent critic as the best ever published on the coast. It was not propagandist in any
line, not exclusively feminist in tone, but varied and
interesting. It lasted twenty weeks.

This fiasco was what showed me my standing in that
city. Mrs. Campbell, who was honored as a distinguished stranger, made some inquiries as to the rather
surprising lack of support, either in subscribers or ad-
vertisers, and was answered, "Nothing that Mrs.
Stetson does can succeed here," and, "You risk your
own reputation in joining her." Said a prominent woman
doctor, "Yes, it is a brilliant paper, an interesting
paper, but after what Mrs. Stetson printed in her first
issue no self-respecting woman could have it on her
table."

And what was the marvel of iniquity which so
shocked as immoral a city as the country owned? It
was a beautiful poem, of a nobly religious tendency—
by Grace Ellery Channing! Such was the San Francisco
mind.

One somewhat important woman told Mrs. Campbell that it was a pity she should lose by this venture,
and that she thought the paper might be supported if
a committee of matrons could be assembled who would

guarantee that the paper should be kept—there were a number of requirements, but the only one I remember was "clean." There was really something exquisitely funny in comparing the moral superiority of attitude in the "society" of that city with the stern stoicism, the passion for social improvement and ceaseless effort to serve, of this earnest woman teacher. The *Impress,* blameless and attractive, was open to all.

One piece of work contributed to California during these years was a share in arranging several annual Woman's Congresses. These brought together the foremost women of the state, showed what progress was being made, and introduced noted speakers from the east. Among these, as I have said, were Helen Campbell and Jane Addams. Also came Susan B. Anthony, that grand leader of the Equal Suffrage Movement. These all became friends of mine. Mrs. Campbell became like a mother to me, Miss Anthony wanted me as a suffrage worker, Miss Addams's championship was most valuable.

I used to delight in planning the programs for these congresses, making a balance of the subjects before we invited speakers; and I contributed one feature which I wish could be adopted by all such assemblages. We held three two-hour sessions a day, for a week, four speakers to a session, with this announcement printed on all our letters of invitation, on the programs distributed in the seats, proclaimed from the platform— "Each speaker will be allowed twenty minutes for the reading of the paper. A bell will be rung three minutes before the expiration of that time, to allow the speaker to close."

Ten minutes of discussion followed each paper, real *viva voce* discussion from the floor, in two-minute speeches. The sharply limited time, the genuine and not tedious discussion, with the well-related topics, made the meetings continuously interesting. Women came from all over the state and farther; remote school-teachers saved, the year through, to attend this stirring convention. Our meetings were crowded, we always had to move to a larger hall before the week ended.

The speakers, however much displeased, stopped on time, they had to. One good lady, from Santa Rosa, was particularly aggrieved, said she knew her paper only took twenty minutes to read—she had tried it! But she had to stop when her time was up just the same. Persevering soul that she was, she withdrew into the audience, and in each discussion period up she popped and read her paper for two minutes until she finished it—amid wild applause.

Another instance of the pleasant attitude of the San Franscisco newspapers occurs to me. There had been a murder, an unbelievably atrocious murder of a poor woman, somewhat intoxicated, by a man, quite evidently a pervert. The woman's husband knew me and my work, he came to me pathetically broken, and begged me to make the funeral address.

"I can't ask any minister," he said, "they'd blame her. You'll know, you'll understand." He told me how her father had been a dipsomaniac, that she had inherited the craving, that a very little made her irresponsible, that she had never meant—"

It was a painfully difficult thing to do, the dreadful story blazoned in pitiless head-lines far and wide, the ghastly details in every one's mind. I had not known her beyond a casual introduction. But I could not refuse the broken-hearted husband.

It was in an undertaker's parlor. One of my friends

went with me, and seeing the blank gloom of the place she bought a dollar's worth of glorious sweet peas— about a bushel of them, and we poured that flood of color over the coffin. There were no mourners but the husband, but there stood like a row of vultures, reporters, ready to make the most of every detail and to make it all as hideous as they could—to keep up the story.

I said what I could, with as much of understanding and sympathy as was possible to me. And the newspapers gave full description of the ghastly scene and stated that I had thrust myself into this congenial limelight for the sake of notoriety....

The summer of 1895 brought my California activities to a close. I had put in five years of most earnest work, with voice and pen, and registered complete failure. Such gain as I had made in England and our eastern states was not known here. Outside of warm support in the labor movement, the best welcome I had met was with a few friends in Stanford University, where I visited a little and addressed the students once or twice. I remember sharply how delightful it was to be among educated people again, bookish people, and to be treated with respect and friendliness. I had warm personal friends, to be sure, but the public verdict was utter condemnation.

Thirty-five years old. A failure, a repeated, cumulative failure. Debt, quite a lot of it. No means of paying, no strength to hold a job if I got one. I decided that it was time to leave. So I gave up the half-house, Mrs. Campbell and Mrs. Tyner having gone east again, and gave away enough of my scant furniture to enable a poor woman who had been living in the basement to keep house in a small way again. I remember how astonished she was at some silver which was part of this outfit. "Why it's *silver!*" she protested. "Well, why not? You need some spoons and forks, don't you? What's silver!" Other things I stored in the house of a good friend.

"I am going east," I announced. I didn't know when, nor where, nor how, but I knew I was going. That summer I visited about among various friends and admirers, and lectured a little here and there. There was one trip over the mountains, when I sat on the front seat of the rocking stage, talking to the driver now and then. We had topped the divide, and began swift descent; a narrow road from which one looked *down* on soaring eagles; and hairpin turns, as we rounded the spreading flanks of the hills. Approaching these sharp turns the driver did not slacken speed, but merely put a big whistle in his mouth and blew to give warning of our approach. But one man coming up must have been deaf, for we whirled around the corner and were upon him—before they could pull up, his horses were trying to climb the side of the mountain and ours had their forefeet over the edge. It was a close shave, but they managed to wriggle out of it in safety, and when we were on our way again I took up the conversation where it had broken off.

The driver looked at me as if I were uncanny, probably thought I was not intelligent enough to be afraid; maybe I wasn't. That evening in the little town where the trip ended I was strolling about to see the place and passed a Salvation Army mission. There on his knees I saw that driver—he knew danger when he saw it, anyway.

There was one long trip up the central valley; from five in the morning to five at night I think it was, ending in Sacramento; and all day long, on both sides of the track, there ran beside us an unbroken ribbon of flowers. On my arrival I was met by two dingy-looking women, and a tall, handsome, well-dressed man, with two offers of entertainment. I had two lecture engagements, thus represented, but felt shy of the impressive man, and went home with the women for the first night; he was to call for me next day. These women were the wife and mother-in-law of a man I had met who had made the first engagement. He had told me he kept a hotel in Sacramento, and asked me to stay with him when in town. This "hotel" I found to have been a most unsavory sailors' boarding-house, now purified by the simple expedient of keeping women out of it— but I was a visitor. We ate in what had been the bar, I think; there were decorations on the mirror and windows, drawn in soap. In my bedroom the window sill was furry with old dirt, the bed I slept on, not in; and the washing accommodations were most insufficient.

But I was glad I went with them, though that night's lecture wasn't much, for the little woman was very unhappy and I was able to help her. My own various distresses gave me *carte blanche* in other people's troubles, it appeared. I found that the closest thing one can say to another is, "I've been there!"

Next day came the handsome, finely dressed man, with a prancing pair of horses, and took me to his fine house. Here I had a lovely and luxurious bedroom with its bathroom all shining, a reading-lamp by the bed, with the latest books and magazines, flowers of course,—it was the most sudden and longest leap from bottom to top that I ever took. It was fortunate for me that I chose the poor place first.

After this I waited a little in a friend's house in San Francisco. Jane Addams had invited me to visit her in Hull House, in Chicago, so I knew *where* I was going. Another friend had asked to meet me on a certain date, and I accepted—as well then as any time—so I knew *when*. But in order to keep that engagement I must leave on a certain Tuesday, and up to the Sunday previous I did not know *how*—for I had no money for the journey.

That Sunday came good Mrs. Sarah B. Cooper, always a friend, with a half-price ticket—as a missionary—which she had somehow obtained from the Southern Pacific! Perhaps they were glad to get rid of me. Perhaps she did not mention who the missionary was. I took it thankfully. Now I had everything but some ready money for the trip, and this I intended to borrow from a man I knew, next morning. He was kind, cordial, willing, but actually hadn't the money—I had asked for fifty dollars.

This was somewhat of a blow, the next day being Tuesday. But I said to myself, "Never mind, I'll go if I have to sit up in the day-coach and eat out of a basket. But I will not try to get it of any one else just now, being a little discouraged perhaps. To-night I'm going to a meeting of The Altrurians, some one there will give it to me. I'll go home and take a nap." This I did, sleeping peacefully.

These Altrurians, named after Howell's recent book, were another of California's thousand little clubs with large purposes. I went, made my little speech, and studied those present with a view to the probability of their having any money. Selecting one who seemed able if willing, and reducing my request by half, I spoke to him as we went out—a total stranger—told him exactly how I was situated, had been disappointed at the last moment, was going anyway, but I'd be glad if he'd let me have twenty-five dollars for a month or two. He promptly produced five little half-eagles, so I had a berth and enough to eat on my journey.

I paid him in due course, paid all those San Francisco debts sooner or later. I remember how astonished the Oakland land-lady was when I turned up, some years after. She opened the door, and stood, staring blankly, as I calmly remarked, "I've come to pay the rent."

That dear lady who had enabled me to pay for Katharine's ticket and move to Powell Street got hers back just after the earthquake and fire, when a little ready money was most useful.

The sense of hope and power rose up afresh as the train rolled eastward. Failures were nothing, debts were nothing—didn't most business have to have credit? I was alive and had my work to do; I was escaping from the foulest misrepresentation and abuse I have ever known, and I had a wholly reliable religion and social philosophy.

On the cars I wrote this, not much as poetry, but strong in purpose:

As the strong sweet light of the morning,
As the strong sweet air from the sea,
As the strong sweet music of the wind among the leaves,
Comes the voice of my goodwill to a weary world that grieves,
    Crying "Be glad! Be free!"

CHAPTER XIII

AT LARGE

ASKED, before leaving the coast that summer, to write my name and address in the visitor's book of the Friday Morning Club of Los Angeles, I cheerfully inscribed, "Charlotte Perkins Stetson. At large." For the next five years that was a legitimate address. Back and forth and up and down, from California to Maine, from Michigan to Texas, from Georgia to Oregon, twice to England, I wandered. There were visits, long and short, even residences, very short, but for the most part there was the railroad train, and no address in my little book to which to send "the remains" in case of accident.

"Don't you feel very much at sea?" some one asked. "I do. Like a sea-gull at sea." And when inquiring friends would ask, "Where do you live now?" my reply was, "Here."

The difference is great between one's outside "life," the things which happen to one, incidents, pains and pleasures, and one's "living." Outside, here was a woman undergoing many hardships and losses, and particularly handicapped by the mental weakness which shut down on her again, utter prostration and misery. But inside her was a conscious humanity, immensely beyond self; a realization of the practical immortality of that ceaseless human life of ours, of its prodigious power, its endless growth.

My "self" I was sorry for. When the suffering was

extreme I would look at my self as if it were a little
creature in my hand, and stroke it softly, saying, "You
poor little thing! You do have a hard time, don't you."
When the burden seemed more than I could possibly
stand I would say, "Huh! You don't have to. It's up
to God and He can stand it."

"He" is merely a survival in terminology. This God
I was so sure of, was not him or her, not limited by
personality, but an inescapable, ever-acting force *to be
used*. Once solidly convinced of this reliable power—
nothing else matters much. That workable assumption
was at the bottom of my cheerful calmness. But besides this basic strength there was a growing social
philosophy which was like a sunrise. One may be contented or reconciled with one's individual life, yet in
misery about the suffering and confusion of the world.

Mr. Howells told me I was the only optimist reformer he ever met. Perhaps because I was not a
reformer, but a philosopher. I worked for various reforms, as Socrates went to war when Athens needed
his services, but we do not remember him as a soldier.
My business was to find out what ailed society, and
how most easily and naturally to improve it.

It might be called the effort of a social inventor,
trying to advance human happiness by the introduction
of better psychic machinery. I was not depressed by
the local and temporary misery I saw in the world, any
more than by the long centuries of worse misery behind us. When humanity is grasped as a growing thing,
one long, unbroken process, one is more impressed by
its new advances than by its old mistakes.

Moreover, I had from these childish years of happy
castle-building, the mental capacity for keen enjoyment
from percepts. To see in my mind a clear, attainable
happiness and the way to get it, was a solid joy. What

I saw in the world was not its foolish, unnecessary troubles, but its splendid possibilities; as a competent promoter sees in some tottering business the success he can make of it.

As I had planned the programs for those Congresses of Women, I planned programs for the world, seeing clearly the gradual steps by which we might advance to an assured health, a growing happiness. If they did not see it, would not do it, that was not my fault; my job, my one preëminent work, was to "see" and to "say," and I did it.

The main output was in lecturing and preaching— there was little difference except in using a text. Once, indeed, in the Unitarian Church in Moline, Ill., gazing at the calm resigned faces of the congregation, I announced, "I am not going to give you any text. If you listen carefully you will know what the sermon is about by what I say." They listened. Furthermore, they paid me a prodigious compliment, by keeping me, after dismissal at twelve, for three-quarters of an hour, to answer questions.

Sick or well, in all the years, preaching was always ready. There was no preparation, simply the choice of some subject in which I was deeply interested—had something to give. I did not use oratory, just talked, talked so that I could be heard without difficulty, understood without effort. Also, being a Beecher, there was plenty of fun, nice little jokes that happened in the soberer part, and at which I chuckled with the audience.

The hearers were always interested, even if they resented the criticisms of present methods and disliked the alternatives offered. I used to love the buzz of excited discussion which followed a lecture, though not assuming it to be favorable. Nor was I misled by the line of handshakers who came up to express approval, but cast my eye upon the far larger group going out, who probably did not like it. To avoid pride, anger, or discouragement, I made it a rule for years never to look at what the papers said of my lectures. This helped to maintain a vivid freshness of presentation. . . .

So I went gaily to Chicago, on Miss Addams's invitation. Jane Addams was a truly great woman. Her mind had more "floor space" in it than any other I have known. She could set a subject down, unprejudiced, and walk all around it, allowing fairly for every one's point of view.

At that time the work started by her and Miss Ellen Starr in Hull House was fresh in the public mind, widely known and honored. The wise kindness with which she took me in for a three months' visit had an immediate effect in counteracting my California newspaper-made reputation. Instead of ridicule and abuse I found myself introduced by sonorous ministers as "One of those consecrated women who have given their lives to the service of the poor and needy." Which was true enough, except for the limited object, my interest was in all humanity, not merely in the under side of it; in sociology, not social pathology.

The change was sudden and great. To Hull House came distinguished people, humanitarian thinkers from all over the country, and from other countries, too. Here was companionship, fellow feeling, friendly society. My verse was known and liked, new friends were made, there were lecture engagements, and presently I was asked to be the head of another settlement, on the North Side, in a place called "Little Hell."

The loathly river flowed sluggishly near by, thick and ill-smelling; Goose Island lay black in the slow stream. Everywhere a heavy dinginess; low, dark brick factories and gloomy wooden dwellings often below the level of the street; foul plank sidewalks, rotten and full of holes; black mud underfoot, damp soot drifting steadily down over everything.

Knowing the unreliability of my health I did not undertake to manage this settlement, but suggested Mrs. Campbell, who was by this time teaching economics in Wisconsin; and she accepted the position. I did live there, however, and helped as I could with the work, still lecturing as opportunity offered. Two young Harvard men who were interested in sociology were also with us, George Virtue and Hervey White, and later a pleasant Miss Vogel.

Helen Campbell was our beloved "Head" and mother to us all. She even cooked special treats for us when the settlement maid was worse than usual; I remember bringing in some delicious gingerbread with the proclamation, "Made by our Ma!—Not marred by our Maid!" It was a pleasant family life, though planted in the midst of misery. Among so many poor why should I worry over my own poverty?

"Social evolution," I wrote on some of those everlasting self-reminding pieces of paper, "is as natural as any other kind. It is promoted by individuals. If I am one of them, and needed at this time, I shall be enabled to function. That means living, and that means money—enough to live on." And though I was many times entirely out of money, there always came some, somehow, so that living went on and some debts were paid. The one important thing was to do the work. As to power, that was God. "There is plenty of God," I wrote. "Enough for us all. We have but to help ourselves to that illimitable force."

So I lectured and preached, wherever I was asked, for my expenses or for what they could afford to give.

"Will they pay you?" some friend asked. "I don't know." "Don't *know*—isn't that your business?" "Oh no, my business is to preach, and I do that whenever I can. It is their business to pay me, that's not my affair."

For years I lived on that basis, as propertyless and as desireless as a Buddhist priest, almost, though needing something more than a yellow robe and begging bowl. Once I preached in Battle Creek, Michigan. My pay was to be the collection. The sermon was on heaven, and never did I give a better one, making them see how near it was, our heaven on earth, how real and practical, how well within our power to make. When it was ended the congregation sat breathless, eager, deeply moved. I gave them a benediction and the meeting was over.

I quite forgot the collection. If I had remembered it, I would not have broken the spell that was on them for any money.

Two good old people were entertaining me, and next morning my host asked me, "Do you believe in missionaries?" I said I did, some kinds. "Do you think they ought to be supported?" I agreed that they had to be. Then he told me that they thought I was a missionary, and his wife wanted him to give me ten dollars. So I was paid, even without the collection.

The social philosophy I was teaching included my organic theory of social economics, later developed in Human Work; the theory of the economic independence and specialization of women as essential to the improvement of marriage, motherhood, domestic industry, and racial improvement; with much on advance in child culture.

I worked for Equal Suffrage when opportunity offered, believing it to be reasonable and necessary, though by no means as important as some of its protagonists held; and for Socialism, feeling the real basis of that system to be right, in spite of the mishandling of Marx. It amazes me yet to see how stupidly, how obstinately, people refuse to consider fairly a proposition because of their violent prejudice against some of its interpreters. It is as if Christianity were to be judged by the Doukhobors!

In January, 1896, I attended a Suffrage Convention in Washington, D. C., as a delegate from California, with traveling expenses sent by their W.S.A. There I spoke, read verses, preached, and addressed the Judiciary Committee of the House of Representatives—while having the mumps! The attack was so light that it was discredited till we heard that my fellow-workers in the Settlement had come down with it, far worse than I.

Most pleasing and important of all the happenings of this visit was meeting Professor Lester F. Ward, quite the greatest man I have ever known. He was an outstanding leader in Sociology, familiar with many sciences, and his Gynæcocentric Theory, first set forth in a *Forum* article in 1888, is the greatest single contribution to the world's thought since Evolution.

He had written me before this, being struck with the poem "Similar Cases," naturally pleased with its scientific background, and now he and Mrs. Ward gave me a reception, where I met many learned and interesting men and women. Having spoken that morning at the Conventions, and in the afternoon at the Capitol, it is no wonder that the day ends, "Am seen home by Dr. Eaton" (one of our delegates) "and put to bed. Says it grip." It wasn't. It was mumps.

Back, rather feebly, to Little Hell, where there were several much sicker than I, and among our neighbors,

worse trouble. "The Marshall baby died last night."
"Visit Mrs. Marshall. Lend shawl for the funeral. Mr.
Virtue lent his coat and other things. We advance
money for the funeral."

Lectures went on. Writing went on. March 10th:
"Feel badly again. Just a cold but pulls me down
much. Better later and write Burne-Jonesey poem." As
a product of Little Hell this is worth quoting:

THE BEDS OF FLEUR-DE-LYS

High-lying, sea-blown stretches of green turf,
   Wind-bitten close, salt-colored from the sea,
Low curve on curve spread far to the cool sky,
And, curving over them as long they lie,
   Beds of wild fleur-de-lys.

Wide-flowing, self-sown, stealing near and far,
   Breaking the green like islands in the sea;
Great stretches at your feet, and spots that bend
Dwindling over the horizon's end,—
   Wild beds of fleurs-de-lys.

The light keen wind streams on across the lifts,
   Thin wind of western springtime by the sea;
The close turf smiles unmoved, but over her
Is the far-flying rustle and sweet stir
   In beds of fleur-de-lys.

And here and there, across the smooth low grass,
   Tall maidens wander, thinking of the sea;
And bend, and bend, with light robes blown aside,
For the blue lily-flowers that bloom so wide,—
   The beds of fleur-de-lys.

As this is one of the very few poems among all my
verses, it seems singularly out of place in that environment. "Wed. 11th. Write 'The Room At The Top.'"

This last taught me something about my "style" which I had never in the least intended. I noticed this verse:

> It is not so hard to stand
> And fight on the broad free land,
> But to climb in the wind and night,
> And fight, and climb—and fight—!

and perceived that all the words were of one syllable. Looking at the rest I found the whole poem had but one or two longer ones. Then among all the others I noted the same unconscious habit, evidently a natural method.

Edward Everett Hale, in his admirable book for young peole, *How To Do It*, gives as an ideal specimen this political speech: "I do not think that I am fit for this place, but my friends think that I am, and if you put me in, I will do the best I can." Perhaps I had subconsciously cherished that ideal.

Meanwhile, my health sank lower and lower, the same old misery and exhaustion. "Sunday Mch. 15. Am so bad that 'mother' sends me over to Dr. McCracken's. They take me in joyfully and keep me. Also they recognize that I am in a serious condition."

This is another instance of the wonderful goodness with which, lacking family, I have been cared for by friends, wherever I went. Good doctors have doctored me for nothing, good dentists have made me a present of their work—Dr. Van Orden of San Francisco gave me a Christmas present of fifty dollars' worth of work, once, and charged next to nothing for more service.

The McCrackens were both physicians. Mrs. McCracken was a member of the Chicago Woman's Club, had often heard me speak; I had given parlor lectures in her house, we were already friends. And now they rescued me from that black house in Little Hell, welcomed me in their own pleasant house on the south side, and the wife-and-mother-doctor slept on the lounge downstairs and gave me her own bed, with her little girl in it. She well knew what it meant to me to have a child in my arms again, a little girl child, about the age of mine when I had her in Pasadena.

Mr. Doctor took me with him when he made his morning calls, leaving me limp and dolorous in the buggy while he was visiting his patients. March 16. "Sit down in office to talk to Dr. and weep dismally. It is really the beginning of melancholia. Am very weak, can hardly sit up, low appetite, mind a heavy dark gray." He tried to cheer and encourage me. "You should not dwell on sad things," he said. "You should think of the pleasant ones—count your mercies."

To which I wearily replied, "Doctor, I am thirty-six, nearly. I have no father—to speak of, I have lost my mother, my brother is unable to help me, I have lost my husband, I have lost my child—temporarily at least, I have no trade or profession, no 'job' and could not hold one if offered; I have no money and am in debt; you know the state of my health,—what do you advise me to think about?"

They concluded that I was on the verge of losing my mind. . . .

But I didn't. I pulled up again, somewhat, went back to the Settlement, and continued to lecture. Between January 2nd and July 3rd of that year I gave fifty-seven or more sermons and addresses, average of more than two a week. In April I went east again, stopping first in New York, where I made this entry: "Sun. 19th. At Father's—first experience." This visit and my later stay there call for a little family history.

When my father was a young man, he became en-

gaged to a pretty and charming damsel called Frankie
Johnson, but the engagement was broken, his mother
acting as intermediary. The slighted lady presently con-
soled herself by marrying James Beecher, my father's
youngest uncle, not much older than he. Thereafter,
the changeable lover married my mother. In years
pursuing, Mr. Beecher died; still later my mother died;
and what should father do but return from California
and marry the love of his youth, now his widowed aunt!
By this combination my father became my great-uncle,
my great-aunt became my mother, and I became my
own first-cousin-once-removed. Furthermore, good
Mrs. Beecher, having no children of her own, had
adopted three little orphan girls, all of them pretty,
two of them twins, and these I used to call my step-
adopted-sisters-in-law-by-marriage!

It was literally the first time I had ever been in my
father's house since infancy, and at that it was only
a boarding-house, kept by my stepmother. She was a
charming little lady, with curly hair and dimples, the
kind which attains vivid attractiveness at sixteen and
remains permanently at that period. She had long kept
a girls' school at Cos Cob near New York, but after
this second marriage she and her three daughters
undertook the boarding-house business—father, unfortunately, was not earning much—if anything. He was
already far from well, though at the time of my visit
he was in Washington, probably trying to arrange for
some employment.

That April day's entry closes with: "Have $15.00
and a little change. Trunk .50. breakfast .20." My
margin was always narrow. I spoke in Brooklyn, the
same night in Providence—after eight years' absence.
It was a pleasure to see relations and friends, and an
astonishment to find their children quite grown up.

"Address the Com. of Sen. and House in the State House." In the evening "Reception and banquet. Speak again. $20.00."

Midnight train back to New York, where I arrived too early for breakfast and beguiled the time by a lovely spring morning walk in Central Park before returning to my stepmother's. Lectured in Brooklyn again that evening: "W.S.A. $20.25."

Again at my stepmother's: "Talk with the boarders a lot, Mr. Funston especially—an interesting man." He was, becoming General Funston in later years.

The lectures of this spring were somewhat scattered: Chicago of course, Milwaukee, Detroit, Evanston, Washington, Philadelphia, Springfield, Ill., Grand Haven, Mich., Aurora, Ill., Brooklyn, N. Y., Providence, R. I., Lynn, Mass., Boston, Kansas City, Mo., Topeka, Kan.—that Kansas trip will bear enlargement. It is an excellent specimen of the kind of work I was doing. Mrs. Addison, a suffrage delegate from Kansas, had planned it after meeting me in Washington.

Thus the diary, June 5, 1896: "Reach Kansas City, Mo. at 9.35 A.M. Am taken to Almon's Hotel, K. City, Kan. and stay there a day. Callers, reporters, etc. nap. car-ride, speak in evening on 'The Goodness of Common Men.' Made good impression. Uncomfortable hotel, very."

Next day to Topeka, and to visit a Mrs. Hull: "A delightful place." Sunday, "Lecture in Hamilton Hall, evening, on 'How to Get Good and How to Stay So.' Well received." Next evening again in the same place, on "The Heroes We Need Now." "Small but pleased audience." Tuesday: "Speak on 'Production and Distribution' in a small hall to a small audience. Good lecture—folks pleased." Also, that morning I had addressed the high school for ten minutes on "Educated Bodies." Wednesday: "Speak in High School, evening, on 'The Philosophy of Dress.' Not very good, was too tired." Thursday, Eleventh: "Spoke P.M. in High School on 'The New Motherhood.' Drove out to Tecumseh in evening to address suffrage meeting, in buggy with Miss Julia Seymour and Miss Miriam Church. Converted Miss Seymour. Very funny time— no one there at first—they don't gather till nearly nine."

Friday Twelfth: "A reception given The Stedman Club. P.M. Spoke on Club Work for Women. In evening Presbyterian Church on 'The Goodness of Common Men.'" Saturday Thirteenth: "Parlor meeting at Mrs. Wheeler's. Spoke on 'The New Motherhood.' Successful. Stayed to dinner. Stupid evening—the men afraid of me. $10.00."

Sunday Fourteenth: "Preached in Baptist Church in North Topeka, A.M. on Love. Very good. Slept all P.M. Speak in Congregational Church in evening on Truth. Get faint and have to stop short of half an hour. Pretty much tired out and bad air in church. A splendid week. $20.00."

June in Kansas is apt to be warm.

Monday Fifteenth: "Go down to Lyndon P.M. and speak on 'The Good Time Coming' for the Sweazys. Drive out home with them and stay over night. Nice folks. $15.00." Tuesday was a day! "Drive over to Osage City and take train for Holton. Stop over in Topeka awhile. See Dr. Harding and Mrs. Hull. Stay at Mrs. Moore's in Holton. Splendid supper. Speak at the 'University' on 'The Heroes We need Now.' Change dress again, midnight 'Hog-train'—ride in caboose—to Valley Falls."

I remember that evening well. They sent me to the

station in a "hack," escorted by an unhappy student from the University. This worthy youth had probably never been up so late in his life. He continually relapsed into slumber in spite of the noblest efforts, so I assured him that I was quite safe in the station and sent him home. Kansas is admirably provided with railroads east and west, but very poorly north and south, and to make my next connection I had to wait for what was described to me as the "night freight." When at last it drew in to that dreary little station, after midnight, behold it was a long, malodorous cattle train!

Car after car jangled by, mooing, baaing, squealing, cackling—and the only place for a human traveler was the caboose at the end, occupied by cattle punchers, trainhands and salesmen. Some were sleeping on the long seat at the side, the others clustered together telling "snappy stories." I slipped quietly in and sat down next the door, looking nowhere at all.

Then was shown the chivalry and courtesy of western men. When one of the sleepers awoke and began to swear as was his wont, he was softly and promptly hushed—"Shut up! There's a lady aboard!" And those jovial raconteurs went on with their stories indeed, but told as about their sisters!

I spoke next day in a little church in Madison, Kansas, and on Thursday; eighteenth went to Eureka, where I was met by my good friend Mrs. Addison, and "a deputation." A reception that night. "Very nice people here, intelligent and progressive." Friday I spoke twice, $17.00. Saturday, June 20th: "Morning train for Howard. Stay at Mrs. McKay's. A vague-feeling place. Mrs. Addison and I have one room, small, and a feather bed!!! We remove it. Speak in

evening in church on 'The Heroes We Need Now.'
Well received. Methodist minister calls. $3.50."

Sunday has a very pleasant happening: "Preach in
Methodist church on 'Whosoever Loseth His Life for
My Sake'—Very well received. A Mr. Barretman—
Co. Supt., put into Mrs. McKay's hand $5.00 for me,
and said 'God bless her, and tell her to keep on preaching that gospel.' Speak to Christian Endeavorers P.M.
a little. Drive to Moline. A dirty mean place. Get
crackers and milk at restaurant. $8.39 (I judge that
included the extra five)."

Monday, Twenty-second: "Stormy night, up at five.
Six A.M. train to Winfield. Breakfast in hotel. Am left
in delicious peace and loneliness at Mrs. Albright's
house. Write. Winfield assembly P.M. Hear part of
Gov. Hubbard's address on Japan. A bombastic, ego-
tistic longwinded fat man."

Tuesday a few words and a poem at the Assembly
A.M. and again P.M. lecture on Woman's Suffrage and
Men's Sufferings. This was evidently the high light of
the tour, judging by the fee, $50.00, and I think it was
also the occasion when, drawing in my breath for some
imposing peroration, I also drew in a fly. It was an
out-door auditorium, airy and pleasant, but free to
various forms of life. The lecture had made a good
impression and was winding up effectively. Should I
let all be spoiled by a mere insect? As a few quiet efforts failed to dislodge the little visitor I calmly swallowed it, and finished in fine style. This quick lunch
had no ill effect whatever.

Wednesday spoke twice, Thursday once, and took
9 P.M. for Concordia. That was a broken journey.
"Chair car to Strong City. Common car to Manchester.
Chair car to Concordia. Hour and forty minutes wait

in Strong City. Stood it first rate. Two good rooms at
boarding house, *alone.* Nap. Write. Say a few words
at Institute. Dine well. Sleep three hours. Speak in
evening on 'The Royal Road to Learning.' $25.00."
Saturday the twenty-seventh, it was "U.P. to Clay
Center, Rock Island to Wichita, Mo. P. to Eureka";
again visiting the Addisons, and preaching next day
in the Congregational church—$4.00.

On Monday the Twenty-ninth was another amusing
trip. Good Mrs. Addison had planned all my connections and arranged for entertainment, so that I had
been met and cared for everywhere; but this was the
last engagement on her tour, and when I reached Yates
Center I found I had no directions whatever. It was a
small, dingy wooden station standing quite alone on
the wide prairie—nothing else in sight. One vehicle,
a sort of carry-all, stood waiting. Into it got the two
traveling men who were the only other passengers
alighting there, and I followed—there was nothing else
to do.

"Where you goin'?" demanded the driver of first one
and then the other of the two men. They told him, and
then he turned to me. "Where you goin'?" To which
I calmly replied, "I have not the faintest idea." But
he had, fortunately. "Guess you're the lady that's goin'
to Mrs. Clapp's"—and he was right. "A nice woman,
Mrs. Clapp. Speak in Baptist church on Woman's Suffrage and Men's Sufferings. Very poor address. Tired
out and an abominable audience, dull and antagonistic."

Next day: "Speak again, evening, on 'Kingdom
Come.' A little better but not much. Leave on one-thirty
train, night. Don't want to see this place again. A person, presumably here, printed on the white satin lining
of my hat 'Better get your face plated.' The exact na-

ture of this I am yet unable to grasp. Y.C. paid
$15.00."

One more stop, in Bedford, Iowa, with a friend's
friends, and an address—$5.45, and so back to
Chicago.

On Wednesday, July 8th, started for England.

CHAPTER XIV

ENGLAND

THIS first visit to England was made to attend the International Socialist and Labor Congress of 1896, to which I was a delegate from California. It was intended that I should go as a Socialist, to which end they sent me the membership card; but when I read that card I utterly refused to sign it; sharply disagreeing with both theory and method as advanced by the followers of Marx.

Among the various unnecessary burdens of my life is that I have been discredited by conservative persons as a Socialist, while to the orthodox Socialists themselves I was quite outside the ranks. Similarly the anti-suffrage masses had me blackly marked "Suffragist," while the suffragists thought me a doubtful if not dangerous ally on account of my theory of the need of economic independence of women. One of the suffrage leaders once said to me, "After all I think you will do our cause more good than harm, because what you ask is so much worse than what we ask that they will grant our demands in order to escape yours."

Not being able to go as a Socialist, I went as a delegate from the Alameda County, California, Federation of Trades, duly accredited. This was the group which had given me the medal for the best essay on the labor question, while I was in Oakland—the others must have been poor indeed!

I left Chicago by train, then by boat from Toronto

down the St. Lawrence, through the Thousand Islands and the rapids, to Montreal, and sailed July 10th, on S.S. *Mongolian,* Allen Line, for $50.00. Before leaving Chicago my diary remarks, "Feel calm and happy. Cash low however, down to $10.00 in envelope. $20.00 in purse. Never mind." And I didn't.

The steamer was a "whaleback" cattle-boat, one "class," pleasant people enough. Our bovine passengers grew steadily more perceptible as days passed, until the dining-room port-holes had to be closed, to keep them out, as it were.

"Get to the foremost prow and the rearmost stern and am happy," says the diary. There is no such chance to be alone with the sea on the big liner. "Sit about contentedly with books, papers and writing things." "Icebergs! Yes, lots of them. Just like the pictures and descriptions." "Pleasant morning alone in the stern. Pleasant afternoon making paper dolls for the chicks." Whose "chicks" I have utterly forgotten, but children were always a comfort. "Crochet a cap, close fitting, as my beloved hat blows somewhat." "Crochet cap for one Mr. Roberts. Three men have lost caps overboard."

It was an eleven-day voyage, landing at Birkenhead on Tuesday the twenty-first, and going to Liverpool by lighter.

There were two jokes on me, this trip. One was the row I made when I found the "outside room" I had stipulated when buying my ticket in Chicago merely opened into a passage, with a sort of skylight there. I was furious, being passionately addicted to fresh air, and wanting to look out at the water. There was no redress, however, and I prepared to suffocate, avoiding both berths and taking the hard little sofa on which

I could have my head right by the open door. The cold sea air poured down that skylight affair in such a torrent that I caught a heavy cold, and became more reconciled to my room.

The other was my becoming a smuggler without knowing it. My method of selling my little paper books was of the crudest. I always carried some with me for the purpose, and I had quite a lot of the second edition in my trunk, which I hoped to dispose of in England. The trunk had not come when I reached the steamer, so I took a cab and brought it from the railroad, and it was hauled on board hurriedly at the last minute.

I spoke to one of the officers, regretting the haste, there had been no time for examination by the customs officers. He reassured me, "There's nothing dutiable that you'd be likely to have, only tobacco and liquor— books." "Books!" I rather gasped. "Oh, not such books as you'd take, Madam, only books to sell." The trunk was in the hold. No use telling him about it now. I would explain when I got to England, and pay what I must.

But in all the bustle of arrival I could not find my keys. I searched and searched, called upon the stewards for help and got none—they seemed somehow amused! —landed, and was met by Alfred Hicks, an English friend I had known in America. To him I explained my predicament, we told the customs officers, and sent for the loose keys they keep for such emergencies; but they were in a hurry, judged us harmless, and I got into England with my contraband, untouched. Then I nobly gave them away, instead of selling!

I stayed with the Hicks family in Camden Town, London, and most kind they were to me. Good Mrs. Amie Hicks, a wise, strong woman, I adopted as my

English mother, and the whole family, with Claire, an adopted sister, became like brothers and sisters.

My first call was on T. Fisher Unwin, my English publisher. He showed me reviews, many and good, was most polite and kind. I found in England a far higher reputation than at home, based on the little book of poems. John Davidson, in his *The Man Forbid and Other Essays,* has an amusing reference to them. There is an argument between two initialed gentlemen, as to whether women can write poetry or not. One is sure that they cannot, that they have not the clear strength of mind or some such requirement. The other then quotes a stanza from the most brutal bit of satire I ever wrote, "The Brood Mare," and his opponent says that proves just what he was saying—no woman could have written a thing like that—"While she is looking for an agate to fit her sling, a man will throw bricks, mud, anything—and hit the mark." I quote from memory, the bit of criticism always pleased me.

For sightseeing I went up into the tiptop of St. Paul's, long familiar from reading. Next day a long row on the Thames with Alfred Hicks, from Richmond to Hampton Court. I surveyed the exquisite neatness, the close-cut velvet lawns, trimmed as with scissors to the water's edge, mile upon mile of lovely decorum. "Beautiful!" I agreed. "Beautiful! But where do you go when you want to get out of doors?" He knew America east and west, and appreciated the difference. But the peaceful cleanness and greenness of England are dear to the heart of any real American.

The Congress was prefaced by a "Great Peace Demonstration," a procession, an enormous gathering in Hyde Park, that Paradise of free speech. I was in one of the speaker's wagons, with August Bebel, Herbert Burroughs, and, as I remember, George Bernard

Shaw. "A drenching rain," says my diary, and "I was the last speaker on the last platform to stay out."

Next day, Monday, the opening, in Queen's Hall, the largest in London. There were distinguished Socialists from many countries, the more conservative Labor group, and many earnest Anarchists trying to secure seats. Tuesday I record: "Fighting still on credentials and 'Zurich Resolution.' Anarchist bodies finally refused admission." But in the evening I went to their meeting and heard Prince Kropotkin, Elisee Reclus, Louise Michel—desperately earnest souls.

Of all the "literature" with which our seats were papered, the funniest of all were the plaints of the anarchists, as to their lack of organized numbers. They said that the principles of anarchism had been taught in England for many years, and that society after society had been formed to further the teaching; but that when differences of opinion arose, as no one would give way to another, they of course divided, and so subdivided until the society disappeared! A better exposition of the essential weakness of that philosophy could hardly be offered.

Jaurés, the great French Socialist, was with us, said to be the greatest orator in France. He was certainly the greatest I ever heard. A stocky man, thick-necked and heavy, with one gesture, a sort of hammering motion with his right hand. As his emphasis increased he pounded the air, harder and harder; his face and neck reddened, his veins swelled and stood out, purple. And in this rising storm of eloquence the great audience was deeply moved, we rose in our seats again and again, fairly gasping with excitement. It was of no importance that the English-speaking crowd did not understand the language, oratory does not need understanding. I was as much stirred as any one, and did not know a word he said.

The Fabian Society, that group of intelligent, scientific, practical and efficient English Socialists, honored me with membership. I sat with them during the meetings, and was delighted to meet some who were known to me already as writers. I saw a good deal of "the great G.B.S." as he was called, Mr. Shaw. He and others of the Fabian group wore knee-breeches, soft shirts, woolen hose and sandals.

Some of these sandals were made by Edward Carpenter, who lived in a small cottage in the country, near a little brook which served as a bathtub, and "Worked with his hands." I was taken to see him, later, and he measured my feet and made me a pair of those strong leather sandals, still in working order.

At a most miscellaneous reception given during the Congress by those distinguished Fabians, Mr. and Mrs. Sydney Webb, I stood talking to two men at once, an English coal-miner and a charming blue-eyed Italian Prince—Prince Borghese.

The Webbs later invited me to their place in the country, near Saxmundham. Mr. Shaw was there at the time, and the Miss Payne Townsend whom he afterward married. There was a tent and a summer-house on either side of the lawn; he sat in one working on his plays, and I in the other with my writing. I remember the little cubes of wood he placed here and there, visualizing the positions of his characters on the stage. The note in the diary: "Some talk with Bernard Shaw on literary work. Very good and useful criticism."

He was kind enough to send to London for "Candida," asking my opinion of it. It did not seem to me at all convincing—the assumption that the puny poet was the stronger of the two men, and that Candida was so superior to her efficient husband. If that impressive lady had had to go out and earn her living she might not have been so impressive.

The kind interest of these people was all due to the little first book of poems. Mrs. Webb had me read some of them, and later ones, to the group of Fabians gathered there for the week-end, and listened attentively. To my great surprise she then advanced this dictum: "You will do critical work but you will never be able to do original work."

I had always supposed that critical work involved more education than mine, and that if my work had any merit it was originality. But as I studied her cryptic judgment I saw at last what she meant—"original" was research work, and critical was pointing out what was the matter with society, no matter how original was the analysis.

"All these men are funny all the time. Miss Townsend listens," says the diary. Conversation, where Mr. Shaw took part, was bitterly brilliant. He made jokes about his sister's grave. Just once I answered him successfully. We were at dinner, and the talk drifted into animadversions on the U.S.A. Presently Mr. Shaw turned to me as I sat quietly beside him and caustically remarked that he supposed I would put all this into the newspapers when I reached home. I assured him that I did not write for the papers, and was not that kind of a writer, anyway.

"Then what were you thinking about?" he demanded. To which I peacefully replied, "About the effect of geography on the mind." After a little they all laughed, and made no more remarks about my country.

There were other pleasant visits, meeting many interesting people, one with Mrs. Stanton Blatch, a daughter of Elizabeth Cady Stanton. At her home I met J. A. Hobson, the economist, and his nice American wife. "Lots of talk on woman's economic evolution. He doesn't like it."

I think it was on this visit that I acquired information upon English topography. A group of us were walking along the smooth country road, and I observed between its crown and the hedge, in a stretch of grass, a quiet piece of water, resembling a small irrigation ditch. In this walked a man in hip boots, hoeing the weeds on the bottom.

Now I always endeavor, in a foreign land, to speak of all its advantages, and say nothing of its disadvantages—till I get home. So I expressed warm admiration at this sight. "How wonderfully neat you are in this country! Just look—there is a man cleaning the bottom of the ditch." "Ditch!" they almost screamed. "That is the river Wye!" Then they piled local history onto that little river till it almost looked like something, but in spite of its battles and ruins I could not feel much respect for a stream I could jump over, a little thing running by the roadside like that.

One short visit with Mrs. Jacob Bright; her husband was brother of John Bright. The address was delightfully English—"The Chestnuts, Woburn near Maidenhead, Bourne End," and more. Among the guests was to be Grant Allen, and when I learned this, it brought me face to face with an ethical problem.

After three years' consideration I had arrived at a definite conclusion as to the duty of the individual in reacting against other individuals guilty of evil conduct. This I held so important that I had recorded it at the time. "July 29, 1894. Hurrah! my puzzle in ethics is solved. It is the duty of the individual to react. We are the environment of one another and we must establish causation by our action and interaction. Write it out briefly."

We do this, sharply enough with legally punishable malefactors, but in many other cases we let pass various offenses without comment. My conclusion was that it was a social duty promptly to show an offender that he was offending—this not involving punishment or retaliation but merely the expression of one's feeling.

The first time I had occasion to try out this principle in public was at a banquet of some sort, in California, when a pretty little W.C.T.U. woman told this story: At an election with some temperance issue involved, she stood at the polling place, offering the temperance ballot to the voters. Opposite her was a saloon representative, with the other kind of ballot. A man approached, already somewhat intoxicated, and she persuasively offered him her paper. He was not as drunk as that, however, and refused it, taking the other. Then she asked him to let her look at his ballot, and when he politely allowed her, she changed it for the one she had, so the man went in and voted for the temperance ticket.

This she related with modest pride as if she had done a smart thing, and had probably told it before, no one commenting. I sat near her, and without saying a word created such a chill atmosphere of condemnation that she looked at me in some alarm, with "You don't think that was right?" All I said was "No," but it carried such depth of feeling that other ladies took heart of grace and also expressed disapproval; and the foolish little lady learned that she had done a horrid thing instead of a commendable one.

Now Grant Allen had been for some time my favorite example of what in my ethics is social treason. His work in popularizing science was of immense value to the world, incalculable; but instead of doing it, he was writing novels, poor novels at that, just for money. But I had never expected to meet the culprit and have to take him to task for it.

Moreover, though this was, to my mind, a social duty, there was also the duty of a guest—I certainly ought not to inject my ethics into a pleasant dinner-party. We had some earnest talk over it in the Hicks family, and one of the girls wisely suggested that while I could not do it at the table, I could if I saw him alone. This was hopeful, but alas! no sooner were we introduced than he invited me to walk in the garden. So there we were, and having decided this thing was right to do, do it I must.

"Mr. Allen," said I, making a tremendous effort, "don't you think it is wicked for a man who does such splendid work as your scientific books"—and I enlarged, honestly, on their value—"to give it up and spend his time writing novels which you yourself admit are not good ones?"

He took it like a lamb, told me he was "congenitally moral," could not do what he thought wrong; that this was no more wrong than if he was jewel-grinding; that a man's first duty was to his family and he could provide more money for them this way.

I said no more. He had a right to his point of view, of course, the ethical question being whether the family or society came first. Almost every one would agree with him. But if we do not "ring true" in showing one another our conduct values, we withhold the force of public opinion. Whether wise or not, what I remember best of that meeting is its difficulty.

A more amusing memory is of staying with some pleasant people in Liverpool, my host a "fruiterer" by trade. He was an intelligent, well-read man as far as

I could see. In the course of conversation he remarked to me that we had no grapes in America. This I took calmly, only asking what he meant by "no grapes." "Just what I say. You don't raise grapes in America."

I thought of the wild grapes of New England—did not the exploring Norsemen call it "Vineland"?—of the grape-arbor in every back yard, of the New York state crop, of "the reeling, wheeling aisles of the vine-yards, miles on miles," in California. But I merely asked, "How do you know?" "How do I know? Why we export grapes to America!"

Then I understood. Hot-house grapes. Cheap coal. Cheap labor. Supplying the steam-ships. "But that's not *grapes!*" I said. Then I told him there was hardly a state in the union without them, of the workman taking home a basket for ten cents, and so on—but alas! he didn't believe me. American brag.

Another of those kind friends who took me in and cared for me so hospitably was Miss Gertrude Roecliff of Newcastle. "Charming," says the diary. "She treats me like a sick princess."

Between visits, in London, I did some of the "ought tos," as "Went to Westminster Abbey and prowled awhile," and "Went to National Gallery of paintings and saw more than I could hold." At the British Museum I was treated with marked politeness by Dr. Garnett, on account of my father, who was widely known as a great librarian. Also I visited the Tower of London and saw the Crown Jewels, or their replicas, of which the most numerous and impressive were the tall, massive gold *Salt Cellars!* Some of them seemed to be a foot high.

One golden opportunity I missed was an invitation to dinner to meet Justin M'Carthy and George Meredith. Laboring heavily under an overtrained conscience, I thought it was not right to break a previous much less important engagement for this one, so I declined, but have since wished that on that occasion I had done wrong!

But I did meet William Morris, both at the Congress and in his home in Hammersmith. Gray and glorious he was, and most kind. I addressed a local group in his little neighboring hall. The most vivid memory of that visit is of Mrs. Morris, the adored model of the Pre-Raphaelite, her rich hair white and splendid, holding up a great silver candelabrum that I might see Rossetti's portrait of her in youth.

May Morris, their daughter, had a little house near by; she became a dear and lasting friend. The Cobden-Sandersons also lived near, and they showed me over "The Dove Bindery," with its strange and beautiful books.

If I had been well and clear-headed all this would have been a vivid and wonderful time. But I was still dragging up from that last collapse, and often had hardly wit enough to get about. Once, while unable to do any kind of work, I was riding on an omnibus, painfully conscious of the minimum of intelligence left me, and had this horrible thought: here were the other people beside me, also able to sit up and ride on an omnibus—perhaps they had no more brains than I did.

My entries are often dismal. "Find that I am really very low again, Oh dear! It is so long." "Am very weak and miserable." "Another miserable day." "Still miserable. Cannot write nor do anything." "Still miserable. I am alarmed at it." "Ghastly tired." "This illness seems more physical than usual. Doubtless sympathetic collapse internally." "I notice, gradually in the past month or two, a loss of my ready control of words."

I do not wish to cumber this story with a hundredth part of such items, but, as in that tedious chapter on The Breakdown, to make clear the interminable handicap under which I lived. Nevertheless, I wrote some, visited variously and spoke often; in halls and drawing-rooms, once on London Docks standing on a chair in the rain, in Liverpool, in the market-place in Shields, in Newcastle.

The most impressive sight of all that English land was the "New Castle upon Tyne." This huge, age-blackened block of stone, in which the rooms are hollowed like holes in cheese—there was a little chapel *in the thickness of the wall!*—stands in the fork of a railway. Signal towers with red and green lights gleamed on either side of it; the trains rushed by; and that thousand-year-old black block stood there like a boulder parting a stream.

As my stay extended I became a boarder with those pleasant friends in Camden. I learned much as colder weather came; as the "feel" of an unwarmed stone house, a house without a furnace. That is why English people so love their great stuffed chairs—the fire in the grate keeps them warm in front, but the room is cold, and the thick chair behind their backs is a needed comfort.

Also, I learned why most English cooking is so "plain." There is the little soft coal fire in the open grate, the oven at the side, the "hob" for the tea-kettle. Food is put in the pot, or in the oven, and thankfully left, there is no temptation to fuss with anything, standing over an open fire. In an exhibition I attended in Newcastle there was shown an "American Cooking Stove." The thing had a sort of shutter in front, with slats, so that they could see the fire; and

it was filled level to the covers with fine anthracite,
almost "pea coal."

Onc unforgetable visit was with Alfred Russel
Wallace, in Parkstone, Dorset. I lectured in a small
neighboring hall, on "Our Brains and What Ails
Them," with Mr. Wallace in the chair. This was one
of the rare occasions on which I have felt modest and
inferior, that world-renowned intellect was an over-
powering presence. We played two games of chess, one
he won, one was a draw—which was better than I
expected.

Immediately after the Congress, J. Ramsay Mac-
Donald called to interview me on the American situation, and engaged an article for their new magazine,
the *Progressive Review*. He was a handsome, brilliant
young fellow, just engaged to a lovely blonde girl, Miss
Gladstone. I liked them immensely, but did not dream
that he would become a premier.

At my first Fabian Society meeting I noted, "Very
exciting. J. R. MacDonald moves to withdraw Tract
70. Animated discussion. The executive wins—tract retained. Mrs. Hubert Bland asks to be introduced and
asks me to dinner." This was the beginning of a most
pleasant friendship with a delightful family. She was
"Edith Nesbit," a well-known author, and her husband, Hubert Bland, wrote for the Manchester *Guard-
ian*. There were several youngsters, all attractive; I
had most enjoyable visits with them, then and in later
years.

Having adopted dear Mrs. Hicks for my English
mother, I now added a Scotch one to my list. A lecture
engagement taking me to Glasgow I went on to Edinburgh, and visited Mrs. Dowie, who had invited me
when she ordered the poems from San Francisco. No
one could have been kinder, and no one in Edinburgh

more competent to show the beauties of that most beautiful city. She was a Miss Chambers, of the great publisher's family; her uncle had "restored" the Cathedral, with other benefaction. She showed me all that I should see, knowing more about everything than the curators; and told me many tales, as of Marjorie Fleming, whose childish boast was, "I put my hand on every chair that said 'don't touch' in Holyrood."

Wednesday, September 16th: "Go out alone between showers and see beautiful Edinburgh from Castle Hill—sunset and moonrise—bugle notes—all glamor and loveliness." 17th, "Get very friendly with my hostess and 'Struey,' a shaggy waggy little doggie." "18th. Mrs. D. shows me over the Castle—herself a living guide book. . . . Am still bed-breakfasted and lunch-napped, most luxuriously. Am improving."

A few days' care had evident effects, for by Sunday, the twentieth, comes this cheerful record: "Up earlier than usual and take 8:30 train for Glasgow, pleasant ride. Able to read and enjoy it. Quiet time in my beloved Hotel Drummond. Lunch, nap, speak P.M. for Labor church on 'The New Religion.' Enthusiastically received. Wanted again. Back on 5 P.M. after a hasty dinner with the Gilchrists. Not tired ! ! !"

Still feeling well next day, and met several people, including "an old Miss Burton who had known Aunt Harriet Stowe." By the twenty-second I hopefully remark, "Third day of feeling well. I believe the tide has turned." Soon I returned to Newcastle, where kind Miss Roecliffe took me in once more—"Everybody is so good to me!" I gratefully record.

October 3rd has a heavy black line. "William Morris died to-day." That was a great loss to the progress of England, of the world. Fortunately he left large work, long years of glorious giving.

Back and forth I went to various towns, for lectures and visits, with another stay in London, and with Mrs. Dowie again. She took me to hear "an eminent archæ-ologist, Professor Hildebrandt"—"insufferably tedi-ous," and to call on Mrs. Maclaren, sister of John Bright. Her son, Walter Stowe Maclaren, M.P., was born while Aunt Harriet Stowe was in Edinburgh, and named for her. Next evening we heard Professor Flinders Petrie, and at a reception thereafter met him, and the tedious Professor Hildebrandt, who wore twenty-three decorations. A very German professor.

Then a week of engagements in Glasgow, of which I remark—"A week of foregone failure, hard work and heavy sledding. Pay $16.25! Stood it fairly well." Tuesday, November 19th: *"Furnessia* sails."

I have not the least recollection of how I got to-gether enough money for the return trip, though it was about $50.00 as before. There are no cash ac-counts during these months abroad, but after reaching home I find December 1st begins: "In hand $9.25," so it was evidently a close thing.

That trip on the *Furnessia* is memorable for my first seasickness and for philosophy therewith. I had a state-room to myself, but it was far down in the lower re-gions of the ship, and poorly ventilated. Having to sleep there at the dock before starting was enough to make anybody sick. I was up and out next morning, but off Movill those long Irish swells were too much for me. So I managed to get back to my berth that Friday morning, and stayed there till Tuesday before I had strength enough to undress.

But those long days were calm (save for unavoid-able interruptions), and meditative. "I'm unable to take my clothes off," I ruminated. "How fortunate it is that they are such as to be quite comfortable to sleep in, and not injured by it. I cannot eat nor drink, but then I do not want to. I cannot do any thing whatever, but again, I have nothing whatever to do. This state-room is small and low down, but how fortunate I am to have it to myself. It is so pleasant to have it all freshly painted white—if it were pale green—! There is only one thing hopelessly bad, that is the air; but the worst that can do is to make me sick—and I'm sick already! So that's no harm." Surely a philosophic invalid.

Presently it was Thanksgiving Day, and I remark: "I give thanks earnestly for a good world, a good God, and to be able to eat dinner again!"

Monday, November 30th, we reached New York.

CHAPTER XV

WANDER YEARS

"ARRIVE," says the diary, "about two P.M. Drive up to my 'Mama's' 20 W. 32nd St. They are glad to see me. Letters waiting. Little upstairs room—will be $7.00 a week. Visit a while first. Very comfy."

It was very comfortable indeed. A settled residence for a while was restful, and some family atmosphere most pleasant. My pretty stepsisters were cordial, the little stepmother affectionate. My father was no longer with them. He had broken down completely.

"Mother gets letter saying Father is worse. Go to see him at sanitarium, Delaware Water Gap. He is much better and seems glad to see me." I stayed overnight, next day: "Little talk with Father. Give him $5."—if from me or mother I do not recall. There were many such visits when I was in or near New York. He seemed to value my coming—so long as he knew me. He lingered on, till the beginning of 1900. Softening of the brain. It is not right that a brilliant intellect should be allowed to sink to idiocy, and die slowly, hideously. Some day when we are more civilized we shall not maintain such a horror.

December was mainly sewing, I made most of my clothes; occasionally some "meeting" where I "said a few words" or read from my verses. As: "Go to Pilgrim Mother's Dinner at the Tuxedo. Read two poems. Great hit. Sold eleven copies forthwith. Go to Social

Reform Club in evening, speak a little on social reform in England. Another book sold. Tired but feel good."

My fellow-boarders were pleasant and kind. One, Dr. Edmund P. Shelby, has remained a warm friend ever since. He and his brother Evan had the big front rooms on the first floor, and in that long, high-ceiled parlor the doctor and I used to play battledore and shuttlecock. We became so proficient as to score over a thousand; we played left-handed, we played with two birds at once, and made 500 at that. With badminton racquets, not the noisy parchment things, it is a charming house game and especially good because it keeps the head up—offsets the stoop of constant reading, writing or sewing.

"Dec. 31. Received the New Year alone as usual. Health and Work!"

Of the many people I met during these years I was particularly impressed by Elizabeth Cady Stanton. To have been with her and "Aunt Susan," as we called the great Susan B. Anthony, seemed to establish connection with a splendid period of real heroism. It amuses me when the short-memoried young people of to-day introduce me as "one of the Pioneers." The pioneers of the Woman's Movement began with Mary Wollstonecraft, early in the last century, and ceased to be such when their message was listened to politely.

The Blackwell family were among my most honored friends, brave progressive people; Elizabeth Blackwell, the first woman physician in England; Henry Blackwell coming to this country and marrying Lucy Stone, one of the first—and sweetest—of our suffrage leaders, in days when speaking for that cause meant real danger as well as abuse; and also a genuine pioneer in establishing a married woman's right to keep her own name. Another Blackwell married Antoinette Brown, our first woman minister.

I visited the Anthonys, Susan and her sister, in Rochester, New York, and lectured there; also preached in the Unitarian church, Dr. Gannett's. This was in January, on my way to a Suffrage Convention in Iowa, stopping to give two or three talks in Chicago. It was a cold trip. When we reached Des Moines, January 25th, it was twenty-two below zero.

On this, or perhaps another midwinter excursion, I learned the force of prairie winds. Being entertained in an isolated farm-house, I was given a bedroom on the ground floor. The little house stood shivering in the snow, and all around its toes were tucked in—it was banked up around the edges. Being violently addicted to fresh air I sought to open a window, and found them all double glassed and fastened for the winter. Just one had a pane in the inner one that opened, and a sliding shutter that covered three auger holes as the only means of ventilation. I was horrified at this paucity of air, but concluded that I should not die of it in one night, opened the shutter to its full capacity, and went to bed.

The wind of the great open spaces came in through those auger-holes in such a streaming torrent that I rose and shut two of them. Even then, from one small hole the "air" I was so desirous of was shot across my bed like water from a fire-hose.

The Convention went off well. My own address so pleased them that the Congregational minister asked me to repeat it in his church. January 29th I spoke in Highland Park College, also in Union College in the morning, and in the afternoon at the Unity Club. Sunday I preached twice. Evidently the impression was

good, for a state Representative forthwith invited me
to "open the house with prayer"—which I did. The
same day lectured at Highland Park College on "Our
Brains and What Ails Them." $25.00. They didn't like
it much I think.

One of those Des Moines days includes a side trip:
"Start for Omaha on 8.15 train. Arrive near two.
Dine at restaurant with Mrs. Ford. Speak at Woman's
Club on 'Women and Politics.' Read 'Mother To Child'
by request. Make an impression. Return on 4.50 train,
arrive 9.30 or so. Walk up to Sabin House. Receive
$10.00 (Trip cost $9.00). Quite a day."

From Iowa back to Chicago, where I had a pleasant
visit with my "Chicago mother," Mrs. Dow, and
another with Mrs. Coonley, giving parlor talks in various houses for ten and fifteen dollars. A lecture in
Dowagiac, Michigan, February 12th, then back to
Washington, D. C., where I spoke for the W. S. A.,
also in the high school and National Park Academy,
reaching New York again on the twenty-second. That
evening I opened a discussion at the Sunrise Club, on
"Home, Past, Present and Future." "Splendid time.
Lively discussion. Make two engagements." My engagements were always the result of previous ones,
not to any agent or advertising.

The next day marks a noteworthy ambition: "Talk
with Mr. R. and Mr. L. and Mother in evening. I must
learn not to talk earnestly in conversation! Awfully
tired." But alas! I never did.

Friday 26th: "Go to hear Mr. Bryan on Bimetal-
lism. Am not much impressed." Before this I had heard
Felix Adler, with the comment, "Not great." Another
day, "Go to Fabian Study Club. I do not take to Marx
as an economist." Here is a cryptic entry: "Wild-
haired opera singer, name of Prentiss, calls to instruct

me in the social problem." And I can't even remember
if it was Soprano or Tenor!

On the eighth of March I called at an office on
Wall Street to look up a certain Cousin Houghton Gilman I had been fond of in 1879. He sat, extremely
busy, writing, suspecting the approaching female to be
a book-agent. I stood beside him and remarked, "You
haven't the slightest idea who I am." Then he gazed
sharply at me and replied, "Yes I have, you're my
Cousin Charlotte." This was the beginning of a delightful renewal of earlier friendship, still continuing.

There were various small engagements, one in Jersey
City, where I gave a parlor talk and spent the night,
with this note, "Very dull and difficult. Sleep ill thereafter. Also for the first time in all my travels I arise
and slay bed-bugs—four fat conspicuous bed-bugs."
Long residence and acquaintance in New York in later
years taught me more charity. Those indestructible insects can live a month without food—this has been
scientifically established by experiments with a bottled
one—they love steamheated flats and transfer their
affection among changing tenants, they are enterprising travelers, and, while not beloved, are discussed
without the horror of New Englanders. One New York
lady, with a studio in an unfashionable quarter, calls
them "Crimson Ramblers."

I lectured for the Photorene Club in Brooklyn, for
$10.00; for the Manhattan Liberal Club, $10.00; for
The Single Tax Club—for nothing but abuse. I have
a real respect for the Single Tax as a useful fiscal reform, though overrated in its hoped-for results; and I
have known many good and noble souls who were devoted to it; but I have noticed that the more narrowly
specific is a proposed reform, the more narrowly intense become its advocates. This was well shown in the

limited ardor of Dr. Mary Walker, who became quite
monomaniac on her one profound conviction—that
women should wear trousers. She was a competent
physician, I understand, and a brave, good woman, but
no human intellect can maintain its balance on so small
a topic as the redistribution of trousers.

With Single Tax Clubs I had many experiences.
Their method was to invite a speaker to address them,
gratuitously, on whatever subject was dearest to him
or her, and then to use that subject and that speaker as
a stamping ground whereon to exploit their own doctrine. In Chicago, in 1896, February 14th I wrote:
"Speak for Single Tax Club. Don't ever want to see a
Single Taxer again." But I did, many of them, some
were among my best friends, so I accepted this New
York invitation to address their club, on "Why We
Work." The record says: "They are horrid as usual,
but Wm. Dean Howells comes to hear me! was introduced—says he is coming to see me! A very jolly and
exciting discussion."

He did call, the next day, and brought his daughter
Mildred, a lovely girl. The day after that came an
Englishman, also impressed by that lecture, to ask me
about the social movement in California; also "A big
Swede, Axel Gustafson, calls to express admiration, in-
terest, and rage at the Single Taxers the other night."

In the boarding-house parlors one evening we had
a little private exhibition of hypnotism, which was as
funny as could be desired. The performer selected four
subjects from among us; a boy of about fourteen, a
young girl, a young man, and a not-so-young maiden
lady. The boy proved obdurate, no impression was
made on his mind. The girl became quite obedient,
tried to eat a napkin when told it was a peach; the

other lady tottered, but did not succumb. "You can not tell me your name," he asserted. "I c-c-*can!*" she declared. "No, you do not know your own name," insisted the hypnotizer. But she did, and with great difficulty got it out at last.

The young man proved the best subject. He was told he could not jump over a walking-stick laid before him on the floor, and nearly fell on his face trying to do it. His arm was stroked down stiffly, with the statement that he could not bend it—nor could any one else. He tried, other men tried, it would not bend. Then he was laid out on his back as stiff as a log, head resting on one chair and heels on another, told that he was unbendable—and that fourteen-year-old boy was set on his body! The hypnotist worked hard over all these stunts and now prepared a glorious finale.

"I will go out in the hall," he said, "and call you to me. You *must* come. There will be three men trying to hold you back—they cannot stop you " So he placed one man in front of his subject and one on each side, withdrawing into the hall. I was standing where I could see him on the stairs, "concentrating," making compelling gestures; but also I could see the man who must come, and his forbidders.

Unhappily for the exhibitor, the man he had placed in front of his victim happened to have hypnotic power himself, and he was not tired. The gentleman on the stairs was "pulling" with all his might. He beckoned and clawed the air, emitting his silent command, "You *Must* come!" But the gentleman in front of the subject made pushing passes, and even more violently emitted, "You *Must Not* go!" The first hypnotizer strove and sweated, the unfortunate young man wavered back and forth like a lily in a breeze, but the second hypnotizer triumphed—and the first one was not pleased. All the rest of us were, however.

With a pleasant home, kind friends, congenial work and a rising reputation, I began to thrive. March 30th: "My health is certainly better. I have been really working for two weeks and feel no worse for it." The friendship of the Howells family was a special pleasure; with them I met Oliver Herford, he too is a friend of thirty years' standing. "Mr. Herford walks home with me, buys two books, wants to make a design for cover, very cordial."

By the twelfth of April I was off on another lecture trip; Wilmington, Delaware, Chester, Pennsylvania,— I think it was here that a worthy Quaker gentleman took exception to my playing solitaire, cards being evil. I agreed with him that gambling, even the smallest, was evil, but maintained that cards in themselves were no harm. But he insisted that they were "the Devil's instruments," that they were used for betting and gambling and therefore should not be used for any purpose.

"Do you feel that way about horses?" I gently inquired, and the conversation lapsed.

Then Lansdowne, Pennsylvania, Wilmington again, and home for a few days. While there there is one triumphal record of a brilliant Easter Sunday, a walk in Central Park with one of the boarders—"Walk six miles, and row half an hour. Feel fine—not tired a bit. I really am well." Stayed feeling well for a while, and was off again by April 21st. A suffrage address in the Legislative chambers at Harrisburg, Pennsylvania, then, twenty-third: "Take 11.30 train for Detroit. Hot day. Fine scenery. Feel well. Write rondeau." During these wander years very much of my writing, both prose and verse, was done on trains.

In Detroit I spoke for the Protective Alliance for Women and Children on "Society and the Child." "Very successful. Mrs. G. says I spoke seventy-five per cent better than last year. Also that she had never thought me beautiful before." As to being beautiful, some thought I was, others didn't. I didn't. My ideas of beauty were so exalted, and I was so vividly conscious of my various shortcomings, that I never got much satisfaction out of my looks. Amusingly enough I am vainer at sixty-six than I was at sixteen—think I make a better-looking old lady than I did a young one.

To Chicago next day. "Feel well and clear-headed. Write 'Ballade of Relatives' and a lot of letters. Arrive at 9.10. Met by Mr. White—bless him!" A pleasant visit with dear Mrs. Dow, and next day, "Nice day. Feel fine. Get lot of letters including invitation to chair in Kansas Agricultural College—$1400.00 a year!"

This looked to me an immeasurable sum. As I had not been to college I was naturally complimented by being asked to teach in one. But I knew too well that I could not hold out in steady work, had no right to undertake it. So I declined, and as in the case of the Settlement proposition, I suggested Mrs. Campbell as much fitter for the place than I. She accepted the position and filled it well. But I have always rather gloated over the invitation.

April 29th gives another proof of improved health: "Quiet evening reading. So good to be able to enjoy reading again." The thirtieth was a busy day: "Press blue dress after its wetting. Write eight letters and five cards. Pack. Lunch. Stop to get watch, take cab at Court House, .50, catch train just barely. Go to Savanna, Ill. Lovely trip. Write two letters and two poems, sestina on 'Homes' and 'How very nice,' in four hours and didn't feel like one. Lovely place in Savanna, Mrs. Depin's, I think, right on the Mississippi—*very beautiful*. Speak in evening on 'What We Need To Know To-day.' Pretty tired. $15.00."

The Mississippi at this point is *blue*, not muddy at all, the Missouri brings the mud in. Just a clean bright river, and the long grassy garden down to the brink, a pleasant memory.

May 1st: "Glorious day. Set forth at 9.30 for Rock Island. Arrive at 11.30, three and a half hours to wait. Take car ride over the river to Davenport. Lunch in connection with a gramophone, parrot and tame squirrel" (A lively restaurant, that). "Another car ride to Moline. Wait twenty minutes. Then to Burlington; wait three hours less five minutes. Keokuk at 11.20. Mr. Bennet meets me. Nice little home. Lovely wife and baby."

I preached and addressed a Young People's meeting next day, and on Monday went back to Chicago, writing triolets on the way. Still with kind Mrs. Dow, and on Sunday the 9th a visit to Henry Demorest Lloyd at Winnetka. There next morning, on a pleasant piazza: "Read, loaf, talk with Mr. Lloyd, and write three poems—Exiles, Our East, and Immortality." These are all in the book, and do very well for one morning's work.

Wednesday, May 12th: "Write fiercely, enraged by 'Margaret Ogilvie,' on what life is for—best one 'Give Way.'" If I owe that poem to Margaret Ogilvie I'm much obliged to her, it is a good one. Thirteenth, "Am feeling rather dull. Read a lot of poems to Mrs. Dow while she sews. I guess I have twenty or thirty good ones for my next edition, twenty or so brand new." Fourteenth, "Finish 'The Commonplace.' Write 'To

My Baby' thing. Write 'Their Grass' and laugh much over it."

Sunday, May 15th, I went to Milwaukee to preach on "Heroes We Need Now," and on the train wrote "Heroism," which is one of the best, and "They Wandered Forth." But I was running down. May 19th: "Am feeling very dismal again." Twentieth, "Very bad day. Can't even sew well. Squeeze out one rondeau, 'A Man Must Live.' " That's a good one, too, bad day or not.

May 25th off to Dowagaic, Michigan, where I spoke twice, and learned something of the exceeding beauty of that state, with its clean hardwood forests and plentiful waters. An excursion was made to Sister Lakes, and to Magician Lake, with its island cottages. "Lovely day and very pleasant time. A beautiful world and lots of nice people in it." Then to Battle Creek where I gave an address in the famous Sanitarium, and preached also; with a ride to Lake Gognac—"Another pretty resort—'the woods are full of 'em.' "

May 31st in Charlotte, Michigan, where I visited some cousins, the Perry family. "Speak in evening on Our Brains etc. Speak *well*. $5.00. Back to Battle Creek, where the Sanitarium gave me a "Complimentary Bath," which I shall never forget. A friend who was there, scanning the menu as it were, picked out the order of exercises. "Footbath, hot water to drink, electric light, shampoo, salt glow, needle shower, massage. Feel fine." The electric part made an indelible impression. Laid out on a stretcher, with only a towel for bedclothes, I was slid under a curtain into a long glittering oven, and even the towel plucked away. My head was outside, but moved by a natural curiosity I parted that little curtain and looked in. Circumambient electric lights, innumerably multiplied by a lining of mirrors—the scene was like that upon which enters a devout Mussulman newly slain in battle!

That night I spoke in Kalamazoo, Michigan, in the People's Church, at a Woman's Club Anniversary, on "Duties, Domestic and Other." "Pretty good. Enthusiastic reception. $15.00." On this occasion I encountered one of the most amusing *contretemps* of a lifetime's lecturing.

I was in full career in my address when the chairwoman, who had been growing more and more nervous, handed me a bit of paper which bore the astonishing request that I stop for a while and give place to a lady who was to sing a memorial hymn to her mother. "Why," I whispered, "did she not come before the lecture?" There was some reason—perhaps she had to wait for the accompanyist. "Why does she not wait till I have finished?" She had another engagement. So I told the audience that there was to be an intermission, that they were to have something they would doubtless enjoy more than my talk, and sat down.

Nothing happened. The audience fidgeted. The poor chairwoman was increasingly distressed. Said I softly, "Would you like me to recite something while you wait?" "Oh, if you *would*—!" So I rose again, with suitable explanation, and gave them some of my verses. Finally the lady with the hymn arrived and sang it, and departed. Then, quite unperturbed, I took up the thread of my discourse, and finished it.

This lecturing of mine, after I ceased to write papers, consists in fresh thinking on some topic in which I am vitally interested. Once in Chicago I repeated an address at the instance of a friend who had heard it once, and who was anxious that I should do as well the second time. I invited her to attend, and when I asked if it was as good as the first time she said it was just as good— "But you didn't say one word you did before!"

Being used to straight, logical thinking it is no trouble to be clear and connected, an interruption does not annoy me, nor does a sudden change in the theme I had intended to discuss. Three times I have had to take up an unexpected topic, with practically no notice, once as suddenly as this:—Seated on the platform at a Woman's Club meeting ready to speak on "Our Brains and What Ails Them," I listened to a very smoothly worded introduction, with the usual compliments, which wound up with—"who will now address you on 'Men, Women and People.' " So between my chair and the front I had to change my subject, and did not mind it in the least.

In Kalamazoo I stayed with the Rev. Caroline Bartlett Crane, the able and beloved minister of the Peoples church, a woman both strong and charming. Back to Mrs. Dowie again and writing. Saturday, June 5th. "Feel some better. Finish Servant Question article and fix yesterday's poems. Lester F. Ward sends me 'Collective Telesis' with reference to Similar Cases in it. Read and enjoy it." Next day: "Send off fourteen poems and Servant Question article.

"Mrs. Dow's daughter, Jennie Harvey, here with two chicks. Lovely children," and next day, "Cry some apropos of Mrs. Harvey's babies." In time I learned not to suffer at sight of mothers with their children by deliberately putting myself in the mother's place, thinking of her pleasure and not of my pain.

Similarly I learned to bear the smell of tobacco, at least with complacence, on top of a London bus. I was there to get fresh air, but the eleven other seats were occupied by men smoking. Said I to myself, "Eleven pleasures are greater than one displeasure," and focused on their enjoyment rather than my discomfort. I do not mind it so keenly now, except in a low-ceiled room or crowded place. When people are all jammed in the narrow alley of a Pullman car, ready to get off, and a man cannot wait to dismount before lighting his cigar; or when in a thick-packed crowd before the ticket gate, in a railway station, men smoke, it shows gross selfishness.

By Tuesday, June 8th, I was off on another Kansas trip; was delayed two hours and a half in Mankato by a washout: "Sit serenely in station and work on novel—arranging chapters, etc." Saturday the twelfth, in Topeka, "Feel very weak and goodfornothing—can't write." Mr. Wyman comes to arrange for my preaching for him." Sunday, "Goodfornothing yet. But manage to give a good sermon on The Heroes We Need Now. Mr. Wyman gives me five dollars that he gets for preaching to the lunatics this P.M."

In Eureka I visited Mrs. Hardy, a dear woman. "Hot, can't work these days." "Talk with Mr. Hardy and learn much about the cattle trade." I also learned what Kansas heat was like; the *wind* was hot, we had to avoid the breeze instead of courting it, it blew from the southwest as from an oven, and the long corn leaves crisped and curled.

In Mankato I acquired $25.00, in Topeka the lunatics' five, Eureka on the seventeenth, $10.00, and on the twenty-seventh: "Speak in evening at Cong. Church on Social Settlements. Was presented with the collection, $3.96." Twenty-sixth: "feel very weak and tired." Twenty-ninth, "Feel weak. Get letter from Mr. Howells about books." July 1st: "Still weak but fall to work in sheer despair on article on economic basis of woman question. Get hold of a new branch of my theory on above subject. Now I can write the book."

Thirtieth: "Send letter and some new poems to Ripley Hitchcock, reader for Appleton's, at Mr. Howell's suggestion." July 3rd: "The Addisons present me with a five dollar bill for a birthday present." Fifth, "Get mail—Katharine's birthday present—a beautiful silk waist made with her own hands! The dear child!" It was enterprising of her, for she was only twelve, and it warmed my heart.

The hot weather continued. "At 4 A.M. it was 80, some one tells me." On the ninth I spoke in Augusta, Kansas, remarking: "Gloomy prospect for lecture. Very Hot, Hall very hot. Ten people come, two pay. I sit down and talk to 'em. Pretty hard work."

From Kansas back to Chicago for a day or two, and then a visit with Mrs. Coonley—now Coonley-Ward, at her lovely place in Wyoming, New York. Mrs. Ward was quite the lady of the manor thereabouts, and had arranged for me to preach in the village church on Sunday, but the minister, a young man, did not like it at all. He listened, disapprovingly, but as I came out he shook hands and made this cordial concession—"You did not make a single grammatical mistake!"

Jane Addams was a fellow-visitor, to my delight. "She is really impressed by the new big idea. To have her see it is a great help." I highly enjoyed the garden, "Pick raspberries, they have 'em black, red and white, and great currants of the same three colors." "Pick colored raspberries in the sunset light."

From there to Rochester, New York, on the twenty-fifth, where I preached in Dr. Gannett's church. "Dr. Gannett left me five dollars but I wouldn't take it. Miss Mary Anthony tried to make it two, but I wouldn't. Mrs. C-Ward gave me the trip ticket—no loss."

After Wyoming I set forth, July 30, for "Summer

Brook Farm," Miss Prestonia Mann's unique establishment in the Adirondacks. Miss Mann I had come to know and like in New York. She was a Fabian Socialist, running a little paper called the *American Fabian,* for which I wrote. Her parents had been progressives in the days of the Abolitionists, and were interested in the original Brook Farm experiment.

So Miss Mann, having plenty of money, had built a "camp" at the head of Keene Valley, of huge logs with the bark on, broad porches, a sunken fireplace where we all sat on the low steps approaching it, and an enormous long west window with a cushioned seat, some fifteen feet long it was. For further accommodation of guests she added a sort of chalet as a dormitory, in later years another yet.

To this agreeable place she invited numbers of interesting people of a progressive tendency; among them was a Mrs. McDaniels, a sister of Mr. Dana of the New York *Sun,* and a member or visitor of the original Brook Farm Group. Miss Mann brought two competent maids with her, who did the cooking, and kept her house in order, but all the rest of the work was done by the guests. We paid for our food materials, in careful division of expense, and then "coöperated," taking turns in our allotted tasks, the men doing the heavier work.

It was immensely amusing, the cheerful good-will and colossal ignorance of these co-laborers. Even the laundry work we did, putting the clothes to soak over night, and attacking them with washing-machine and wringers next day. Good Mrs. McDaniels and I were the only ones present who knew how to wash, and we exchanged sad glances to see gallant college professors and high-minded poets toiling at the wringers while buttons flew away and spots remained.

One day there was a happy excursion up Mt. Hurricane. "Four hours up. Two and a half down. Splendid time." Most joyously recalled is the blueberrying—a pleasure I had not had since youthful days. Huge ones they, hanging thick and easy; that night when I shut my eyes I saw blueberries, a dense pattern, like wallpaper.

Mr. Radcliffe-Whitehead, that nice Englishman who had heard me lecture in New York and called afterward, was at the other end of the valley, at St. Hubert's Inn. He called, and arranged for me to give a lecture at the Inn, which I did, to a dull crowd of expensive people who had no use for it. That impressive man of learning, Professor Thomas Davidson, had a group of his own up there; we went to hear him, and I remark, "Listen for an hour and a half, and take notes—great gain for my head." Entries are scarce. "Go blueberrying." "Iron some." "Iron some more." It was not an exciting life, but immensely beneficial.

By August 14th I was back in New York, met at the station by my Cousin Houghton and—Katharine! She was to be with me for a few days before starting for Europe with her father and second mother. Rules or no rules, she fled past the gatemen and came flying down the platform to meet me....

Twelve years old, and a darling ... Houghton and I took her to Bedloes Island next day, where she went up the inside of the Goddess of Liberty, then to the aquarium. Monday we went shopping together, Katharine and I. Tuesday: "A fine long day in the park with Katharine. We do everything pretty much, and she has a very good time. Is especially delighted to learn to row, which she does in astonishingly quick time." Wednesday: "Put in a few stitches on Kate's

"But I haven't," I explained. "It is a temporary arrangement. While I am unable to maintain her as well as her father can. He has a right to some of her society certainly, and she to his. If I was keeping her in a boarding school would you say I had given her up?" "No, that would be different." ... It was a little odd that in this extremely "advanced" group should be the only such misjudgment I had found east of California.

So I spoke, as requested, on "The Social Organism," just as willingly, and note on the next day: "Much call for 'The New Motherhood.' Agree to give it to whomever will come." I started in that afternoon, and on Saturday: "Talk a lot to various people, from 10:30 at Miss Chamberlain's cottage to a big group, all day to others until 8 o'clock—all but meals and a few moments rest. About nine hours talk!" There was more next day, so I got "The New Motherhood" over pretty generally. August 30th: "Am paid by the hotel clerk, for Miss Farmer, $16.50" (plus expenses I think).

I distinctly remember that day's talking. Instead of exhaustion I had a triumphant feeling of having at last had a chance to say all I wished to on that topic— for once. From Greenacre I betook myself to Laconia, New Hampshire, visiting Mrs. Hackett, a good friend of Grace and Katharine—they had visited there before me.

Here, on Tuesday, Auguest 31st, record: "Begin my book on the *Economic Relation of the Sexes as a Factor in Social Development.*"

CHAPTER XVI

COMING UP

THE nineteenth century, now so contemptuously discredited as "Victorian," was distinguished not only by its large achievements in practical science and mechanical invention, but by such swift strides in psychic progress as set it high among the most important since our historic birth. Alfred Russel Wallace placed it highest of all.

The development of the theory of Evolution alone was enough to give glory to this age; practically the entire range of the Woman's Movement was within it; think of belittling a century when women began to rise! In our belated freeing of the slave we see the end of one economic period, in the rise of Socialism the beginning of another.

In my youth the world was full of "Movements," of an eager massing together to work for "causes." There was the Labor Movement, the Temperance Movement, the Woman's Suffrage Movement, the Dress Reform Movement, a general movement toward better methods in education, from the Kindergarten to University Extension, and a broad, deep, liberalizing of religion. There was the Society for The Prevention of Cruelty to Animals, and another to protect children —the state reaching out at last to recognize the child as a citizen, not the property of the parents. There was the Organization of Charities, steps in Prison Reform and in the Care of the Insane; a demand for right teaching of children as to sex, and for an equal standard of chastity, equalized up, not down; there was that wide-spread educator, the Woman's Club.

Full of the passion for world improvement, and seeing the position of women as responsible for much, very much, of our evil condition, I had been studying it for years as a problem of instant importance. The political equality demanded by the suffragists was not enough to give real freedom. Women whose industrial position is that of a house-servant, or who do no work at all, who are fed, clothed, and given pocket-money by men, do not reach freedom and equality by the use of the ballot.

So after years of thinking, with the progressively illuminating effort of teaching others as far as I could develop the theme, I now set to work on my first book, in prose, named by the publishers, *Women and Economics*. The first day I wrote 1700 words, and "some planning." The second day 2400 words; the third, 3600; the fourth, 4000. "Doing finely," says the diary.

I well remember that 4000-word day, the smooth, swift, easy flow—it was done in about three hours and a half—the splendid joy of it—I went and ran, just raced along the country road, for sheer triumph.

The stay in Laconia lasted till September 6th, then a night in Boston and a little visit with Cousin Mary Phelon in Providence. September 8th, "Write 2800 words." This record does not involve laborious counting. It was all hand-writing, of course, and ran one hundred words to the page very regularly. The amounts were not great, three thousand words in three hours is my usual output when well. Friday the tenth, "Some re-writing of Wednesday's work and finish 5th chapter."

It was a pleasure to be in Providence again, and see relatives and old friends, but by Wednesday fifteenth I returned to Boston, and visited my dear friend Martha Luther Lane, in Hingham. Here I worked on the sixth chapter Thursday, and Friday seventeenth, "Write more—no good." Saturday, "Write about 2000 words—goes better," and Monday, twentieth, "Write fine chapter seven, real good." Next day another chapter, a short one.

Wednesday twenty-second was an interesting day in Boston. I met Sylvester Baxter—a friend already through my verses; he took me to the *Atlantic Monthly* office, "Introduces me to Mr. Walter Page. Very cordial. Also to *New England Magazine* office and Mr. Edwin D. Meade. Also to Small, Maynard and Company—Bliss Carman is the 'Company.' He was there! They want to publish my poems. All very friendly and polite."

These young publishers had been to England and knew my reputation there, I think. Appleton's also offered to take the book, but I chose the new men just starting, partly because they were beginners, partly because they made the proposition entirely without recommendation. In later years when asked how I made my "market" so to speak, I explained that it was by giving away my work until it made an impression.

Then a little visit with dear Aunt Emily Hale in Roxbury, and Thursday twenty-third: "Write on book A.M." Friday: "Write on book." Saturday eleventh: "Call on 'my publishers'" (it did feel good to have some real professional ones!) "Bliss Carman has now read my poems and approves. Good. See only Mr.

Small this time. They want to do the poems and also to look at the book. Good." I had given them a brief and impressive account of that book, which I was in the midst of writing, on my previous call.

So I went away happy and made my first visit to Norwich, Connecticut, staying with Mrs. Jean Porter Rudd, a friend of Grace's and of mine, a widow, a brave, strong talented woman, admirably bringing up a family of small children. She wrote, wrote more than well, but life gave her small time for that work. My Cousin Houghton was visiting his aunts in Norwich at the time; he called on me and Mrs. Rudd, and took me to see his aunts in the old home. The diary says: "Nice people, nice house." Little did I think I should come to live in it!

New York again by October 2nd, and by the sixth, "Write on ninth chapter of book." Thursday seventh, "Begin Chap. 10. Am feeling very well these days, strong, cheerful, hopeful." Friday, October 8th: "Finish book, 356 pages. That is finish first draft. Date and arrange the separate chapters as written in different houses, and do it up."

This first draft, some 35,600 words, was rather less than half the book when published; but it contained the argument, it showed method and style, it was the manuscript the publishers accepted. It was done in seventeen days, in five different houses, on this little string of visits.

I settled down at my stepmother's boarding-house again, contentedly. Made a little visit to the married twin, in Ridgewood, New Jersey. "Step-adopted-brother-in-law very polite." My principal work at this time was the careful copying of poems for the publishers. I began to run down again, as was my custom. A series of bad entries, 'til November 3rd: "Bad night. This is really a very low time, worst since England."

Already it has been tedious enough, all this record of recurrent incapacity and misery, but I wish to have it clearly understood that the spurts of energy and accomplishment have been fragmentary compared with the helplessness and distress; they *show,* however, and the misery doesn't.

Pulled up again somewhat, spoke in Wilmington, Harrisburg, Brookline, Cambridge and Boston. November 8th: "Notman, photographer, asks to take my picture. Cheerfully let'em. Take my book to the publishers and leave it to be read. Talk poems. By Wednesday, November 10th: "Call on publishers. Small, Maynard & Company, 6 Beacon St. They take book. Give me new Whitman. I feel fine over the book."

In New York by the thirteenth, and, sixteenth: "Begin on book again." "Not strong yet but doing much better." On the twenty-first I had a game of chess with Houghton: "But Oh I cannot *play!* Tires me much. Read him the new chapters of the book. He begins to be really impressed. Good."

Here is an idea I deemed worthy of putting down, Tuesday, November 30th: "Woke up with big thought —the sense of duty is developed in proportion to our specialization—Ethics is only *conscious physics.*" This "duty" means social duty, not the arbitrary religious sentiment. Ethics is the science of social relation, as is physics of material relation.

December: "Feel fine. Houghton comes. Read last three chapters—ten done. He is more and more impressed." I read some of it at Mrs. Richard Hovey's— "Great excitement, all much impressed."

Wednesday, December 8, was memorable. Jane Addams was in town, back from a tour in Europe, even

Russia, where she visited Tolstoi, and I had the honor of introducing Mr. Howells to her. "And they talk about Tolstoi—she brought a message from him to Mr. Howells. Very interesting." That was another of the times when I felt modest.

The book was finished on December 14th. Mr. Small called on the sixteenth and took it away. Twenty-three days' work this time, total of forty.

He called again on the nineteenth. "Is greatly impressed with the book, wants it as soon as possible, print in January." The Macmillan Publishing House now wrote me, asking to read the poems with a view to publication, which pleased me. By December 27th I set to work on the final copying and revising, well content. A very quiet Christmas, with the closing note of the year: "Health pretty fair now. Am able to work. Literary reputation steadily increasing. Things look bright."

New Year's Day came a letter from the *Illustrated American,* asking for articles—at one cent a word. I remember how large this looked to me. I fell to work with calculation of how much it would be at my rate of 3,000 words a day, six days a week, throughout the year, and felt rich indeed—$9,390.00! Poor little idiot.

Sunday, second: "Copy chapter V, five thousand words. Also finish Fabian article, a page or two only. Houghton comes, Reads 5th chapter. We go through the whole five and correct errors. A big day's work—must not do it again. Very tired."

January 3rd: "Very poor day, only sixteen pages of an easy chapter." The copying went on, usually a chapter a day, to January 15th: "Still fairly well, finish chapter 15th, the last. Tired though. Some battledore with Dr. S., 900 and something. Have to get out some knitting for amusement." Sixteenth: "Am pretty weak-headed" but seventeenth: "Ah! Feels like vacation. Loaf. Guess I don't break down this time." The last chapter went to the printer that night. The entire time spent on that book was fifty-eight days—just inside of two months. . . .

A little lecture trip to Boston, Lynn, and Newtonville, January 19th to 29th, netted me about $45.00, and involved pleasant visits and seeing old friends and new. One of these was Frederic Peabody, who heard me lecture and took me to his home: "Splendid baby. Dine and talk—good talk." More important was meeting William Lloyd Garrison, another link with the Great Lifters of earlier days.

Back in New York on the twenty-ninth, and settle down comfortably to sewing, writing, and seeing people. Also to the evening games of battledore—"Over 200 with my left." February 3rd, a friend called for me and "We spend the rest of the morning with Annie Russell, the actress. She wanted to see 'The Pretty Idiot.' I stop on my way home and get it, of Maude Adams." Grace and I hovered always on the brink of great hopes for our plays, but they never materialized.

Went with my Cousin Houghton to my first opera, *Die Walkure*. Didn't like it. Never liked any grand opera. The drama has its conventions and limitations, but they are to my mind more rational, more possible, than those of the opera. No acting, no singing, can make a middle-aged, portly woman like Madame Nordica, leading a tame old white horse of which she is visibly afraid, look like a Valkyr. When two people supposedly in the throes of desperate passion, and quite able to fall into each other's arms, stand at a distance and sing at each other instead, it becomes

comic. When poor Valentine in Faust, run through
the lungs and dying on the ground, cheerfully raises
himself on one elbow and sings—the effect is farcical.
Those who know enough and care enough for music,
seem able to overlook these flagrant absurdities, but
music is the one art in which I am wholly incompetent.

Proof-reading was my principal occupation for a
while. My good publishers had engaged a competent,
scholarly young woman, a Miss Rollins, to correct
my manuscripts, and how she did plane smooth all the
cheerful eccentricities of my style! But I was to have
the last word—February 7th: "Feel well. Read proof
and correct Miss Rollins' corrections." Most of her
work was genuine improvement. I was never a careful
writer.

The poem proofs were coming in, too. Even in
verse I was not fussy in details. When the *Atlantic*
wanted to make some little change in "The Beds of
Fleur-de-lys" as a condition to taking it, I let them.
"Do it as you like," I said. "When it comes out in the
book I'll do it my way." Those publishers of mine were
so much pleased with my imitation of Maeterlinck in
"The Impress" that they reprinted it in a little magazine they ran for a while; also they made a booklet
of "The Yellow Wallpaper."

Life ran on pleasantly enough in the boarding-house.
My charming sister May had a crowd of admirers
dancing attendance. Occasionally I visited the other
twin, now a mother. February 19th: "Talk to Peg, and
hold the baby—nice baby. Feels good to have one in
my arms again."

The writing of articles went on all the time, but
most of them were for magazines which did not pay
anything. There were ups and downs in health, pleas-

ant friends, interesting meetings. One of these was funny. A social group in Brooklyn, the Merickawyck Club, had invited one they thought a violent Socialist to address them. He was unable to keep the engagement and I went as a substitute. Houghton accompanied me. They looked for a wild-haired "Red," and behold! a lady in a smooth-flowing "princess dress" of dark plum-colored satin, and a gentleman in irreproachable evening clothes.

The talk was on "The Principles of Socialism," which, properly presented, reach almost every one. One of the members, sitting by me during the refreshment and discussion period afterward, told me, "I came prepared to deny everything that was said, but you haven't said anything but what is true."

Friday, March 18, 1897. "Poems out."

By March 20th: "I find I am really very low—don't feel up to a walk, even." Twenty-first: "Feel very weak and low—unable to work. Down to the crying stage." And so on for a while.

My kind little stepmother, who had far more sense of hospitality and generous affection than of business, now became a Christian Scientist. Varied teachers of that faith enjoyed her excellent rooms, and paid their board by giving absent treatment to my poor slowly dying father, which was of no advantage to his health or her business.

One of these healers had a room next mine, with only a casual board-and-paper partition between; mine was the "hall-room" thus made. There was a door in this partition, securely fastened, against which stood my narrow couch, on which it was my custom to take a nap, or try to, after lunch. Each of us could hear everything which went on in the other's room, and as his treatments were oral, I got a fair idea of the method.

Rather brisk and brief with poor persons, he was; much more prolonged with the richer. There was one deaf old lady who came often from quite a distance. To her he read from his precious book, in a loud, penetrating voice, assuring her that she could hear perfectly. "I can hear you," she plaintively admitted, "but I can't hear any one else." One day there called on him a lesser light in the same field to consult him on points of practice. This visitor admitted that he had a "claim" of pain in his chest, when coming from Boston on the boat. Being unable to "demonstrate" its unreality, he had summoned a steward and besought a mustard plaster—with beneficial results. This my neighbor gravely commended as wise under the circumstances.

Then the caller opened his heart to him. "When I —pass over" he seemed to minimize the event— "There is no death! Nothing real dies! All that is real is in the mind—I take it with me—am I right?" He was assured he was perfectly right. "I do not lose my wife nor my children. There is no matter, there is only mind. They only exist in mind—I take them with me in my mind!" This conclusion was also fully agreed to as correct. "Then," cried he in logical triumph,"why should I keep up that life insurance?"

It did seem a reasonable question, but his host was equal to the occasion. He was a practical man, as his method of paying board-bills showed. "Wait," said he. "Does your wife share in your views? Would she see it as you do?" The man admitted that his wife and children would very likely not feel that they had gone with him in his mind, but would probably insist that they were alive on earth. "Then," said the teacher, firmly, "you had better keep up that insurance."

March 30th was a happy day. The married twin was in town. "Stay in and tend Margie's baby, from 8 to 10.30 or so. . . . A delight to be mama a little."

By April I had the pleasure of receiving six copies of *In This Our World* from the publishers. One copy they had bound in soft dark blue kid for me. I literally wore it out, carrying it about to read from when lecturing. April 15th: "Letter from English publisher asking for manuscripts, to examine." That pleased me, too. In this petty and personal account of daily happenings I step aside on April 21st to remark, "War with Spain becomes a fact."

My purpose in diary-keeping, since girlhood, was not at all to make revelations of feeling, though, or of incidents not readable by other people. As I go over it now, for the first time since it was written, I am surprised by its fullness of small detail, and amused by its paucity of material which might be eagerly looked for by—well, by a newspaper-minded person.

There were three lectures in April, $10.00, $5.00, and $10.00, and, twenty-eighth: "Mr. Small sends the advance I asked for, $25.00." Next day, some one "opportunely returns the $20.00 I lent him last summer." Thus enriched, I went forth and added to my wardrobe: "Buy a little black hat. $1.98, and dark blue Danish cloth, 11 yds. $1.44."

It was fortunate that I could "compose in cloth" and loved to sew. How I ever managed to travel and lecture far and wide, and present a decent appearance, on so little, is astonishing. Those debts of mine, from California days, were being steadily reduced, by bits, but my earnings were ridiculously small.

May 30th I was off again: "Good-bye to New York and my family-by-marriage." First a little visit with Claire Beecher near Baltimore. May 2nd: "They want me to stay, but I don't—the Grandmother is ill, an aunt arrives—I take the 5.30 by Bay Line, SS. Georgia, to Norfolk." So to Goldsboro, North Carolina, where I had a pleasant stay with Mrs. Clara Royall, who had boarded with us in New York. She was a tall, beautiful woman, graceful and charming. One of the admiring young-men boarders told her one windy day, "You were the only woman on the avenue whose skirts blew right!"

While there I attended the most amazing "entertainment," a concert given by a neighboring lunatic asylum—colored. The performance was by the least crazy ones, those next crazy sat around us, and in the guarded background howled the most violent. I was told that insanity had increased greatly among the Negroes since they were freed, probably owing to the strain of having to look out for themselves in a civilization far beyond them.

There were lectures, four; given in the court-house, total receipts $37.50. Goldsboro was a pleasant little town, the people kind and friendly. I have spoken in every one of the Southern States, and was struck from the first by the vigor and efficiency of the women, as well as by their progressiveness. Naturally I met that kind, but they were a good percentage.

May 21st: "Advance sheets of book at last! Letter from Grace and one from Katharine. Very happy day." One Sunday I was taken to the Presbyterian church, where I heard a "Mission Day" sermon. The man, wishing to rouse us to generous contribution, enlarged on the terrors of damnation, and then gave the exact numbers of those so doomed! His calculation was simple: take the population of the earth, subtract the number of Christian Protestant church members—and all the remainder were damned! I did think he might have given the Roman Catholics a chance—they are certainly Christians—but no, his Heaven was most exclusive. How that kind of Christian can worship a Deity who plays such a poor second to the devil I cannot see.

Another sermon there made an impression. This was Easter Sunday, and the preacher told us that the miraculous conception of Jesus, his virgin birth, his wonderful life, his divine teachings, his martyrdom itself —all together were of no avail without the resurrection! Good fundamentalists, these.

May 23rd I wrote a poem, "Up and Down," quite the highest and farthest I ever reached.

By June 1st off northward again, to Mrs. Blankenburgh in Philadelphia. Her husband was a German, a good one, afterward mayor; her mother, Dr. Longshore, was the first woman physician in the city. The old lady told me how when she began to practise the prejudice against women physicians was such that druggists refused to handle her prescriptions, or put them up incorrectly to bring discredit upon her. She was treating one sick woman, whose daughter was entertaining a suitor, and the young man told the girl that he would withdraw his suit if her mother employed a woman physician!

It is easy to forget, to-day, the contemptible tactics employed by our natural protectors to keep women out of the professions. In medicine, where one might have expected decency, those who taught in medical colleges deliberately employed obscenity in their lectures to deter women students. One of these records that she fairly starved herself that she "might not have blood enough to blush with."

Mrs. Blankenburgh and I went to Longwood, that old-established meeting of progressive friends who have encouraged all manner of daring reforms from days when Abolition was new. I lectured on the Principles of Socialism so convincingly that they passed a resolution in favor of those principles and their gradual adoption. It is a very great pity for our true economic progress that this legitimate policy in business administration should have been so misunderstood by Marx, and made so repulsive to the American mind by its alien protagonists.

Preached in Longwood Sunday the fifth, was back in New York next day, Wednesday, June 8th, having accumulated $85.61, I sent off $40.00 on debts. On the twelfth I set forth for Cold Spring Harbor, Long Island, where I was to spend the summer. "Letters from Grace and Katharine, they may be here any day." And the very next Houghton brought my daughter out to me. "Katharine is tall and lovely, sweet-mannered and strong. It is good to see her!"

Such a happy time! Katharine was delighted with the pond across the road. I taught her to swim, which she greatly enjoyed. She could float like a cork, but found it difficult to dive, being so light. It must have been large lung capacity, she was thin enough. I have seen her stand vertically, one arm held straight up above her head, and go down quite a way, but the arm remained up,—she could not sink to the bottom. There was an ancient boat, in which we used to go hunting for turtles. We were in bathing suits, Katharine at the bow watching for her prey while I rowed—youth at the prow and pleasure at the helm as it were. If the turtle dived so did Katharine, we accumulated quite a pile of them. Then, having enjoyed the pleasure of the chase, we tossed them all back in the water. Turtles do not seem to be nervous beasts, and we did not hurt them any.

"She is so good to be with!" says the diary.

Nevertheless, I was "down" again, though writing the best I could. The Biological Station at the Harbor brought us a new boarder, Francis B. Sumner, another lasting friend. He was a most pleasing addition to our party. Henry Linville, another biologist and still older friend, was the one who had first told me of the place.

Monday the eleventh: "Owe to-day two weeks for Katharine, one for self"—the last cash entry, on June 27th, being: "In hand $3.26." This is not surprising. Through the month it is still "Miserable" and "Very miserable, no work," till the twenty-fifth. "Feel much better," and also "Paid up to-day"—perhaps that was the reason. On the twenty-eighth a kind friend of whom I asked a loan of fifty dollars sent me a hundred, so I felt quite wealthy again.

In August down again, far down. But sick or well I wrote, sometimes selling, more times not. "I row dismally on pond and dismally converse." "All bad days and nothing in 'em." "Drag around generally."

By the end of August we returned to the city, and I took Katharine to her father and other mother, now on their way back to Pasadena. If I had any settled home, any settled income, any settled health, it would have been "my turn" now—how gladly my turn!—but I could hardly keep myself, even with many visits, much less keep two, so it was another good-by. September 1st: "See Katharine off. . . . Go home and collapse."

Saturday second: "Ride on 5th Ave. bus . . . have to give up and come home." This was the hottest week of that summer; there were sixty-seven deaths in New York. I returned to Cold Spring Harbor for a while, still far from well. "These are long heavy days, head thick and weak, body weak too." On the twenty-fifth I went for a short visit to Miss Lillian Wald at the Nurses Settlement on Henry Street. She was called the

"Jane Addams of New York." Then I engaged a room at the 32nd Street house again.

September 30th was my last visit to my father. "Carry grapes. Knew me for awhile. Probably cannot see him again.". . .

Another visit in Boston early in October. My publishers showed me the reviews of *In This Our World* —"very fine." There was a pleasant little parlor talk in the house of a friend, now long grown dear, Mary Hutcheson Page. Just a few earnest women who were interested in my theory of domestic economics. They were "stirred and not frightened," and under the new stimulus admitted things, feelings, they had never dared mention before, hardly acknowledge to themselves.

Speaking of the supposed sanctity of family meals, one said, "Breakfast really isn't so pleasant at our house. There are the children in a hurry to get off to school—there's my husband in a hurry to get off to his business—there's my husband's mother, who is a little out of her mind, and her attendant—" And another owned that when she was left alone with her first baby there were times when she felt like saying, "Take it! Please take it for a little while—somebody, anybody!"

Funds remained low, the record for October 15th is $1.15. There were some addresses but no fees set down, may have forgotten to do it. Was pretty well along here, yet so reduced one day as to remark, "Get very tired after dinner and can't talk." That was being tired, indeed. "Call at Small and Maynard's and get $25.00. Still more due me—really mine!" So it appears the books were beginning to pay something.

November 5th went to Wellesley College, with Dr. Ellen Hayes, and talked to the Agora Club girls. It

was a very pleasant time, some of the professors were
much impressed with my views on early education,
and urged my writing on that topic. Sunday sixth, spoke
in Newton and lunched with Mrs. Kate Gannett Wells.
"They've read the book (W. & E.) and like it—she's
an anti, too."

November 11th off again westward, via Michigan
Central, and saw Niagara Falls—no remarks. One of
the best comments I remember on that great cataract
is the Irishman's, who quite refused to be impressed.
"But look at that vast body of water pouring over
there!" they cried, to which he only said, "And what's
to hinder it!"

A pleasant little visit to Mrs. Corbett in Detroit,
then to Battle Creek, with those good Turners who
thought me a missionary. Dowagiac next, with Mrs.
Lee, and addressed the Woman's Club on Social Progress. Arrived in Chicago late one evening: "with
woman and child, bags and birdcage on my hands. Good
Mr. White meets me, with his friend Carl Linden, and
sees to the woman."

That was the beginning of a long stay with dear
Mrs. Dow, Mr. White coming daily to work with me
—we were collaborating on a play.

It was always a pleasure to be with that kind
"mother," in her large house standing in a good-sized
lot of its own—with their own cow in it. There were
plenty of old friends and new ones, Dr. McCracken
thought I was doing well; at Hull House I met George
Herron, Hamlin Garland, Keir Hardy, N. O. Nelson
the profit-sharer and coöperator, and "Golden Rule
Jones," the most Christian Mayor of Toledo. A lecture in that town; a little trip to Grinnell, Iowa, with
several talks. For this last there was a gift of fifty dollars from Mrs. Rand, whose daughter Mr. Herron

afterward married. "So I clear $28.00—surprising and pleasant."

By December 20th we had finished our play, first draft, of which achievement nothing ever came. Mrs. Dow went to her daughter's in Geneva, for Christmas, but arranged to have her excellent servants prepare dinner for Mr. White and me. So there we sat, two homeless wanderers, eating a Christmas dinner in a house where we had no connection but friendship. He had the grippe, and couldn't eat. I was having a "low" time and couldn't eat, either—it was a funny meal.

That year wound up creditably—December 31st: "Finish all the letters I had to do, 12, and 9 post-cards." Must have been feeling stronger. The New Year opened, as so often, with a sort of "confession of faith." As these represent a definite attempt to state and restate my belief and purpose I quote this one:

To live, letting God do it. Spread self-consciousness into con-cern for others. Leave one's self an open door, a free uncon-scious channel, for the deep rushing flood of life to pour through. To make sure in one's own life of what one teaches others—"say 'come' not 'go,'" be what they ought to be. To tell and tell forever humanity's great secret—that each one *is all the rest*—and each "can do," himself, the world's work, so made easier for all. A calmness born of the immeasurable Power which moves us. A rich Peace, seeing that life is good. A Joy, deepening daily as we understand. And Love—the love that all things live in—to feel it and give it, to Give it, Give it, Give it everywhere. . . .

Another good dentist befriends me, "Gold crown $10.00," and a Christmas present of just that amount made it nothing. January 7th to Toledo, where I visited "Golden Rule Jones," and spoke in the Hall of that name, on the "Social Organism." Also preached

there next day. Monday in Wauregan, Ohio, on Socialism, "Collection, $5.00." Further: "Mr. Jones
gave me $25.00 and offered a lot more, but I thought
best not to indulge. Back to Chicago again."

Presently I set off on a southern trip, from which I
hoped much as an escape from cold—my years in California having left me with a settled distaste for winter
weather.

The first stop was with N. O. Nelson, in St. Louis,
or rather in the model village of Leclaire, just across
the river. Mr. Crunden, the librarian in St. Louis, was
much interested in my books. I spoke for the Wednesday Club, for The Pedagogical Society, twice for Mr.
Nelson's group at Leclaire. "There are lots of nice
people here," I note. January 20th, a talk in a private
school; twenty-second preached in Unitarian church
A.M. and in Congregational church in evening; twenty-
third, spoke at a "Christian" ministers' meeting, and
addressed a colored Woman's Club at their church;
there were a kindergarten meeting and a settlement
meeting, too. For all these I got $90.00, of which
$40.00 was from the Pedagogical Society.

Then I set forth, February 26th, for Ruskin, Tennessee. Ruskin was another of those sublimely planned,
devotedly joined, and invariably deserted Socialist
colonies. Only ignorance of the real nature of social
relation can account for these high-minded idiocies. A
city, a village, a settlement of any sort, is not based on
"Go to! Let us live here and behave so and so!" That
Socialists, so convinced of "economic determinism,"
should overlook the necessity for a legitimate local
economic base and relationship, is especially sad, but
they do. The result is that those of their membership
who are capable of serving the larger organism of
city, state, or country are drawn away by the pull of

pongees, pack her valise and take her down to Hotel Albert."

There I saw my dear Grace, and had a chance to do a few errands for her. They sailed on the *Wester-land.* ...

My little stepmother went off for a three days' vacation, and I kept house for her. "Fri., Aug. 20th. Quiet day, mend tablecloth. Entertain boarders." By the twenty-third I was off again, to no less a place than "Greenacre," Maine, where Miss Sarah Farmer had a species of summer school of a metaphysical sort. Dharmaputra, a Buddhist of Ceylon, was there. I remember him enthroned in a rocking-chair, surrounded by admiring women who stood. He discoursed also under the pines, all squatting on the ground about him. All who were able, that is; one elderly spinster was much chagrined because she had to have a camp-stool.

Following upon the Congress of Religions at the World's Fair in '93, there came to us many of those swarthy preachers, who were attended by crowds of devout women as if the preaching was something superior to Christianity, which it was not.

I had been invited to that place by Miss Farmer, who wrote, "Give us your best thought," so I had arranged to speak on the "New Motherhood." But after arrival I was told by a friend that there was opposition to my giving this address. Miss Ida C. Hultin, a Unitarian minister from Moline, Illinois, objected on the ground that I was not a fit person to lecture on motherhood— that I had "given up my child." Miss Farmer came to me herself to ask me to change my topic. Being forewarned I was calm, and asked the reason for the change. She was obliged to repeat the charge—that I had given up my child.

that larger service; those who remain are of the sort who need to be taken care of, not world-builders at all.

January 27th: "Tennessee City at 6:40 A.M. Cold. Get breakfast there and take the 'mail coach' (!) at 9:30. Six miles to Ruskin. Roads awful." Well I remember that trip; we forded the winding river over and over—no bridges at all. Arriving, I found one large wooden building, with some heating apparatus, much needed; with some smaller ones, and a general look of undertaking things. I was fortunate enough to be in the heated building, whose comfort was also appreciated by various more than friendly rats.

Twenty-eighth: "5:30 whistle! Make surreptitious coffee over lamp. Miss C. providing cup, etc.—I brought the coffee." Monday it snowed. Tuesday it snowed. "Cold. Spend my strength in putting up with the difficulties of this place." February 1st: "Twelve below zero they say." "Wrote 'The Rats of Ruskin' for the paper." Third: "Lecture on 'Ethics and Socialists.'"

From this uncomfortable resort I went to Nashville: I found me a boarding-house, 302 N. High Street. "Small cold room. $.25 per day—all right." I cheerfully remark.

But I was being painfully disappointed in my hopes of escaping the rigors of a northern winter. "Awful," says the diary. "Below zero." My room was over a porch, board floor merely. The only means of heating it was a gas stove, and the meter froze in the cellar. I slept in and under all my clothes, with a blanket around my head, like an arctic traveler. In the closed wardrobe, in a closed traveling bag, in my little inkstand—glass, tin, leather,—the ink froze.

Wednesday, February 8th: "Still awful. Still below zero," and "it is a terribly cold spell, a fortnight nearly." Thursday, "Worse and worse." Friday, "Still severe, still below." But I went to Memphis that day, visited a Mrs. Anderson, and there I had a room with a fire in it. But it stayed cold. "This is preternatural weather. We all sit shawled and hug the fire." In spite of fires the milk froze *on the mantelpiece,* and our hot food was dead cold before we could eat it. The suffering all over the unprotected South was dreadful, the poor Negroes died like flies. It was thirteen below at Memphis, and at New Orleans sunk to only four above. Below all records, for a fortnight or more.

I spoke once in Nashville, four times in Memphis, then in Birmingham, Alabama, and so to Atlanta, Georgia, February 21st. Here I had a charming time, staying with Mrs. Lowe, then president of the General Federation of Women's Clubs. I lectured for their local club that night: "Tremendous crowd—standing —lots couldn't get in. Went well. Great enthusiasm. People fainted, went out, recovered and returned."

They were wonderfully kind to me in the South. One soft-voiced lady, introducing me, said, "And to think that a niece of Harriet Beecher Stowe should come down here and make us all love her!" There was a week of this cordial enthusiasm, with six addresses and a sermon, to say nothing of "entertainments." At one of these I had a little encounter with an earnest temperance advocate. It was a sort of garden-party reception, we sat about at little tables for our refreshments, a smiling spring having followed that arctic period.

There was coffee, hot, strong and delicious in fragrance. I like coffee better than almost any eatable—or potable, rather, but take it only for breakfast, having a high respect for its stimulating powers. Also, there was punch, a pale pink punch for ladies, the barrel-oflemonade-and-bottle-of-claret kind. But it was cool and wet, and I took some. Came and sat opposite me a majestic woman, full-bodied, glittering with black beads or spangles which rose and fell on the expanse before her.

She ordered coffee, gazing on me with unconcealed displeasure. "I see you are not a temperance woman!" quoth she. "How do you see that?" I countered. "You are drinking an alcoholic beverage!" she declared triumphantly. "Bless you," I gently explained. "There's not enough alcohol in that to hurt a six-month's-old baby." "It is not a question of effects," she replied with unction, "it is a question of principle."

She drank that coffee—and O how good it smelled! —and ordered another cup. "I see you are not a temperance woman," said I. "Why—what do you mean!" "You are taking two cups of a strong stimulant in the middle of the afternoon just because you like it." "But it has no intoxicating effect," she protested, to which I calmly replied, "It is not a question of effects, it is a question of principle." The conversation lapsed.

Another visit in Goldsboro, North Carolina, followed, with my friend Mrs. Royall, for a month this time; there were some lectures, a good deal of writing, and a pretty bad "low" period. While there I received a letter of invitation to address the International Council of Women meeting in London that summer, and cabled "Yes." This was my fourth voyage for fifty dollars or near it, for Houghton telegraphed me about first-class passage on SS. *Furst Bismarck,* $55.00! I began to write for the *Cosmopolitan,* having been pursued by eager letters from James Brisbane Walker, its enterprising owner and editor. Also the Philadelphia *Saturday Evening Post* wrote me, asking for

short editorials, of which I wrote a good many—till
they left off having any from outside the office.

So northward again, speaking in Wilson and Ral-
eigh, North Carolina, then Washington, Baltimore,
Newark, New York, Cambridge and Boston; also at
Bryn Mawr College. While in New York I attended a
"dollar dinner" given for Mr. Wm. J. Bryan—
"Mayor Jones of Toledo escorts me to the platform,
Mr. Bryan gives me his seat, all very grand."

Father McGlynn, a Single Taxer, was unfortunately
allowed to speak before Mr. Bryan, whose "dinner" it
was, and whom every one wished to hear. This fiscal
enthusiast, quite ignoring the wishes of the audience or
any sense of politeness and fairness to the speaker of
the evening, poured forth his special theory so long as
almost to break up the meeting.

Not Single Taxers alone are guilty of such conduct.
In London, at a great peace-meeting, Archbishop Ireland chanced to be present, and was politely asked to
make a few remarks. He talked for over an hour, and
broke up the meeting, people went out in platoons.
The brutal rudeness of speakers in disregarding others
deserves punishment.

Mr. Walker continued to make urgent demands for
the *Cosmopolitan,* wanted me to work on it regularly,
to send him everything I wrote—was most urgent. But,
going there to see him, and observing how he treated
his editors, I declined, though readily agreeing to fill
certain orders.

On the fourth of May I embarked for England, this
time to attend the Quinquennial Congress of The International Council of Women. My first-cabin accommodation proved to be one bed of four, in a state-room
on a low deck, the other berths being occupied by three
German Jewesses.

CHAPTER XVII

OVER THE TOP

THE International Council of Women is a federated body, composed of many National Councils and a number of other groups, some of great size, as the W.C.T.U. and the W.S.A. It was an important part of the world-wide stir and getting-together of women which so characterizes the last century, representing millions of women, and the noblest upward movements of the age. Fancy the juvenile ignorance that scorns an age in which half the world woke up!

Women had claimed and won equal education, from the public schools to the universities; professional opportunity, and had made a place in medicine, law, the ministry, and all manner of trades, crafts and businesses; equal suffrage, and had made much progress in that demand. But the most wide-spread and in a way the most important of these various associations was the Woman's Club, which reached almost every one, and brought her out of the sacred selfishness of the home into the broader contact and relationship so essential to social progress. Once in five years this International Council held a Congress, to which came leading women from many nations, of many religions and purposes; they came together from all parts of the world and learned to know each other and their common needs.

London was very kind to us. Great houses were opened, invitations poured in, royalty itself was polite.

I went as a free lance, invited personally as a speaker, my visit not limited to the Congress. So I went out to Hammersmith, where my friend May Morris lived, and engaged board in Carnforth Lodge. Miss Starr of Hull House had told me of this place, she stayed there while studying book-binding with "The Dove" experts.

This was a square old manor house, now a home for nurses, which added to its resources by its "paying guests." It stood in a large garden, and bore high upon its stately walls a broad band of white, going all the way around, with this inscription—"The Hammersmith and Fulham District Association for Nursing the Sick Poor in Their Own Homes Supported by Voluntary Contributions Only."

I was glad to be in England again, to renew friendships made in 1896 and to make new ones. I've been there five times, and every time I like it better. Furthermore, since the War, when the various nations stood out so sharply in their true colors, England rose higher than ever in my esteem.

People were more than kind. I was made a member of the Sesame Club, an international woman's club of a purely social nature. Of the Fabian Society I was still a member, and saw something of them. Having tea with May Morris, "J. Ramsay MacDonald calls and invites me to dinner." "Feel pretty low," as but too usual.

On a fine May Sunday I visited Mrs. Henry Norman. She was the daughter of my dear Edinburgh friend, Mrs. Dowie. "Very cordial and nice. A lovely country, pure picture. Sleep at Ivy Farm, another picture. I hear and see the skylark, hear the cuckoo too." Nevertheless, on Monday, "continue very low and miserable," and Tuesday, "lie flat on the daisies and buttercups and weep—very low indeed."

Again in Carnforth Lodge, there presently appeared as fellow-boarder a distant cousin, Miss Foote by name, also studying book-binding. She was a very pleasant companion. We enjoyed the beauties of England together, and smiled as strangers may, at some of its—differences. There came a spell of extremely hot weather, cruelly hot, horses died in London streets. We two Americans sought for ice, and found none. No ice for sale anywhere. Finally we were told, dubiously, "You might find some at the fishmongers."

By the fifth of May I proudly record, "Women and Economics has come." Small and Maynard arranged with Putnam's for their English publishing. Mr. George Haven Putnam remembered me as a small child in Mrs. Swift's boarding-house in New York; he was a friend of my father's. There was a demand for my book, but some inefficiency at the American end delayed its coming. Mr. Putnam complained to me that while there were so many books he could not sell it was pretty hard to have a waiting list for mine and not be able to get it.

Meanwhile I was writing, always writing, or trying to; with little visits, dinners, and so on in between working days. Presently I met Dr. E. A. Ross, the sociologist, whom I had known at Stanford. He and his pretty wife had a tiny flat in London for a while, and they were intensely interested in *Women and Economics*. He asked why I had not put in a bibliography. I told him I had meant to, but when it came to making a list of the books I had read bearing on the subject, there were only two! One was Geddes's and Thompson's *Evolution of Sex,* the other only an article, Lester F. Ward's, in that 1888 *Forum*.

Then they were anxious to know how long I had been at work on it, said they thought it must have been ever since they had seen me last, some four years. "If I tell you you will never respect me or the book any more," I protested. But they were determined to know, and I told him that the first draft, the manuscript the publishers accepted, had been written in seventeen days, while visiting in five different houses. This was a blow to the scientific mind.

The book was warmly received in London, with long, respectful reviews in the papers. What with my former reputation, based on the poems, this new and impressive book, and my addresses at the Congress and elsewhere, I became quite a lion.

The Congress opened on June 26, with its week of many meetings, addresses, reports, and so on. Noted women were gathered there from all quarters of the world—which had any. Other women, as yet distinguished by the interest in progress and the courage that brought them, came in their native costumes; the "golden lilies" of high-born Chinese ladies, the Hindu sari, the veils of harem women.

The most pressing matters of importance to women, to children, to the home, to the peace, purity and health of the world, all were discussed in stirring papers and speeches, and listened to by great and enthusiastic crowds. Most hospitable entertainment was offered us, large cards of invitation, such as I had never seen before; a reception by Lady Battersea at Surrey House on Park Lane, a garden-party at Fulham Palace—"Lord Bishop of London and Mrs. Creighton," and another at Gunnersbury Park, Baron Rothschild's place. "Very gaudy bright and splendid," says the diary.

The grandest of all was the opening one given at Stafford House by the Duchess of Sutherland. For this, I learned later, our much-impressed American women had prepared with awe, wearing their best and newest, with large outlay. It was an impressive occasion; Stafford House was called the finest private house in London, and as for its Lady—when they asked me, "What has impressed you most in England?" I promptly answered, "The Duchess of Sutherland." She was so big, so progressive and intelligent, so nobly beautiful.

If I had been well—if ever I had had a clear, strong head—all this would have been a vivid and pleasant memory. But I moved through meetings and entertainment with a groping mind, doing what I had to do as well as I could, in my usual dreary twilight. It was always a struggle to get necessary work done, to keep up in some degree with the flood of engagements, to try to recognize and remember people. This last effort I have long since given up. I do not, can not, hold in mind a fraction of the innumerable people I have met. In the everlasting traveling, lecturing and being "entertained," it was my custom, after the lecture, to look feebly about and ask, "Where is the lady I belong to?" Originally a personal limitation, doubtless; added to by the long ruin; made incurable by the professional life.

Came to me one morning during a session a busy Mrs. Leo Hunter, eager to have me come to dinner. I looked in my little engagement book—"Yes, I can come, thank you," and I asked the place, the hour, the name. "Don't you know my *name?*" she cried amazedly. I owned that I didn't. "But how can you come to dinner with me if you don't know my name!" "You asked me to," said I. If she had but known how many kind persons were nameless to me!

Before the Congress opened a luncheon was given by the Society of American Women in London, to which I, among many others, was invited. In the waiting-room I saw and admired a particularly English type, tall and generously built, so unlike our slender, nervous American kind, with large blue eyes and glorious hair, heavy golden masses. Presently I learned that she was born in Salem, Massachusetts! The Countess of Warwick was there, and I was warned by a careful lady that this nóblewoman "was not a proper person to meet." I had heard something of the reasons for criticism, and cheerfully replied that so long as the Prince of Wales was in good society I had no objections to meeting the Countess of Warwick, which presently came to pass.

"*Would* you mind sitting on the other side of the Countess of Warwick?" asked a worried mistress of ceremonies. "Mrs. Frances Hodgson Burnett has taken your place by mistake." I truthfully told her that I did not care in the least where I sat, but was amused when we passed behind the chairs to see that a very large place-card on the President's left, standing up against a goblet, bearing my name in conspicuous letters, with Mrs. Burnett sitting cheerfully in front of it. On the President's right was the Countess, and I sat next beyond, pleased to study so closely "the most beautiful woman in Europe."

The President held her in converse, and it worried me to see swift waiters taking away her food before she had time to eat. A particularly good plate of chicken was about to be torn from her and I could not bear it. I touched her arm, with some warm commendation of the chicken and protest that she was not getting anything to eat. This seemed to please her as a matter of good-will, we talked a bit, and she asked me to visit her at Warwick Castle—which I took to be merely a general expression of hospitality.

Next I met her at her sister's reception, which deserves more description, being high-water-mark in the matter of gorgeousness of all I ever attended. Our

delegates went to it in all the state they could muster,
in jeweled glory. I went alone on a two-penny bus, having to get off in Piccadilly and scuttle around behind St.
James's Park in the rain and darkness, ducking under
the heads of the horses crowding in. Here was mighty
Stafford House, here were long lines of knee-breeched
liveries, and here was I, giving my waterproof and
rubbers to these functionaries as if it were the coat-
room at a church fair.

My dress, the only one I had for evening wear, was
a dark plum-colored satin which I had made to suit
myself, a "princess dress," fitted smoothly down the
front like a medieval lady's, with a square neck,
trimmed with plain bands of velvet of the same rich
color. It cost me about fifteen dollars, and at this writing I am still using some of it—I was fond of that
dress. One of the reporters, dilating on the glittering
costumes, spoke of "Mrs. Stetson in a plain black
dress, with no diamonds but her eyes," a gentleman
reporter, that.

In the dressing-rooms I saw a woman I had known
in Oakland, rich, elderly, accustomed to social occasions, yet looking strangely timid. She was one of those
persons who love to patronize budding celebrities, but
apt to drop them suddenly upon disapproval. She had
been kind to me during some of my Oakland experiences, had dropped me with sudden violence, and when
I left the state considered me a wholly objectionable
character. Naturally I did not approach her. To my
great astonishment she greeted me with effusion and
hung upon my arm, that I might take her about! Circumstances alter cases.

But my most characteristic performance at the reception was as follows: On entrance we were passed
along that imposing line of footmen, and our names

were cried aloud from man to man as we approached
the grand staircase on whose first landing stood the
ladies receiving. Drawing near the stairs I saw two
members of our Congress, plainly dressed and looking
timidly up at the array of tiaras on the landing. They
said they had no one to introduce them. "Come on,"
quoth I, serenely, "tell me your names and I'll introduce you." One was Susa Young Gates, daughter of
Brigham Young, who became a lasting friend, the other
Emmiline Wells, I think, another Mormon lady. And
so I introduced them to the Duchess of Sutherland,
gloriously tall and beautiful, to the Countess of Warwick, her sister; and then, turning to the third, I cheerfully remarked, "This one I don't remember."

Which was true, and quite habitual with me, but on
this occasion most unfortunate, as the third hostess was
Lady Aberdeen, the President of The International
Council of Women! She was very pleasant about it but
I think not unnaturally displeased—who wouldn't have
been!

The most distinguished honor offered to the delegates was an invitation to take tea with the Queen at
Windsor Castle. With glowing anticipations the women
of all nations prepared for this supreme opportunity.
I was as usual very tired, always too tired to meet the
demands of these great gatherings; and I shrewdly
suspected that this would not be a wholly enjoyable
affair, so I did not go. Afterwards I heard that they
all had to stand about for two hours in a stone court-
yard, which for a woman like Susan B. Anthony and
others near her age must have been a serious tax on
their strength. At last Victoria appeared, in the carriage named for her, and drove slowly about. Lady
Aberdeen knelt on the step and kissed her hand, then
presenting one only of the delegates, a lady from

Canada who had a title, and the Queen drove out again. After which august spectacle tea was served by flunkies; as a matter of boasting all the others could proudly state that they had been to tea with the Queen, but I could proudly state that I'd been asked and wouldn't go.

They told a somewhat similar story of our Antoinette Sterling, the great contralto, who was a popular favorite in England. Her magnificent voice was so renowned that Victoria summoned her to sing before her. Mrs. Sterling, who had arranged to sing for some charity on that day, replied that she had another engagement and could not come. The Queen, who approved her putting charity first, repeated her invitation for another date. The musical Quaker replied that she could not come because she never wore décolleté gowns as required at court, and the patient Queen told her to wear what she pleased. So Antoinette went at last, and sang so gloriously that her majesty gave her a silver tea-set;—I tell the tale as it was told to me.

It appeared the friendly Lady Warwick really meant her invitation. She repeated it at that reception, and somewhat later sent me a telegram three pages long— sixty-three words, a letter, really, urging me to come and address some pen-workers from Birmingham whom she was trying to organize; and to spend the night; so at last I went.

It was but one night, but memorable for the fairy-tale of that cream-walled castle by the shadowy Avon; the white peacocks on the velvet lawns; the harebells on the battlements—I went up there and picked one so I know. My bedroom was liberally decorated with crests and coronets, on the writing paper, of which there was a plentiful supply; on the chinaware, the towels, the water-cans, the sheets and pillow-cases—even the soft, thick rose-colored blankets had a massive one like an inverted soup-plate. It made me think of a steam-boat.

The baronial hall was a revelation in size; three distinct parties might have been held in it without disturbing one another. In the deep embrasure of one window stood a knight in armor on horseback, life-size,—and he made no more impression than a rubber plant.

Any one could visit Warwick for a shilling a head, but when the "trippers" were being shown about by the austere exhibitor, I felt amusingly superior, being on the other side of the rope! Childishly ignorant among all this gorgeousness was I, and when asked about breakfast in bed cheerfully replied that I preferred to get up. So I came down in the morning to that huge dining-hall, with the great Vandyke—or was it Velásquez?—at one end. It seemed depressingly empty, no one else eating but a remote governess and her charge, the few footmen coldly disapproving. Evidently one was not expected to get up to breakfast. The Earl of Warwick was at home, and also the Countess's mother, Lady Roslyn. She was much pleased with my poems and asked me to visit her at Roslyn Castle. Also Lady Warwick urged me to come to them at their summer cottage, and, later, the Duchess of Sutherland asked me to visit her—that was on account of *Women and Economics*.

None of these things did I do, reasons quite forgotten, but I really wanted to accept the last invitation, because when my Grandmother Perkins had been in England with Aunt Harriet Stowe they had been entertained by the former Duchess of Sutherland, who was a special friend of the Queen. She was unable for reasons of state openly to receive Aunt Harriet as she wished to do, and made this arrangement with her friend instead. However I didn't go.

As an offset to all these grandeurs let me describe my reception by Miss Purdie's maid. Miss Purdie was a fine, liberal-minded Scotch lady, who had me give a parlor lecture in 1896, and now, when entertainment was being planned for the foreign visitors, had asked for me. I had mostly forgotten the former meeting, and went to spy out the land and see if I wanted to be with her.

I never had any impressive clothes, and in England it makes far more difference than it does here. I trotted about in my very ordinary raiment, with my everlasting little black bag, just as I would at home, and so attired rang Miss Purdie's bell. The door was opened by a severe Scotch maid.

"Is Miss Purdie at home?" "She is." "Can I see her?" "What do you wish to see her for?" "I wish to call upon her," and I offered my card. The card mollified her somewhat, but not much, for it had no crest, no name of house or address, not even "Mrs.," nothing but Charlotte Perkins Stetson.

She let me in, grudgingly, and started up the stairs. I was uncertain of what was expected. "Shall I come up?" I asked, "or wait here?" This admission of ignorance she considered most damaging, and sternly replied, "If you are *really a caller* you may come up!" I came up, was received with open arms by Miss Purdie, and spent a week there very happily. Doubtless that worthy watch-dog took me for an agent—why shouldn't she?

Like a few pictures out of a big book too hastily turned in a dim light, are these memories. There was one urgent luncheon invitation from a Lady—Grove, I think it was. I was torn between my habit of always seeing people who needed me, and increasing weari-

ness, and wrote as much, saying that unless she wished
to see me imperatively I could not come. The answering demand was most imperative, so I went; finding a
large, handsome lady with two admirers (one of whom
was George Eliot's second husband, Mr. Cross), who
talked with her incessantly, and a spare elderly husband who talked not at all—and myself, evidently only
an exhibit.

The Congress over, there remained many friends to
see, and always work to do. I wrote an article for
Ainslee's Magazine and another for the *Arena,* about
the Congress, and extremely poor stuff it was. With
ease and freedom and some merit, I write thoughts,
ideas, reasoning, yes, and feeling too, but descriptive
work, such as makes a war correspondent famous, is
beyond me.

One delightful visit was with the family of Mrs.
Bland (Edith Nesbit), at Well Hall, Eltham, Kent.
The earlier mansion, built for Margaret Roper by her
father, Sir Thomas More, had been burned, and replaced by this one which they said "was only Georgian."
Behind the house, just across a little vine-walled bridge,
was a large rectangular lawn, surrounded by thick-
grown trees and shrubs, outside which lay the moat
that once guarded the older building. Here, in absolute privacy, those lovely children could run barefoot,
play tennis and badminton, wear any sort of costume;
it was a parlor out of doors. We all joined in merry
games, acted little plays and fairy-tales, and took
plentiful photographs.

There was another visit to Edinburgh, where I lectured for the Summer School, for the University, on
Castle Hill. My dear Mrs. Dowie was staying at
Levenhall, Musselbirgh, near by, and I spent a few days
with her, most happily. From there back to Newcastle,

where I renewed friendship with Miss Roecliffe, my kind entertainer of 1896.

In these English travels I found no difficulty whatever either in audiences or in personal contacts. Hearers laughed at my jokes just as they did at home; one man told a friend, "I'd give half a crown any day just to see that woman smile." Also, my personal work went on. Strangers confided in me as at home. One old gentleman with whom I fell into converse on a train in Scotland, pulled himself up at last, protesting in surprise that he never talked with strangers! I explained that I was not a stranger, and I wasn't—people were people anywhere and my service was for all. So they told me their troubles as usual, and I helped as I could, finding always that the losses and sufferings, mistakes and misdeeds of my own life gave me the key to the hearts of others.

While in Newcastle one unexpected amusement was going to the circus—Barnum and Bailey's—in England! Very popular it was, too. Back to London and my favorite Midland Temperance Hotel on Guilford St., a little last shopping and calling, and then I prefaced my departure by trying Brush's Remedy for seasickness. Sailed on August 31, SS. *Menominee*. "Room 8. Berth 4. Nice sofa bed under porthole. Am not sick." And next day, "Blessed be Brush! Am not sick at all."

As to ocean travel in general, I dislike it intensely. There is no privacy except in bed, and not then unless one has a whole stateroom. Planted in a steamer-chair, the strip of deck before one's face is a promenade, a ceaseless procession of humanity. As to "sea air"— unless one can get to the very prow, or bear the full blast of the wind, what one gets is *ship air,* and if any beast has a fouler breath than a ship, I have not met it. Anywhere to the leeward it pours out from every door that's open, and from those slow-whirling ventilators which reach down to the very bowels of the ship—and distribute its odors. An ocean steamer is a big, inescapable garden-party, reception, afternoon tea—a constant, swirling crowd. Sorry, but I don't like it.

Landed Monday, September 11th, and back to mother's; one dollar in my pocket. But by Friday came the check from *Ainslee's*, $125.00! the most I had ever received up to that time. Things were going well now. There were many "downs" during the summer, but now the little book says "Feel fine," "Do good morning's work on letters and papers and am not tired." But by the twenty-first. "Feel so badly P.M. that I try to take a ride on the cars and have to come back."

Presently Mr. Small, my publisher, called. He came eagerly up the stairs and greeted me warmly, anxious for other books. "We quite understand," he said, "that further arrangements will have to be on a different basis." *Women and Economics* was a success. The discrepancy between its really enormous vogue and its very meager returns I have never understood. It sold and sold and sold for about twenty-five years. It sold widely in England, so much so that Putnam's brought out a seventh edition with a new introduction in 1911. It was translated into French—but alas! the translator couldn't find a publisher!—into German, Dutch, Italian, Hungarian and Japanese. From none of the translations did I get anything, save the Italian. That was done by the Contessa Pironti, and she sent me $30.00—noblesse oblige!

The reviews were surprising, numerous, respectful, a most gratifying recognition. So Small agreed to take my next book, *Human Work,* which I proposed to spend the winter in writing. They offered $500.00 down, 15 per cent to 5000 and then 18 per cent; I was launched.

Lecturing also began to go well. For two in Boston I got $87.00, for another $25.00, and from the *Saturday Evening Post,* for several editorials, $48.00; from the *Puritan,* $25.00. By October I record a grand total of $231.56. But next day I sent Katharine $25.00, and to various creditors $50, $38, $30, $50, $20—there was never much surplus.

From a pleasant Boston visit with the Blackwells, always so good to me, I was off, October 19th for Toledo, staying again with the family of Mayor Jones. Here I did my first "campaign speaking"; did not take to it much. But there was one funny incident while there. I was hurrying to a down-town meeting when the horse-car was stopped by an altercation between the slender young conductor and a big, elderly man who insisted that his transfer was good, and refused to pay another fare as demanded. The conductor threatened to throw him off, but the passenger got in behind the brake—the back platform was only open at one end— and defied him. The driver looked around grinning, the complacent Americans inside looked on in amusement—but I was in a hurry. So I rose with a most philanthropic air and came forward with, "Let me pay this poor man's fare." "Oh no, Madam, no indeed!" protested the insulted disputant, out came his purse and on went the car—it was a mean trick, but the car should not be so delayed.

Then to Indianapolis, October 25th. "Address Contemporary Club on 'What Work Is.' Rather hard sledding but struck some kindred notes." Especially in a youth who turns out to be Booth Tarkington. As I delighted in and deeply honored his work, it was a pleasure to find how agreeable he was personally—I called on him next morning and we had a nice talk. Back to

Toledo, more speeches, and preached twice on Sunday. Then to St. Louis, visiting the Crundens', and speaking for the Pedagogical Society again. "Big house, went well." So to Chicago, and dear Mrs. Dow.

November 3rd: "Go down town and see my manager, Mrs. Laura D. Pelham." I had known this lady in Hull House, she and her husband were connected with a lecture bureau. She came to hear me, and then this bureau offered me $250.00 a week, net, if I would work for them. This was large money, but what of that? I felt sure that they overestimated my drawing power, knew that I could not do good work in six lectures a week right along, and also I was on my way to California to spend a quiet winter writing the next book. Furthermore, I had plans for the next year that brooked no postponement. In June I was to marry again, and the chances of a year's time, when one is near forty, are worth more than millions of dollars. So that golden opportunity was passed by.

But I lectured "on my own," in Chicago, in Milwaukee, in Sioux City, Iowa, and Sheldon—"Big crowd but it went badly. They don't like it. Hard sledding." But next day some ladies called. "They like me and want me again. . . . Can't always make a good impression."

Back to Chicago, more lectures, one in Fond du Lac, Wisconsin, where my title was rendered, "Our Brains and What's the Matter of 'Em."

Thursday, November 16th: "Letter from Russia—a man has translated my book—one Kamensky."

In Evanston, at the Northwestern University, I had the honor of taking the place of Mr. Howells, who could not keep his engagement, and lectured on Ethics. Went well—I was really pleased. So were they, the

professors and such. Then in town and take Wisconsin
Central at 2:00 A.M. and off to Minneapolis.

There was one occasion in this city when I met what
is called "social attention" in a conspicuous form. I
think it was later, but will tell the tale while I remember it. A friend there had arranged a lecture for me.
This is no light work, as any one who has done it knows.
The tickets were fifty cents. Certain ladies, knowing
me by reputation, insisted that I must have some social
attention. Pay fifty cents to hear me lecture they would
not, but got up a lunch party in my "honor" at a hotel,
where they all paid a dollar for their food, and expected me to address them, for nothing! I arrived about
11:00 A.M.—there was a coal famine, a blizzard and a
strike, all at once, and such hindrance and delay that I
had had almost no sleep. And here I was taken to this
hotel filled with buzzing women, for this luncheon.

"Have you engaged a room for me?" I asked wearily. No, they had not thought to do that. I suggested
that I should like a room and a bath, which was presently furnished, to my relief. And all through that
chattering lunch I sat thinking how to tell them, without being rude and grossly ungrateful, that to expect
a speech for nothing, of a professional speaker, was—
well, shall we say unbusinesslike? When women really
grow up they will be more fair-minded.

On westward I went, stopping at Kansas City, at
Denver and Greeley, Colorado, and to Ogden, Salt
Lake City, and Provo, Utah—where I lectured in the
Brigham Young Polysophical Academy!

Mrs. Susa Young Gates, the greatest child of her
great father, Brigham Young, one of the friends I
made at the London Congress, has remained so to her
death. She was a remarkable woman, herself a writer
and speaker, an organiser, an editor, and mother of

eleven children. I always visited her when in Utah. There were a number of lectures this time, and I had a chance to see my brother's second wife and my nephew Basil, a dear boy.

Another friend in Ogden, Mrs. Coulter, took me to the Aglaia, apparently a literary circle. "Hear Lamb discussed—with faint—final—reference to his possible sense of humor!" By December 8th I am in San Francisco, first time since ignominious departure in 1895.

I love to reach the coast by the U.P. The long, upward pull to the divide, two big engines tugging and puffing like live things. Then, as we go over, the sudden change in the sound of the wheels, easy, swift, as we roll down, passing degrees of latitude in minutes almost, snow, evergreens, deciduous trees, the rich, sweet air, the growing warmth, and all at once oranges, palms, roses, California! I love that state (geographically) from end to end; love the whole Pacific Coast for that matter, but California especially.

The mountains, the valleys, the brilliant sea, the endless profusion of rich foliage and flowers and fruit, the long, sweeping contours of the topography, the blessed calmness of the air—all these I love. Yet, when it comes to people, never have I been so misliked and misunderstood as in that state. However, those people are mostly dead by this time, and I have fulfilled my determination when hounded by evil-minded news-papers—have made a wide and good reputation in spite of them.

All this comes up in my mind as I recall that first revisit to San Francisco. But I had friends there, too, and now saw some of them. There I called on one well-remembered, Dr. Van Orden, and paid a bill four years old; called with Harriet Howe on my Oakland

landlady, and paid her $140.00, a long over-due rent
bill. She was indeed astonished. There was a gas bill,
$20.00, a note in full, $70.00, another $25.00, and a
little milk bill, $5.00—he was astonished too. Little
by little, I was clearing things off.

Before going south I visited the E. A. Rosses in
Palo Alto, always a pleasure; and then to Pasadena.
December 23rd—"Katharine to meet me—dear girl!"
Up in the foot-hills, by Mt. Brown, is "Las Casitas,"
a little mesa all to itself, "developed" in a boom period,
but at that time a boarding-place kept by friends, Mrs.
Viall and her daughter, Mrs. Evans, whose child
Priscilla was one of Katharine's playmates. Here I
stayed all winter, writing *Human Work,* the first
attempt.

This is the greatest book I have ever done, and the
poorest—that is, the least adequately done. It is a
piece of social philosophy, as to the nature of human
life and its economic processes; its theories, if accepted,
and better carried out by later thinkers, will completely alter the base of our economic science, and so
our conduct. So far it has made practically no impression. Neither did the work of Mendel, for some time.
It is a matter of many years, and of successive con-
tributive thinkers, to establish any large and basic
change in human thought, and this is a very large one.

It was a grief to find in Pasadena some close friends
of former years now cold to me on the ground that I
was an "unnatural mother." This has always puzzled
me, yet it should not, knowing, as well I do, how most
of us do not think, but merely feel. If they had thought,
surely it should have been clear that it would have been
of no benefit to her to keep that dear child away from
her father and a pleasant home, to drag her over land
and sea on lecture trips, or board her with strangers

while I traveled. That might have been "natural," but not good for the child.

I suppose one reason for this long misjudgment was failure to allow for that permanent nerve-ruin, that recurrent paralyzing weakness which prevented any steady work. I plunged about the world, a species of humanitarian prophet, giving my message as best I could, and collapsing with distressing frequency, but at no time did I earn enough to make a home for one, much less for two. And surely a boarding-school would have been inferior to a father.

This was a very happy season for me. Katharine was close by, and spent a good deal of time at Las Casitas with me. We tramped the hills together, read, played games—it was a joy.

The book grew slowly. Day after day I sat out in the bright air, on a little hilltop near by, with the two dogs of the household one on either side, as close as they could crowd. The big bull-dog, Jack, Mrs. Viall said would go with me; that he thought it was his business to take care of the boarders; but Tommy, a little Skye, "is my dog," she said, "he never leaves me." But Tommy came every day, and added to his recusancy by lying outside my door when I was upstairs in my room.

The last note of the year is "Get well! Get well! Get well! And do good work. Pay all debts if possible," and the new diary opens as usual with a restatement of faith and purpose:

Because God, manifesting himself in Society, calls for ever fuller and more perfect forms of expression, therefore I, as part of Society and part of God owe my whole service to the Social development.

For 1899

For this New Year—and last,
Of the century nearly past—
   Help me to grow!
Help me to fill the days
With deeds of loving praise
   For the splendid truths I know.

Help me to finish clear
All claims of the old year—
   And all behind;
And to meet all duties new
With loving service due
   And a steadfast mind.

A clear and steadfast mind!
Help me, O God, to find
   Such hold on you
As may dispel disease,
That I may work in peace,
   Work deep, work true.

Slowly so long—and dark!
Down at the lowest mark—
   The light grows now!
God! I am seeking still
To learn and do your will—
   Still show me how!

CHAPTER XVIII

THREE FLATS AND A HOUSE—1900-1922

ON April 13th of the new century I left that lovely spot on the foot-hills of the Sierra Madres, for San Francisco, where I visited for a little and had some necessary surgery done. This required boring through the upper jaw, ether being used for the anesthetic. Cheerfully imbibing the same (I have always delighted in anesthesia: it is the only complete rest I have ever known) as the soft tide of unconsciousness arose, as I "died," it seemed to my departing faculties that it was necessary to make a confession of faith; so I cried in a loud voice—or thought I did!—"I believe in God and Life is good!"

From there to Ogden, Salt Lake and Provo, lecturing again among my Mormon friends. That perforation in the jaw was not a good traveling companion, nor did it help in lecturing. Various friendly doctors had a hand in it, almost literally, but mostly I attended to it myself—had to. Dr. Van Orden had equipped me with a few delicate implements, surgical gauze, and medicine, and I rather enjoyed fussing with it. In Denver, April 30th, the diary says, after the usual "Very tired," "Am taking strychnia to keep me up, bromide to sleep on, and in my mouth peroxide of hydrogen, zymocide, borolyptol, iodine and iodoform gauze. Also cocaine on cotton." Not all at once, these! That wretched hole made me a good deal of trouble for a long time but ultimately got well, and a neat pivot replaced the previous incumbent.

Eastward to Chicago, where I rented a room for a while, near my kind Mrs. Dow. There was a short visit in Fargo, North Dakota, with the family of Judge Charles F. Amidon—among the dearest people I have ever known. Poor as I was in some ways, none was ever richer in friends. As I look over these old diaries, and see how many were kind to me, in how many places, it becomes understandable how I lived so long on so little. Complete absence of personal desires, and absolute confidence that I should be taken care of, made lack of money a matter of laughable indifference.

Monday, June 4th, in Milwaukee, I attended the Biennial meeting of the General Federation of Women's Clubs. The Plankinton was their headquarters, a hotel frequently used for political conventions. As those fine-looking, well-dressed women from all parts of the Union filled the halls and parlors, and the streets, too, going bareheaded in streams between hotel and theater where they held their sessions, the men of Milwaukee gazed and wondered. They stood packed in the passages leading to the barber-shop or the bar, staring and silent. Never had they seen women, en masse, going about by themselves, not with, for or to any man, but "on their own" entirely. It amazed those German men.

At these meetings, well-conducted though they were, I was impressed anew with the callous indifference of speakers to the rights of others, so much that I wrote a bit of caustic verse on the subject!

The Speaker's Sin

It was a lovely lady,
With manners of the best;
She was finely educated,
She was exquisitely dressed.

With a topic philanthropic
She arose to fill her place
In the program which was builded
For to elevate the race.
She arose with highest purpose
Her noble best to do—
There were seven other ladies
Who were on the program too.

The lady read her paper
Till her hearers wore a frown;
The chairman was a lady
And she would not ring her down.
And when the chairman hinted
That her limit long was o'er—
The lady with the paper
Asked for just a minute more.
The hearers all were ladies—
What could the hearers do?
There were seven other ladies
Upon the program too!

And those seven other ladies
Had to summon grace sublime,
To smile and wait in silent state
While the speaker stole their time.
Eight papers in a two-hour space
Gives each a fair amount;
Could not the lady read the score
Of those who also claimed the floor?
Could not the lady count?
Did she imagine that her theme
Was the only subject there?
Or that her treatment was the best
And no one wished to hear the rest?
Was it that she forgot their feeling
Who had to lose what she was stealing?
Or that she did not care?

I returned to Chicago June 8th, and on the eleventh went to Detroit, as usual to the house of a friend, where I was met by my cousin, G. H. Gilman of New York, and we were married—and lived happy ever after. If this were a novel, now, here's the happy ending.

The Episcopalian pastor of my friends there naturally refused to perform the ceremony, but we found a Unitarian minister who said—"Charlotte Perkins Stetson? Why certainly, she has preached in my church."

A few pleasant days in Detroit, then a trip to Toronto, and down the rapids and through the islands to Montreal. Here we saw a ghastly game of lacrosse, wherein, directly against the rules, men broke one another's heads with their long sticks. A victim of this foul play would be carried off bleeding, come back sewed and bandaged, and those courteous antagonists would hit him again *in the same place!* It was a very important game between a Canadian team and an Irish, with a perhaps differing sense of honor.

Down Lake Champlain we drifted to Caldwell, charmingly quiet at that early season; we were the only guests in a large hotel. The beauty of this honeymoon was somewhat marred by my trying to read *Human Work* to Houghton! He bore it nobly. If one marries a philosopher or a prophet there are various consequences to be met; Xanthippe loses her temper over it, Kadijah does not, I believe, complain, but it never is wholly easy.

For all my winter's labor the work was by no means ready for publication, so it was postponed and I undertook something shorter. *Concerning Children* was to be the next book. We spent the rest of the summer at Cold Spring Harbor, Houghton commuting.

It was a lovely summer. The little pond across the road gave us our morning bath, cool, still, soft wisps of white mist still curling here and there in the smooth dark water, and the early sun striking long, down-slanting shafts of light between the trees on the high eastern slope. Katharine joined us at the end of July. It was my turn to have her now.

We had a happy time, all of us. The work went on pretty well, though the "downs" still frequent; nothing, not even happiness, gave me back my brain power. Still the book was finished by the twenty-fifth of August; it was not a large one.

At various times I went in town house-hunting, and by August 23rd I was able to note: "We are to have the top flat in The Avondale, 76th st., and Amsterdam Ave. Good!" It was good, too. That house was built by an intelligent Scotchman, our excellent landlord. There was light on all three sides of our end of the narrow building, seven rooms, with grated fireplaces in two of them.

We moved in on August 31, with only the rudiments of furnishing, picnicking till things could be got together. Our rent was to begin with October; in those days they used to give the tenant a month free! September 1st I note: "A rather sleepless night on account of the noise." Noise! There was not even asphalt on Amsterdam then, it was stone-paved. Huge, endless lines of telegraph poles with their thick network of wires obscured the view. Seventy-sixth Street was pleasant enough, but those Amsterdam corners had a saloon on each one except ours!

While living there I was horrified to find myself taxed, on personal property. My husband explained that it was the method in New York for the assessor to guess at the possessions of a citizen by his location;

that since my name was in the directory—which by
the way a married woman's is not unless she insists on
it—he had concluded I was a widow living on 76th
Street, and estimated accordingly. The further process
was for the overtaxed person to go down to the assessor's office and "swear off" the over-charge, which I
found much amusement in doing. When he found by
solemn questions how pitifully scant was my personal
property, how minute my income, the whole tax was
remitted.

We presently secured table-board at the end of the
block, next door to Columbus Avenue where ran the
"L" on which Houghton went and came. This house
was kept by Mrs. Barthelmess, a handsome, able
woman, who before long gave up that business and
went on the stage. She had some success there, and
her son, Richard Barthelmess, is now a well-known
"movie star," an actor of real power. Then he was a
darling child, evidently not liking the boarding-house
life at all.

But we liked it. We had "a home without a kitchen,"
all the privacy and comfort, none of the work and care
—except for beds and a little cleaning. We all went out
together to breakfast, then Houghton went to his office and Katharine to her school, while I had the morning for my work. I met Katharine for lunch there, and
at night we met Houghton at the train and dined together in peace. We had a table to ourselves, but
found much entertainment in the talk of the other
boarders. When we had a visitor all that was necessary
was another $5.00 a week, no trouble at all. That was
all it cost in 1900—$5.00 a week for good table-board.
Our monthly rent was $40.00.

My further life in New York covered twenty-two
years. Before this I had tried it repeatedly, boarding at

mother's, had been as well there as anywhere else, and as happy. I came to it as a settled home with cheerful enthusiasm. Here was home at last, a very pleasant one, the best of husbands, and at last my daughter— I was very happy. I brought to the city a large, undiscriminating love of Humanity, without a shadow of race-prejudice or preference. I had much to learn.

Work opened well. My publishers were grieved at my change of name—"You will lose money by it," they explained, and were not impressed by my protest—"Do you think I would keep one man's name after I had married another, just for money!" I had kept the name of Stetson after getting my divorce, on Katharine's account, having no faintest intention of ever marrying again. It would have saved trouble had I remained Perkins from the first, this changing of women's names is a nuisance we are now happily outgrowing.

The new book went well, was warmly received and widely noticed. I had plenty more coming, and still *Human Work* to do, on which I soon reëmbarked. Also, there were magazine articles from time to time. In sheer bulk of material I have written much more than the twenty-five volumes I hope to see on my shelf some day; but then there are plenty of newspapermen who have done far more.

Such writing as I have done in those years of free delivery was easy work. An average article, about three thousand words, took three hours to do, a day's work. Sometimes I would have to copy it, or change a little, but usually it was written and sent—like a letter. This is not, in the artistic sense, "literature." I have never made any pretense of being literary. As far as I had any method in mind, it was to express the idea with clearness and vivacity, so that it might be apprehended with ease and pleasure.

I had a little talk once with Mary Austin, the beauty of whose writing is well known, in which I disclaimed any pretension to literature, but said I thought I had "a style of my own." She demurred, hardly thought it style, but granted distinction, adding kindly, "I do think, however, that if you gave your mind to it, you could write." This was certainly encouragement. And presently for my own amusement I made a little parody, which, if one recognizes the original, surely proves her judgment correct.

Human Work, however, was not to be reeled off like my usual stuff. Here was an enormous change of thought, altering the relationships of all sociological knowledge. As in astronomy we had to change from the geo-centric to the solar-centric theory of our planetary system, with complete revision of earlier ideas, so here was a change from the ego-centric to the socio-centric system of sociology, with wide resultant alterations in prior concepts. Furthermore, it was a treatise so large in scope as to cover all human life, and in the four times I did it over I never knew where to begin.

I worked over it all that year, still it would not do. A third, and I was not satisfied. Each time I began in a new place, with equal uncertainty. J. A. Hobson, the English economist whom I had met over there and told about this theory, was in New York and came to see me. He was eager to hear about the book. I spent about an hour on it, going over the general argument and its buttresses, while he walked the floor in growing excitement. "You must publish, you must bring it out," he insisted, "we have nothing like it in sociology." I told him it was not done, that it did not suit me. "It never will suit you," he said, "you must bring it out anyway."

He was quite right. I worked on it a fourth year, was still unsatisfied, and did publish it, in 1904. Again I tried to do it better some ten years later in my magazine the *Forerunner*, but that was worse. So it remains, merely a starter, later thinkers must make it plainer.

In the meantime, during those four years, I had written *The Home*, which is the most heretical—and the most amusing—of anything I've done. To quote from another later work:

> You may talk about religion with a free and open mind,
>   For ten dollars you may criticise a judge;
> You may discuss in politics the newest thing you find;
> And open scientific truth to the reluctant mind,
>   But there's one place where the brain must never budge!

> Oh! the Home is utterly perfect!
>   And all its works within.
> To say a word about it—
> To criticise or doubt it—
> To seek to mend or move it—
> To venture to improve it—
>   Is *the* unpardonable sin!

The two new books came out together, this time through the McClure Publishing House. They did not want *Human Work;* I did not suppose they would, but *The Home* looked promising. We made an arrangement by which I was not to get any royalties from *Human Work* until after a certain number were sold, and as they, apparently, never sold that many, I got nothing from it. Neither did the other sell as I had really hoped, for the topic was not of universal appeal, and the stuff was funny, if not orthodox. But

McClures' brought out Wagner's *Simple Life* that year, it struck a popular note, and they very naturally pushed that for all it was worth, perhaps for more.

It seemed to me that the two could have been profitably advertised together, as opposites, reaching different readers, but then I'm not a good business person. At any rate little came of these books, the plates were sold to Doubleday, Page and Company, and in after years I bought them in—plates of *The Home,* that is. I didn't buy the plates of *Human Work* because I was always hoping to rewrite it, do it better.

Small and Maynard I had given up on account of repeated delays and mistakes, all of which they explained by blaming their book-keeper.

We lived in the first flat four years. Some pieces of furniture which were left in California I sent for. Some we bought, some were wedding presents. One kind offer among these was for a set of books or a sofa. I chose the sofa. Being invited to specify, I described a long, flat, smooth lounge covered with imitation leather. What arrived was a short, curved-up-at-the-end, deeply tufted couch, covered with real leather! To sleep on it a chair had to be added to the foot.

Katharine went to school for a while, a pleasant little one, kept by Miss Murphy and Miss Gaylord, rather near us. I kept on lecturing of course, our kind of housekeeping made it easy. On one long absence my dear Helen Campbell was mother for me. A reliable woman came once a week to clean; it was a peaceful and easy home for all of us.

Having met Mrs. Campbell and installed her with Katharine and Mr. Gilman, I started early in November, 1900, for a six weeks' trip which is a good sample of my professional life. "Pack for six weeks in two bags," says the diary. Never did I bother with a trunk on such journeys. I've gone to Europe with those two pieces of hand-baggage, and been thankful.

This tour began with some Federation meeting in Racine, and continued variously. I cannot cumber these pages with repeated description of such trips, which have continued all the rest of my life, but this seems an admirable sample.

Starting on Monday, November 5th, on Tuesday, between Detroit and Chicago I wrote an article for *Success,* 2500 words. Wednesday, lectured in Racine on "Our Brains." Thursday, mailed first article and began another, 2000 words, mailed Saturday in Chicago. Monday, the twelfth: "re-write 'Private Home and Public House'—2500 words." Thirteenth: "re-write 'Celibacy in Domestic Service,' 1700 words." Fourteenth: "Write part of 'Man as a Factor in Social Evolution.' (This is a chapter in *Human Work.*) Fifteenth: "Finish 'Man as a Factor,' and begin 'Persistence of Primitive Types in Domestic Relation.'" Seventeenth: "Write in cars 'A Word for Tommy.'" Eighteenth: "A little more on Tommy." Nineteenth: "Prepare and send off 'Private Home and Public House' to Bazaar, and 'A Word for Tommy' to Dial." Twenty-second: "Finish 'Persistence.'" Twenty-third: "Begin 'As an Investment.'" Twenty-fifth: "Begin 'The Social Service Bureau.'" Twenty-sixth: "Work more on 'Social Service,' recasting beginning." Twenty-seventh: "More on S. S.—goes well."

As to lectures, sermons, and talks, there were four up to December 2nd, the long wait in Chicago filled with writing, boarding the while; and then I rushed about, in Wisconsin and Minnesota, speaking in Monroe, Mankato, Minneapolis, Menominee, and another in Chicago, December 13th, eleven in all. As to re-

turns, "Clear about 130 dollars on this trip. On debts
$135.00." Not much profit, was there! As there was
considerable traveling involved, and a lot of "entertainment," as well as seeing real friends, it was a busy
time.

On my way home, encountering a blizzard, with confusion and delay, I sent from Buffalo a careful telegram to my husband as to arrival. I had always prided
myself on my telegrams, concise but clear, business-
like and direct. So now I studied the time-table, consulted the conductor, and produced this masterpiece;
"On train 13." (I thought it particularly clever to give
the number of the train, so that he could ask at the
station, "Is No. 13 on time?") My wire continued,
"Hour late. Arrive about seven, Central Station."

When that telegram reached him it read, "On train
thirteen hours late," and the rest, but as my "about
seven" did not specify A.M. or P.M., it left much to be
desired. I have put on no airs about telegrams since
that one. "So glad to be home again!" on Saturday
15th, but there was another lecture in Chester, Pennsylvania, on the eighteenth, back same day, and it is
not surprising to read on the nineteenth: "Collapse
after supper. Very tired."

We had a jolly Christmas that year. It appeared
that Houghton had never had a Christmas tree himself, though "attending" many. I determined to remedy
this lack forthwith and fully. On a huge piece of heavy
pasteboard I drew a spiral from center to circumference
in widening curves, and along it, at intervals, inserted
bits of spruce, from a single twig in the center on in
graduated numbers to the last, with as many twigs on
it as he was years old at the time. Then gifts in number
as the years were attached to the "trees," from a great
soft "parlor ball" on the first, up to twinkling multi-

tudes of little things on the more numerous branches.
It became increasingly difficult to find them, too, but
steel pins, rubber bands, paper-clips and such, with
clustering gum-drops and chocolates, filled out nobly.
He expressed himself as entirely satisfied with retro-
active Christmas trees!

We had a real one for Katharine of course; she had
fifty-seven presents. I read her Dickens's *Christmas
Carol,* the Scrooge one. In later years she used to read
it over every Christmas. By the thirty-first we all went
to Norwich to see the aunts, for New Year's.

The year closes! "I am happy and content
Houghton—Katharine—Home." With: "May I grow
stronger and do good work in spite of my happiness!"
Final cash account: "$5.20 left."

In 1901 the first mark of note is "Sewing machine
comes!" A Wilcox and Gibbs, a beauty, and a constant
friend since. I had two to sew for now, and enjoyed it.

Among other efforts at earning I had a "Thinking
Class" at my house, but it did not last long, I was
not up to the kind of teaching I saw the need of. In
April of that year: "Bad news about Mrs. Campbell
—her mind is wandering—and so is she." From then
on was a growing grief and care for that dear
"mother" who had been so kind to me.

My health showed no real improvement. Between
bits of work there were long blank spaces, no entries
in the diary, nothing done, the same old helpless gloom.
I met at the house of a friend that remarkable woman,
Dr. Mary Putnam Jacobi, one of our first to study
medicine. Charles Reade refers to her in his *Woman
Hater,* I think—or was it in *In Propria?*

She was deeply interested in my case, the long continued misery and exhaustion. It must have come upon
me pretty severely about this time, for the diary goes

blank from April 17th to June 6th, when I lectured in
Longwood, Pennsylvania; and again to July 3rd:
"Went to Norwich," and Sunday, 7th, "Returned to
New York much rested and improved." That is all to
the first of August when we all three went to Summer-
brook in the Adirondacks, to visit Prestonia Mann.
That was a pleasure and a gain but after coming
home I went down again, and dragged through an un-
easy autumn. On the seventh of December Dr. Jacobi
wrote, asking if she might try on me a system of treatment she had devised for such brain trouble as mine.

I was more than willing, and prepared for her better
understanding of the case a long "fever-chart" sort of
thing; with parallel lines showing normal, one super
and several sub, down to melancholia; the years
marked off with brief notes as to condition; and a
wavering red line along the stretch of it, with a few
peaks and many deep valleys, the average generally
below normal. She found this helpful, and began a
course of treatment which lasted several months and
did me much good.

The distinctive feature of her method was to set
that inert brain to work under her direct suggestion
and supervision, on small, irrelevant tasks; this to re-
establish the capacity for action, without demanding
any effort from me. We began with kindergarten
blocks, just building things, for slowly increasing periods of application, but before she was through with
me I was reading, still at her desk and under her direction, Wilson on *The Cell*.

All this intelligent care helped me much. I accomplished a little scattered work, and by the end of the
year was glad to state that my legal debts were reduced to less than a thousand dollars, with a few other
claims which I meant to meet when I could. Continuing

to improve, I began to do something on *Human Work* once more, in January, 1902, and did some lecturing in near-by states. Indeed I grew strong enough physically —the trouble never seemed to affect my body much— to join a basketball team of women, playing in Barnard college gymnasium. Katharine belonged also, and I took great pride in a Mother-and-Daughter game in which forty-two and seventeen did equally well.

By February 7th I proudly set down: "Really work a little on book." And I made once more a schedule for my day's work, as I had done at intervals since my strong girlhood when I made and kept them: "Rise at seven. Dress, breakfast, etc., to 8:30. Housework to 9:30. Write to 11:15. Walk to Dr.— to 1:45. Lunch, rest, visit, sew, etc."

But by February 13th: "Can't read Cell book, brain won't hold it. Very tired evening and can't do anything." Seventeenth: "Still low. Do nothing. Dr. sets me back to kindergarten blocks again." But on the whole I gained, and had begun to feel quite steadily well, when, on February 26th, my dear daughter came down with pneumonia.

Almost recovered from pneumonia, she developed pleurisy. Before recovering from that there was a sudden turn for the worse, and by March 18th I have set down in red ink: "Scarlet fever! ! ! Oh dear!...." That dear child who had always been so well—. It was May 12th before I joyfully write: "Katharine is moved into the other room! Hurrah!"

Having scarlet fever in a small flat is not easy. A disinfected sheet was hung at her door, all precautions were taken. There were trained nurses good and bad, till Miss Mendel arrived to bless us— "Tall, beautiful, cheerful, vigorous, calm, quiet, agreeable, capable —a treasure."

Houghton, going to his business, had to be shielded from the faintest chance of contagion, and as for me, when I did have to go forth: "Take cleansing bath, bi-chloride bath—wash hair in bi-chloride and comb it with new comb, put on entirely different clothes even to garters and hairpins, disinfect watch, and walk across park to lecture."

This misfortune also records the end of our easy boarding-house life. "Go and buy some kitchen things. Home and get lunch." One can hardly hire servants with scarlet fever in the family. "Miss Mendel is an angel in the house. I settle down and do the work. Wash fifty pieces or so." "I take to coffee and housekeeping very contentedly." April 13th: "Get splendid dinner—roast chicken, etc."

But there are few entries during that three months' stretch of illness, anxiety and housework, and then none at all till the end of September. We spent most of that summer in Twilight Park, in the Catskills, Dr. Shelby still keeping an eye on Katharine, and by that time I was as weak as she. September 27th: "Katharine sails for Italy." Her father and her other mother were in Rome, and she went to stay with them for a while.

October 2nd, more red ink—"Begin work!" and on the fifth: "*Paint* a bit—first time in many years, not a good picture, but a hopeful sign." That work was in the line of articles and the Home book, but November 23rd again in red: "Begin *Human Work* again! write some eight pages, arrange and plan. Not tired."

My good friend Mrs. Susa Young Gates cheered me much by telling me how well *Women and Economics* was going in Germany, and that they wanted me there for the next quinquennial, 1904. "More than any one else except Miss Anthony." By December 31st: "Consider the book done—the first draft."

These diaries are a nuisance. Page after page of those dismal "downs" with the cheerfully welcomed "ups." Record of writing, record of lecturing, record of seeing people, record of housework. After 1903 I gave up the fat three-by-six kind, with two days to a page, and took to thinner ones, with seven days on a page, or rather on two, for they run right across, with the right hand page for cash account. These are big enough to set down engagements, train time, and such necessities.

Lecture trips long and short continued. There was a suffrage meeting in New Orleans, and another in Portland, Oregon, any and everywhere between. There are now but four states in the Union where I have not spoken, and those I have been through—South Dakota, Wyoming, Arizona and New Mexico. To have traversed one's country from side to side, top to bottom and corner to corner, for thirty-six years, gives one a fair working knowledge of it. Being entertained by intelligent people in hundreds of cities, and meeting representative women from all parts of the country in these various conventions, is another open door for learning the needs and hopes of all sections.

Inheriting a far-focused mind and educating it in a general study of humanity which takes in all races and all times, this wandering life of mine has increased the natural breadth of vision and constantly added to its power. Never having had a settled home, but always feeling perfectly at home anywhere, in this country or others, I have been better able to judge dispassionately and to take a more long-range view of human affairs than is natural to more stationary people.

Also, the lack of happiness in personal relationships in all my early life, enabled me to judge those relationships more impartially than if they had been perfectly satisfactory. Deprivations bring a sort of freedom useful to the social student.

The new period of personal happiness, opening with the century, with the forced reversion to housework, brought its own joys. Work of any kind I always loved, and in this kind I was specially proficient. For intimate comfort there is nothing cozier than a well-appointed flat. There is no outside care or labor, inside everything is convenient, and one's vertical neighbors are no worse than horizontal ones; that is if they are decent.

We stayed six years in that first apartment, the longest residence of my life so far. Then, with joyous courage, we took a house, 313 W. 82nd.

This was a charming house, big, well-built, comfortable. We could by no means furnish the great place, nor pay the rent alone, but a good friend, possessing furniture, took one floor and boarded with us, and several others had rooms and also shared our table. We had two servants, with accompanying vicissitudes, but the boarders seemed to like my menus; there was always a waiting list.

Katharine was with us part of our three years there, then returned again to Italy. Our delight in those great rooms, house-wide, and long in proportion, was intense, after the sense of compression which grows on one in narrow flats. Three years we lived there, and then moved to what was then the height of our desire—an apartment on Riverside Drive. It was the top floor, between 94th and 95th streets, near to a broad, lovely part of the Riverside Park. There was a huge boulder, quite near us, where people used to sit and watch the sun set, as if it were in the country; trees that we could lie under and look at the stars.

If that flat had had suitable closets, and if the other inhabitants had not encouraged New York's little traveling pets, it would have been about perfect. As it was, the sheer beauty of the prospect so filled me that I began to write poetry about it, a descriptive set, called "River Windows." I had hopes of these, but they were not shared by editors. Here's one of them:

Blending

Sometimes that long, high-lying western wall
Grays up into a bank of evening cloud,
Blending and dim; vague river to vague sky;
Only pricked lights—too regular for stars—
To show the margin between earth and heaven.

Again three years (the leases ran that way), and then, still moving northward, we took another flat on 136th Street, again top floor. This was a "walk up" one, about seventy steps in all. I used to walk to the "elevated" with Houghton, to the 135th Street station, and meet him there at night, which involved going up and down the steps of St. Nicholas Terrace, at that point numbering 131. So I had about four hundred stairs a day, quite good exercise for the heart.

These morning and evening walks of ours established our reputation in the vicinity as a model couple!—so we were told by a neighbor. As to neighbors in any sense of visiting acquaintance, we had none, save once or twice in the flat next us; and always excepting a few real friends who chanced to live near. For a while my dear Grace had an apartment similar to ours in the next building, and Katharine a small one on the same floor.

They had returned to this country together after Mr. Stetson's death in Rome.

Katharine had long since chosen her profession, she was an artist like her father. Now she had her studio down-town and her little home, near both her mothers. While living on 136th Street she made a sudden step and began to work at modeling as well as painting, doing marvelously graceful little reliefs, as well as figures in the round. She married F. Tolles Chamberlin, a painter and sculptor, a man of fine talents and a record of achievements. They live in her old home, Pasadena, and with two small children and the housework, she manages to keep up somewhat in her art.

This third flat proved to be a long-abiding place. Ten years we lived there, degradingly comfortable. There is an insidious drugging effect in spending one's time waiting on one's own tastes and appetites, and those of dear ones. There is a picnic jollity in buying just what you want to eat, cooking it exactly to your taste, eating it with satisfaction—and washing the dishes in your own superior manner. It is comfortable, but not elevating. The insidious effects were somewhat mitigated by recurrent lecture trips, and during this New York period there were three more across the ocean.

CHAPTER XIX

CONVENTIONS, EDITORS AND THE "FORERUNNER"

WOMEN AND ECONOMICS was translated into German by Frau Marie Stritt, of Dresden, president of the German National Council of Women. It had a tremendous vogue and a wide sale, but never a cent did I get for it—I forget the excuses given. At any rate it gave rise to a call for my attending the next Congress of the International Council, held in Berlin in 1904, which I gladly accepted, meeting with a warm welcome. Not even in London in 1899 did I have such an ovation. My present feelings about Germany have not the faintest personal basis; never was I more cordially received, more warmly appreciated.

My addresses were in English. The year before I had tried to learn German in preparation for the trip; only to realize anew how permanent was the weakening of my mind, how completely I had lost the power to study. But the educated Germans all speak English, and they said they could understand my English better than the other foreigners' German. So popular was I that great crowds followed me from one hall to another; and the impression was such that arrangements were made for a lecture trip in the following year.

One pleasant expression of good feeling was given by an ardent, blue-eyed young gentleman, who approached when I was eating in a restaurant, bowed till I could see the whole back seam of his coat, and presented me with a large bouquet!

The Congress was most successful. There were said to be three thousand foreign women in Berlin, and the amazement of the German men at these multitudes of *"frauen personen"* was amusing. Some of them were truly exotic, as delegates from India, China and Japan; and one tall, handsome Turkish princess, followed about by what in the *Arabian Nights* was called "a great black."

As in London, we were royally entertained; the Kaiserin receiving Aunt Susan and other leading delegates. There was a reception by Mrs. Charlemagne Tower, wife of the American Ambassador, a garden-party by the Grafin von Bülow, a dinner, to some of us, given by Herr Koch, who was at the time famous for his researches in tuberculosis. Grandest of all was a banquet given to the Congress by the city fathers of Berlin, an honor we were told that was appreciated even by the Kaiser. It was in a high, great hall, there was an unbelievable quantity and variety of meat, as well as some other edibles, and by every plate stood the Bear of Berlin, full of chocolates.

From the crowded glory of the Congress, where I was surrounded by admiring friends from all countries—*Women and Economics,* in German had been read in many lands—and all that rush of full sessions and fuller entertainments I whisked off to Italy speeding through Switzerland in the night, alas!—and joined my daughter in Rome. She had been living there with her father for a while, and was to return to America with me.

But there were ten days in Italy, she was eager to show her mother the beauties of her second country, and had arranged an itinerary of appalling completeness. Those ten days, to my exhausted mind, seemed a sort of beautiful nightmare. I stopped over night in

Florence, to call on our friend Mrs. Hackett, in whose house *Women and Economics* had been begun; and to call on "Vernon Lee" in her villa near by, who had written an introduction to the Italian edition. In a few full days I was shown something of Rome, then Naples.

The contrast was sudden and severe. I was exhausted beyond usual depths by that incessant whirl and rush in Berlin, and naturally somewhat elated by international admiration, and now in the twinkling of an eye I was precipitated into another country of whose language I knew not a word, and became a complete dependent on my charming daughter. In age I served as a chaperon, but in all else she commanded the expedition.

We saw things—the Baths of Caracalla, the Forum, the Catacombs, the Colosseum, various galleries and palaces, the Vatican, yes, and the ball on the tip-top of St. Peters—we went up there! All is vague and blurred. The tremendous bulk of the Colosseum did not make as much impression as the photograph of it in the hall at Aunt Harriet Stowe's in Hartford, when I was a small child. I remember the Catacombs because of the ill behavior of the monk who showed us about. He tried to frighten us by suggestion of putting out his light, he actually laid hands on me, seizing me by the wrist, which surely is not allowed to clericals. But Katharine and I refused to be alarmed, assuring him that our friends would promptly follow us if we were delayed, and he brought us to the surface again in safety.

The Bay of Naples is also confused in my mind with many pictures, Vesuvius under its smoke cloud was but too familiar, and as to the Blue Grotto—the memory of being in it is not half so clear and lovely as what I have read of it. Capri the beautiful has stayed, however, that long, upwinding road, the oleanders on the terrace, the far blue sea. But the vividest memory is of Pompeii—being *in it*—walking those dead streets!

We came home together, to that first apartment, to the pleasant home life with its small housekeeping, to local lectures and the writing of articles, but by February, 1905, I was off again, to England first, then Holland, Germany, Austria, Hungary. This was as tiring as any trip I ever tried. In London a very crowded list of engagements in February weather, though I was most beautifully cared for by Mr. and Mrs. Stanton Coit with whom I stayed; then a few days in Holland, where I stayed with Dr. Aletta Jacobs, who had translated *Women and Economics* into Dutch. *Concerning Children* was there also, done by Martina Kramers. I spoke in Amsterdam and Rotterdam, and so eastward, on this itinerary: Saturday in Dresden (I did go and see the great Madonna!), Sunday in Budapest, Monday and Tuesday in Vienna, Wednesday in Munich (got an opera glass there), Thursday in Heidelberg, Friday in Mannheim, Saturday in Wiesbaden, and Sunday in Hamburg—where I quite gave out with a severe attack of bronchitis. That was "going some."

The last European trip was in 1913, to attend the International Suffrage Convention in Budapest. Mme. Rosika Schwimmer had translated *Women and Economics* into Hungarian, from the German—I'm not sorry I cannot read it!—and again I found a most warm and appreciative reception. If only I could recall the names of all the kind and friendly women I have met! Women from all over the world, fine women, thoughtful progressive women! And of all the homes where I have been taken in and cared for so generously! But since I cannot remember old friends at home I certainly cannot new ones abroad—not all of them.

I think it was on this trip that I had a unique visit at the house of May Morris. She had, meanwhile, been in America on a lecture tour, and we delightedly kept her with us as much as we could, making our house—that time it was the flat on Riverside Drive— a sort of headquarters to go from and return to. She is a most charming home companion; we all loved her. As it happened she was in Spain or somewhere when I arrived in England, but urged me none the less to "make her house my home." To this end she left a most proficient housekeeper with a husband to wait on me, and I had a most restful little visit, even without a hostess!

The year after that—the War.

So much for conventions—that was my last big one. Now for editors. I have had so many good friends among editors that I can by no means remember all of them. Even in California there were some I wrote for—the *Pacific Rural Press,* for the *Stockton Mail* (I think that was its name). There was James Barry of the *Star,* and Charles Lummis who was on the *Los Angeles Times* and afterwards editor of *The Land of Sunshine,* besides being a distinguished archæologist and writer of books.

In Chicago Mr. Browne of the *Dial,* and when I came to New York on the wave of the *Women and Economics'* success, there were ever so many who asked for my work. James Brisbane Walker of the *Cosmopolitan,* before it became Hearst's *Cosmopolitan,* was more than cordial; Margaret Sangster of the *Bazaar,* before it became Hearst's *Bazaar,* was very kind; Mr. Towers, of *Good Housekeeping,* before it became

Hearst's *Good Housekeeping,* was greatly interested in my stuff. When they asked for contributions, afterward, I always explained that nothing would induce me to appear in anything of his. A very nice young man came to see me about continuing to work for one of these, the *Cosmopolitan,* I think it was, and could not understand this attitude. "You would not have to see Mr. Hearst," he explained—as if it was merely some personal dislike; and he offered good prices, in vain.

Hamilton of the *Independent* used to have a good many things of mine; Samuel Merwin, when on *Success,* was friendly and appreciative. Arthur T. Vance, on the *Woman's Home Companion* and later on the *Pictorial Review,* which he built up so tremendously, used much of my stuff. There were others; scattering articles far and wide, and various larger undertakings which somehow fell through. One enthusiast, starting a new magazine, engaged me to write a serial novel for him, but was punished for his rashness by the prompt failure of his venture.

I worked steadily enough, writing whether I sold or not, unless, as was far too frequent, I was unable to work at all. For all my happiness at home and various glories abroad, I remained through all these years more sick than well; that is, there was more time spent in dull distress of mind and dreary helplessness than in my natural cheerful activity. In this long uselessness, I took up solitaire as a sedative. It is just next to doing nothing, and occupies the mind enough to avoid thinking, not enough to tire.

As years passed and continuous writing and speaking developed the various lines of thought I was following, my work grew in importance but lost in market value. Social philosophy, however ingeniously presented, does not command wide popular interest. I wrote more and sold less.

Theodore Dreiser, then on the *Delineator,* as I remember, looked gloomily at me over his desk, and said, "You should consider more what the editors want." Of course I should have, if I had been a competent professional writer. There are those who write as artists, real ones; they often find it difficult to consider what the editor wants. There are those who write to earn a living, they, if they succeed, *must* please the editor. The editor, having his living to earn, must please his purchasers, the public, so we have this great trade of literary catering. But if one writes to express important truths, needed yet unpopular, the market is necessarily limited.

As all my principal topics were in direct contravention of established views, beliefs and emotions, it is a wonder that so many editors took so much of my work for so long.

But as time passed there was less and less market for what I had to say, more and more of my stuff was declined. Think I must and write I must, the manuscripts accumulated far faster than I could sell them, some of the best, almost all—and finally I announced: "If the editors and publishers will not bring out my work, I will!" And I did. In November, 1909, I started the *Forerunner.*

This was a small monthly magazine, written entirely by myself. There have been other one-man magazines, but smaller and confined to one kind of writing as a rule. Mine was not very big, but its ten-by-seven pages, twenty-eight of them, seven hundred and fifty words to a page, made some twenty-one thousand to the issue. It equaled four books a year, books of thirty-six thousand words.

Each issue included one instalment of a novel, also of a book published serially; a short story, articles of various length; poems, verses, allegories, humor and nonsense, with book reviews and comment on current events. For a time it carried some advertisements, which I wrote myself, honestly recommending things I knew from experience to be good. One friend offered some advertising, I told him I did not know his stuff. He sent me some samples, I did not like it, and therefore declined it. This attitude did not make for business success.

The cost of publishing this work was $3,000 a year; its price, a dollar. If I could have achieved three thousand subscribers then I would cheerfully have done the work for nothing, but I never had sense enough—business sense, that is, to get them. About fifteen hundred was our income, and the rest of the expense I met by doing extra work in writing—outside of the "four book" demands of the magazine, and as usual, lecturing.

It was an undertaking, especially on long trips, as when abroad, or on the Pacific Coast, to keep up with the manuscript, and see that it reached the printer. We had a most sympathetic printer, a good German, Rudolph Rochow, who was very patient with my efforts at proof-reading. He liked the magazine so well that he subscribed to it! Which reminds me of an early compliment on *Women and Economics*—that the very type-setters read it and enjoyed it.

The range of circulation was all over this country, quite widely in Europe, and as far afield as India and Australia, but scanty in numbers. What I had banked on in starting was my really wide reputation, the advertising possibilities of continued lecturing, and the low price. But I found to my amusement that among women ten dollars for a hat is cheap while one dollar for a magazine is an unwarranted expense. One woman in a town would take it, and then proudly tell me how she circulated it among all her friends—thus saving them the cost of subscribing!

It seemed to me that out of, say thirty states, there would be a hundred women in each who cared enough for my teachings to pay a dollar a year for them, and I think so still. What was lacking was enough capacity on my part to manage the business properly. However, one cannot have everything. Production is easier than distribution, to some kinds of people at least.

As to engaging a business manager, there was not enough money in the thing at its best to pay a capable man for pushing it. I had a good advertising man for a little while, but he explained to me that for less effort he could sell a page of *Scribner's Magazine* for several hundreds than a page of the *Forerunner* for $25.00, and left.

Similarly, I have never had a good lecture agent or manager for any length of time. Such a person, to succeed, must have a strong conviction of the value of my work, *and* business ability. These do not coexist. There have been many who were profoundly impressed with the importance of the work, but they were not good press-agents, and good press-agents do not care to promote small, unpopular undertakings. Also, can a press-agent be imagined who would work for a woman who would not allow the least exaggeration or misstatement?

However, regardless of difficulties, I wrote and published the *Forerunner* for seven years. This meant seven novels (by which I definitely proved that I am not a novelist)! and seven other books, of considerable value, as *The Man-made World* (widely translated in

Europe). *Our Brains and What Ails Them, Social Ethics, The Dress of Women,* and others; enough verse for another volume, and all the rest of the varied material.

It was an immense task to get the work done, to write more than I could ever have done without some such definite compulsion, and to say exactly what I had to say, fully and freely. If possible I hope to see a "library edition," some day, with the best of the *Forerunner* and all my other books, this autobiography trailing along at the end.

The real "income" from that magazine was in the letters of deep personal appreciation I received. Some I used to print in the *Forerunner,* without the names; some were too touchingly deep-felt to be used for business purposes. Some were funny—as when I wrote this bit:

ALIMONY

Alimony is the meanest money that is taken—by women. It is bad enough to marry for money, it is bad enough to maintain an immoral marriage for money, but to give up this mercenary commerce and then take money when no longer delivering the goods—! There is only one meanness to be mentioned in the same breath, taking "damage" for "breach of promise."

Some hold it is a man's duty to "support his wife," on the ground that her position as his wife prevents her from earning her own living. When she is no longer his wife this does not hold.

Some say that a man should provide for his children, "his" children, note. They are also hers, surely. But even if he should have the whole burden of their maintenance, that is not "alimony." Divorcées without children, young women, quite competent to earn their livings, eagerly claim alimony, take it and live on it, never giving a thought to the nature of their positon.

But a woman's health is often ruined; she is in no condition to earn her living, is urged. Very well. If a woman is really injured by her marriage she should sue under the employers' liability act. She should claim damages, not alimony.

This brief opinion so pleased a man who saw it, that he sent me an approving letter, and a subscription —for his ex-wife! I hope she liked it.

Another funny letter was received when I was sending out a bit of preliminary advertising, a tiny leaflet, something to this effect: "If you are interested in the work of Charlotte Perkins Gilman, or know any one who is, it may be had in monthly form in her magazine the *Forerunner* for $1.00 a year." This was sent to all the names in my address-book, and others, but one name was evidently misplaced, for I received the following admirably expressed answer from a woman doctor in Boston: "I am not interested in the work of Charlotte Perkins Gilman, in monthly or any other form, nor do I know any one who is."

It has always seemed to me something of a joke on the American critics of this period that not one of them, save one woman who was already a friend, should have recognized this literary *tour de force* by an established author as worth mentioning. Without any question as to its artistic merit, it was certainly a unique piece of work, worth recording. But that is not the first joke on critics, by any means.

In regard to the general attitude of hearers, readers and editors, toward my work, I have met a far wider and warmer welcome than I ever expected. Not aiming in the least at literary virtuosity, still less at financial success, I have been most agreeably surprised by the acceptance of so much of what I had to offer. One cannot undertake to alter the ideas, feelings and habits of the people and expect them to like it.

Consider the theses this one woman was advancing

against the previous convictions of the world: in religion a practical, impersonal Deism, seeing God as a working power which asks no worship, only fulfilment:

> God is a force to give way to—
> God is a thing you have to Do!

with no concern for immortality or salvation, merely a carrying out of the divine will. In ethics its presentation as a wholly social science, applicable to every act in life, the measure of merit being the effect on social advancement. In economics, a change in the basis of that science, as with ethics, from the individual to the group, involving a complete reversal of most of our previous economic theories; and in what is of far more interest to most of us, our domestic and sex relationships, the claim that we as a race of animals are oversexed—abnormally developed in that function from long centuries of excessive indulgence, and that it is disadvantageous to social progress to have the feeding of humanity and the care of young children carried on by amateurs.

This last is the view which has been most violently opposed. The food habits of a people are extremely difficult to change, and as to the care of young children, the obvious need and value of the mother have blinded us to her as obvious deficiencies. The position as to sex is most amusingly in contradiction of our present theory of its dominant importance, a theory which claims as "natural" an indulgence absolutely without parallel in nature.

Being so universal a heretic it is much to the credit of our advance in liberal thought that my work has been for the most part well received. The slowness and indifference of the public mind was of course to be expected, and its very general misunderstanding; the only thing I have to complain of in the way of ill-treatment has been from newspapers, and even among them there has been much, very much, of fair and helpful recognition.

So general an attack upon what we have long held incontrovertible must needs have met misunderstanding and opposition. If the world had been able to easily receive it then it would not have been necessary. The clear logic of the position, the reasoning which supported it, made small impression on the average mind. Reason is the least used of our faculties, the most difficult—even painful. That is why successful orators do not need it.

This is also why my little *Forerunner* had so few subscribers, at least one reason why. There were some who were with me on one point and some on two, but when it came to five or more distinct heresies, to a magazine which even ridiculed Fashion, and held blazing before its readers a heaven on earth which they did not in the least want—it narrowed the subscription list.

The magazine came to an end with 1916. For a while I did little writing—I had said all I had to say. Then presently I undertook a new game, writing short bits of daily stuff for a newspaper syndicate. "Could I keep it up?" anxiously inquired the gentleman who engaged me. I told him what I had been keeping up for seven years, and he was satisfied. But alas! though I tried my best to reach and hold the popular taste, I couldn't do it, so after a year that effort came to an end. It was the only time in my life when I had a "pay-envelope," and that was most enjoyable.

Another experiment was with one of the smaller Chautauquas, a six weeks' trip among very small towns in rather backward regions mostly. With the lecturer went a "Revue," a group of girls who danced and sang and otherwise pleased the audience. This I rather dreaded, the traveling in company with a lively bunch of young ladies of that sort, but found them as pleasant and likable as any girls, excellent company; I grew quite fond of them. And they of me it appeared, for they honored me with the title of "Good Old Scout," and on our last performance together, those dear girls presented me with a bouquet and a nice little speech of appreciation, which went to my heart.

As a Chautauqua lecturer I was as much of a failure as in the pleasant platitudes of newspaper syndicates. Giving the same lecture night after night has never been within my powers, that is to do it well, and to do it at all I must have an audience some of whom, at least, are interested. I am a teacher, though sometimes amusing and impressive while teaching, and what is required in this work is an entertainer.

These audiences, in little mining towns and remote villages, were generally like this; in the two or three front rows a collection of squirming children; in the last two or three rows another collection of lads and lasses, with much shuffling and giggling, peanuts and chewing-gum; in the middle rows those dumb ranks of tired housewives, miners or farmers. I did not please, and never wanted to try that kind of work again.

During these New York years there was often some speaking to do, even after I had been forced to stop speaking gratuitously for the many Socialist groups and associations always asking. Slowly, very slowly, I have raised my lecture from a minimum of nothing to a minimum of $100—holding the privilege of making it much less, when necessary, for educational and religious bodies, and for the Forums which are doing such good work all over the country—and also getting more at times.

It has taken a long time for our Women's Clubs to outgrow the habit of being served for nothing. There came to me once a lady from a large Woman's Club in New Jersey, who wanted me to address them for $15.00 (all I asked at that time was $25.00). She said their budget would allow no more, that it was in her department. I had been told of the size and character of this club beforehand, so I questioned her gently— was this a small, new, struggling club? No, indeed. It was the largest and longest established in the city. Was it a reformatory association? By no means— social and educational. Were the members poor working women? They were not, not at all, they were ladies of the highest social standing. Then, I calmly inquired, can you tell me of any reason why I should address your club for less than my usual charge? She could not think of any, and they raised the gigantic sum I asked.

Another time came two ladies from Metuchen, New Jersey. Does that name seem impressive? I had heard that Mary Wilkins Freeman lived there, but that was all. They wanted me to make an address at some sort of civic performance, for nothing. Vainly did I explain that I was a professional speaker, that my rates were so and so, that I could not make distinctions for all comers. They seemed grieved at my conceit, urged their plea most earnestly, and finally brought to bear this irresistible argument—"We think it would benefit you to be known in Metuchen!" I had not sense enough to appreciate this priceless boon, and as far as I can tell, am completely unknown in Metuchen to this day.

In the Forum held by the Rev. Percy Grant I loved to speak, for he had real *viva voce* discussion from the floor. Written questions are safer in the long run perhaps, but it is much more vivid when they come hot from the protesting hearer. On one occasion there my speech was being violently attacked by a whiskerous foreigner, during the question period. Mr. Grant checked him, said it was the time for questions, not counter-attacks, would he please put his remarks in the form of a question; to which with some effort he replied, "My question is that I disagree with the speaker!"

New York abounds with dinner clubs and lunch clubs, with speeches. I used to enjoy the old Twilight Club, to which the original conditions of membership, they said, were the possession of a clean shirt and a dollar—or was it half a dollar? But after they assumed the name of the Society of Arts and Sciences, to which they had not the faintest shadow of a claim, and the purpose of which was but too obviously to induce visiting foreigners to accept their invitations to speak for them, for nothing—I have declined to meet with them.

There was a small woman's lunch club called the Heterodoxy, started by that brilliant and beautiful woman, Marie Jenney Howe, and composed of various ultra-heretical thinkers, or doers, or those wishing to be so considered, which I found interesting for a while, but when the heresies seemed to center on sex psychology and pacificism, I wearied of it. Another much pleasanter one was the Query Club, the well-managed pet of another brilliant and beautiful woman, Claire Mumford. This consisted of professional women of ability; their lunches were always vivid and amusing. Unfortunately they smoked all the time, smoked before the soup—with the soup and all the time, smoked worse than men do—and there are still some people who do not like the smell of tobacco, especially with food. So I dropped out of that.

Then there was the Gamut Club, mothered by Mary Shaw—that well-loved great actress who has done so much for the American stage. These were professional women too, largely actresses, kinder and not so smoky.

In great cities where people of ability abound, there is always a feverish urge to keep ahead, to set the pace, to adopt each new fashion in thought and theory as well as in dress—or undress. So in New York swept in with a rush the Freudian psychology, with all the flock of "psycho-analysts."

Always it has amazed me to see how apparently intelligent persons would permit these mind-meddlers, having no claim to fitness except that of having read certain utterly unproven books, to paddle among their thoughts and feelings, and extract confessions of the last intimacy. Men and women with no warrant in professional education, setting up offices and giving treatment—for handsome fees—became plentiful.

One of these men, becoming displeased with my views and their advancement, since I would not come to be "psyched," as they call it, had the impudence to write a long psychoanalysis of my case, and send it to me. My husband and I, going out in the morning, found this long, fat envelop with our mail. I looked at it, saw who it was from, and gave it to Houghton. "I don't want to read his stuff," I said. "You look it over and tell me what it is about." This he did, to my utter disgust. "Burn it up, do," I urged. "I haven't the least curiosity to know what this person thinks is the matter with me."

Fancy any decent physician presuming to send a diagnosis to some one never his patient, and who on no account would have consulted him! The joke is on him, in that his arrow never reached the mark, but the joke is on me because with a mind of that sort nothing could make him believe that a woman could have so little curiosity.

CHAPTER XX

HOME

TWENTY-TWO years in New York. Twenty-two years in that unnatural city where every one is an exile, none more so than the American. I have seen it stated that there are but 7 per cent native-born, of native ancestors, in that city. Others give a larger proportion, perhaps 15 or 20 per cent. Imagine Paris with but a fifth of its citizens French! London with but a fifth English —Berlin with but a fifth German! One third of the inhabitants of New York now are Jews, and we know of the hundreds of thousands of Italians, Germans, and others.

One summer we went to the coast of Maine for a little. I could have hugged the gaunt New England farmers and fishermen—I had forgotten what my people looked like!

The petty minority of Americans in New York receive small respect from their supplanters. Why should they? What must any people think of another people who voluntarily give up their country—not conquered —not forced out—simply outnumbered and swallowed up without a struggle. After a speech of mine in Cooper Union a scornful German demanded from the floor—"What *is* an American?"

A good answer which I did not think of then would have been: "An American is the sort of person who builds a place like this for you to enjoy, free." But my real answer is this: "Americans are the kind of people

who have made a country that every other kind of
people wants to get into!"

One of the bitterest lacks in that multiforeign city,
that abnormally enlarged city, swollen rather than
grown, is that of freedom in friendship and neighbor-
liness. People of similar tastes huddle in little local
groups, narrower than villages, as in the vaunted
pseudo-artistic settlement, Greenwich Village. Dwindling islands of earlier inhabitants cling to Murray
Hill or some other spot, and do not "call" beyond certain limits.

As I always tried to live where I could at least see
out of the crowd, where Central Park or, better, the
river, rested the eye and gave air to the lungs, we
moved farther and farther up-town. The result was
loneliness. Few indeed are the people in New York
who will go to see a friend unless they are fed. It is
not lack of friendliness, it is lack of time; and also that
ridiculous inability to step outside of their villages.

Some few dear friends we had, friends I love and
am proud to know. Yet even these I saw but little of.
My husband and I, not being afraid of distance, went
a-calling from time to time, but seldom indeed did
people reach 135th Street and climb five flights of
stairs to see us.

Yet I remember with joy the able and delightful
folk we knew, though we saw far too little of them.

The War came and passed. It left with me principally a new sense of the difference in races and the use
of nations in social evolution. I was forced to see that
the "next steps" in social progress in England, America, or France, were not those most needed in Uganda
or Tibet. This recognition has brought new light in
my studies of further social progress; there is still so

much more before us—so little to be satisfied with in all our recent advance.

This new century, now past its first quarter, has seen the achievement of many of the things so ardently striven for in the last, but it is like climbing a mountain range, each surmounted peak only shows more and higher ones. For instance we have attained full suffrage for women. This was never to me the *summum bonum* it was to many of its advocates, but I did expect better things of women than they have shown.

They remain, for instance, as much the slaves of fashion as before, lifting their skirts, baring their backs, exhibiting their legs, powdering their noses, behaving just as foolishly as ever, if not more so. I have no objection to legs, as bare as faces when necessary. The one-piece bathing suit is precisely as right for women as for men. It is an exhilarating sight to see men and women, swimming together, walking or running on the beaches together, free, equal, not stressing sex in any way. But these gleaming "nudes," in the street-car for instance, have no *raison d'être,* are merely an exhibition, neither timely, nor by any means always attractive. I have seen legs, yards of them one might say, with knee and thigh in full evidence, which so far from being desirable were fairly repellent.

The fine women who were making such advance in all manner of business and professional achievements are going on, in increasing numbers. More and more our girls expect to work, to earn, to be independent. But on the other hand, the "gold digger" is as rampant as ever, as greedy and shameless.

There is a splendid stir and push among our youth, what is called a "revolt," against pretty much everything that was before good, excellent, necessary—but what have they to propose instead? So far there has not been put forth by all this revolted youth any social improvement that I have heard of. Much is heard of the advantage of repudiating tradition, superstition, old legends, dogmas, conventions. Little is heard of any clear, newly established truth.

There is now nothing to prevent women from becoming as fully human in their social development as men; and although just now they seem more anxious to exhibit sex than ever, the real progress in humanness is there and will gradually overcome this backwash of primitive femininity.

It is amusing to find in this "advanced" period, some survivals of the mental attitudes of our decorous ancestors. For instance, I made myself, within a few years, a dress for the platform. Behold this aged amazon, stark and grim, covered from neck to wrist and ankle. Allow also for six layers of covering, the lace, the silk, the "slip" and so on inward.

Yet I was told confidentially, for my good, that people had criticized this costume as indelicate! They said it "showed the outline of the bust"! Two women and one man, it appears, had made this objection, with the added reproach, "At your age." When one considers the "outlines" now freely shown on our streets and in our parlors, to say nothing of the limitless exhibition elsewhere, and then looks at this grave and voluminous robe, such objection as this surely shows that there are still with us persons of a pure-mindedness difficult to fathom.

The Labor Movement, for which I worked as earnestly as for the advance of women, has now gone so far, achieved so much, with reduced hours, increased wages, and better conditions generally, that sympathy has given place to admiration. Further, there is a growing question on the part of the consumer as to where he comes in for advantages. The coal-miners fight for themselves, the coal operators fight for themselves, and the price of coal continues to go up.

Socialism, long misrepresented and misunderstood under the violent propaganda of Marxism, has been fairly obliterated in the public mind by the Jewish-Russian nightmare, Bolshevism. That "public mind" was never very clear on the subject, as was natural under the kind of talk they mostly heard; people used even to confuse Socialism with Anarchism—which are absolute opposites; and now there is such horror at the crimes and such contempt for the stupidities of the Russian Tyranny, that it is impossible to get a fair hearing for the most simple and advantageous steps in social progress if they seem to savor at all of Socialism. It may be years before that legitimate and gradual social advance can be presented with any hope of understanding.

One of the most important and most hopeful of all lines in advance is the rapid growth toward better education. From the post-graduate to the baby this gain is shown, and the baby end of it is most important. That intensely valuable period of life, the first four years, is at last recognized as deserving better care than can be given by solitary mothers and hired nurse-maids. We have now a name for this young person, "the pre-school child," and under this title earnest study is now being given to those first years and the best treatment for them. I sit and chuckle to see the most conscientious mamas proudly doing to their children what I was called "an unnatural mother" for doing to mine. Maternal instinct is at last giving ground a little before the resistless march of knowledge and experience. All this is good to see.

In our prehistoric status of "domestic industry"

there is some progress, but not much. The increasing cost and decreasing efficiency of domestic servants teaches most women nothing. They merely revert to the more ancient custom of "doing their own work." But the double-pressure goes on; more and more professional women, who will marry and have families and will not be house-servants, for nothing; and less and less obtainable service, with the sacrifice of the wife and mother to that primal altar, the cook-stove. This pressure, which marks the passing of the period of domestic service and the beginning of professional service—cooked meals brought to the home, and labor by the hour—will gradually force that great economic change.

For some thirty-seven years, with voice and pen, I have endeavored to explain and advocate this change, and the gain made in that time is probably all that could be expected in so deep-rooted a custom as that of to-every-man-his-own-cook. It would seem to one not accustomed to measure the glacial slowness of social progress, as if a change which would increase the income of a family and decrease its expenses by half, while at the same time greatly improving our health, would attract the most ordinary intelligence. But reason has no power against feeling, and feeling older than history is no light matter.

In politics there seems no great improvement. Our democracy is still the world's standard for commercialized government, for pitiful inefficiency. We cannot enforce our own laws. Private individuals have to hire bravos to defend their property, as if we were still in the Dark Ages. Armored cars defend the transfer of pay-rolls, not always successfully. Groups of "hilarious" law-breakers make a joke of recent legislation. Worthy citizens evade taxation, and complacent assessors aid them by underrating the value of property. The "melon" and the "plum tree" continue to be the desirable fruits of political success.

In the first years of the century there was a burst of protest and exposure in many magazines, "The Shame of the Cities" was shown up. But with astonishing thoroughness these "muck-rakers" were put down, they and their magazines with them, and the protest ceased.

Physically we seem to be improving. There is far more knowledge about health, more interest in hygiene and exercise, the death rate is being lowered, we are getting ahead of some diseases. In this line of progress there was no orthodoxy to be overcome.

Religion is in a very healthy commotion. The Romanists were perfectly right in foretelling that if we once began to divide we should keep on dividing. We have. That is the law of growth, the growth of living things. From the first step, the division of the fertilized cell, all the way onward, growth means division.

Also, the stony-minded orthodox were right in fearing the first movement of new knowledge and free thought. It has gone on, and will go on, irresistibly, until some day we shall have no respect for an alleged "truth" which cannot stand the full blaze of knowledge, the full force of active thought. We no longer— meaning educated people in general—believe as our forefathers did; and the uneducated, who probably know more than the educated of a few centuries ago, refuse to submit to dogmas and commands.

The religious need of the human mind remains alive, never more so, but it demands a teaching which can be *understood*. Slowly an apprehension of the intimate, usable power of God is growing among us, and a grow-

ing recognition of the only worth-while application of
that power—in the improvement of the world.

As to ethics, unfortunately, we are still at sea. We
never did have any popular base for what little ethics
we knew, except the religious theories, and now that
our faith is shaken in those theories we cannot account
for ethics at all. It is no wonder we behave badly, we
are literally ignorant of the laws of ethics, which is
the simplest of sciences, the most necessary, the most
continuously needed. The childish misconduct of our
"revolted youth" is quite equaled by that of older
people, and neither young nor old seem to have any
understanding of the reasons why conduct is "good"
or "bad."

Perhaps the most salient change of the present
period is the lowering of standards in sex relations,
approaching some of the worst periods in ancient history. In my youth there was a fine, earnest movement
toward an equal standard of chastity for men and
women, an equalizing upward to the level of what
women were then. But now the very word "chastity"
seems to have become ridiculous. Even if complete promiscuity is avoided, there is a preliminary promiscuity
of approach which leaves little to be desired.

The main influence accounting for this is the psycho-
philosophy, the sexuopathic philosophy, which solemnly
advocates as "natural" a degree of indulgence utterly
without parallel in nature. A larger knowledge of
biology, of zoölogy, is what is wanted to offset this
foolishness. In the widespread attacks upon marriage
it is clearly shown that the attackers do not know that
monogamy is a "natural" form of sex relationship,
practised widely among both birds and beasts, who are
neither "Puritan" nor "Mid-Victorian." These uneducated persons seem to think that all animals are either

promiscuous or polygamous; and to add to their folly, forget that even such creatures have their definite season for mating.

These things I have seen happen. None of them give cause for as much anxiety, to an American, as the rapidly descending extinction of our nation, superseded by other nations who will soon completely outnumber us. This, with the majority rule of a democracy, means that our grandchildren will belong to a minority of dwindling Americans, ruled over by a majority of conglomerate races quite dissimilar.

But since it is no new thing in history to have a given nation fail, give way and disappear, while the progress of society continues in other hands, we should perhaps contentedly admit our failure and welcome our superseders. Perhaps they will do better than we.

Leaving New York with measureless relief, I came in 1922 to this old Connecticut settlement, Norwich Town. It is so beautiful as to have won the title, Rose of New England. This is my native state, and while the town is not my ancestral home it is my husband's, and in the larger sense of similarity in people and in tastes and habits, it has more of the home feeling than such a nomad as I had ever hoped for.

After New York it is like heaven. It is true that two-thirds of the population are aliens, but they are not so overwhelmingly in evidence as in the great city. The people I meet, and mostly those I see in the neighborhood, are of native stock. One may speak to them, to workmen of any grade, and get a cheerful man-to-man answer.

Here people can be friends, can see one another as often as desired without making a social function of it;

here I can take my knitting or sewing and "run in"; or
I can stop on my way down-town or up, for a little
chat. Being a Connecticutter by birth, and my husband's family well known and loved here, I have been
welcomed more than kindly.

Such nice people! Such well-educated, well-read,
well-intentioned people! I had more accessible friends
here in one year than in New York in twenty. Our Norwich Town is the early settlement; Norwich, now the
city, is a later growth. The town lies to the north of it,
a narrow strip between wooded hills and the Yantic
River. The long streets are lined with trees, New England fashion, and the majestic old houses stand back
under their great elms, a succession of noble pictures.

The most conspicuous religion of the place is ances-
tor worship—at least it looks like it. The town is
labeled with the names of long-dead residents, not
merely on gravestones, but on neat white signs hung
on old houses, nailed on trees, set on the ground here
and there. These were first put up in honor of the
two hundred and fiftieth anniversary of the settlement,
and have been piously maintained ever since. One somewhat irreverent friend suggested that I write a limerick
on this local habit, with this result:

> So proud of our grandsires are we,
> Each old house wears a sign, as you see;
>   If a house we have not,
>   Then we label the lot,
> And hang up the sign on a tree.

One of these signs commemorates "First child born in
Norwich." Another prouder and more explicit, records
"First male child." Our ancient mansion I found deco-
rated with two, on either side the front door, one a

list of ancestors, the other announcing, "Lydia Huntley Sigourney born here." The general effect of all these white records is of a sort of mural graveyard.

In the real graveyard, the old one, are truly interesting memories. In one place there is a touching group of tricolors around a big marked stone commemorating a number of French soldiers who died here during the Revolution. One table monument bears pleasing recognition of the advance of science—So-and-So, at such a time, "died (very suddenly) of a disease known to the medical faculty as *Angina Pectoris.*"

Home-like and lovely as it is, no one with a sense of historical perspective can live in a New England town and not suffer to see its gradual extinction. Those noble houses, pillared porches, fanlights over rich doorways, wide sweeps of lawn under majestic elms, are no longer built. The old people who had sufficient wealth to live in those gracious mansions pass away, and the young people who have sufficient wealth prefer to spend it in other ways, in other places. Down go the gracious mansions and up spring the close-set "bungalows"; a different kind of people are taking over the place. But as yet there is dignity and beauty and peace, and I enjoy it with the delight of a returned exile.

Our own place is a lovely one. What is left to it is only an acre, but on two sides spreads wide a pleasant park, Lowthorpe Meadows, once the "mowin' lot" of the family. So there is green distance, wide open space to rest the eye, secured to us. On our acre is a big-enough flower garden, and some nine thousand square feet of vegetable garden, which Mr. Gilman and I cultivate with our own hands.

Never before did I have a garden to care for. In Rehoboth I was too young for anything but a bit of flower-bed; in California too sick and overworked for such enjoyment. But here there is plenty of honest-to-goodness physical labor, in which I exult. A somewhat reluctant husband does most of the hardest, but I do a good bit, as for instance in digging a four-foot-deep trench to prepare for sweet peas. That was great fun, to stand breast-deep and pitch out shovels full of dirt as I've so often seen men do in the street. We raise about thirty kinds of vegetables—with varying success.

Admiring friends urged that we write a book about our experiences and Mr. Gilman suggested as a title *Two Gumps in a Garden*. This would be a most legitimate name, for neither of us "knew beans" when we began. The psychology of gardening is interesting and varied; on the one hand there is an almost maternal tenderness for the little seedlings that grow so rewardingly; and on the other one may find expression for ferocious rage and cruelty in uprooting weeds.

As to my work. . . . After seven years of the *Forerunner* I had no impulse to write for some time. I had said, fully and freely, the most important things I had to say. But there were occasional magazine articles, and, after coming here, another book, *His Religion and Hers*. This seemed to me rather a useful and timely work, treating of matters of both lasting and immediate importance—sex and religion. Unfortunately my views on the sex question do not appeal at all to the Freudian complex of to-day; nor are people satisfied with a presentation of religion as a help in our tremendous work of improving this world—what they want is hope of another world, with no work in it.

Magazine articles continue, now and then, mostly then.

But lecturing goes on, I am glad to say, better than ever. I do not mean more of it, but that it is stronger, clearer, more impressive, as it should be after thirty-seven years' practice. Much of it is Forum work. This does not pay well in money, but is splendidly worth doing on account of its wide reach among the people, and particularly enjoyable in being largely discussion. These discussions are always interesting and sometimes funny.

Audiences are always better pleased with a smart retort, some joke or epigram, than with any amount of reasoning. In the discussion after a Forum lecture in Boston, an address on some aspect of the Woman Question, a man in the gallery, who evidently took exception to a dull rose fillet I wore in my hair, demanded to know how women could expect to equal men "so long as they took so much time fixing up their hair and putting ribbons in it"? There was some commotion, and cries of "Put him out!" but I grinned up at him cheerfully and replied, "I do not think it has been yet established whether it takes a woman longer to do her hair than it does a man to shave." This was not an answer at all, but it seemed to please every one but the inquirer.

Something should be said as to the effect on a life-philosophy of some fifty years of thinking and teaching. There must be growth, there is likely to be some change.

The basis, the reliable religion founded on fact, has held firm through all the years and all the difficulties. The socio-economic philosophy is also still satisfying, with its comforting long-range convictions as to our accelerating improvement in spite of all our foolishness. We still hinder social evolution, but not so successfully as we used to. The cheerful sense of our immense immediate power to better our conditions is unshaken; that we do not fully use it is a pity, but it is there none the less; and we are doing more and more with each succeeding year.

Our wide-scattered, irregular efforts are much nearer to an orderly, synchronized advance than they were in 1887 for instance, when I planned a paper on "The Inutility of Sporadic Reform." This too-impressive title was scornfully translated by Dr. S. W. Mitchell into "The Uselessness of Spotty Work." Our work of social improvement is not nearly so spotty as it used to be.

The most marked change which has been wrought by a lifetime's experience is in regard to the recognition of different stages of growth, different kinds of growth, in the different races of men. The general love of humanity remains, with the continuing desire to help it onward, but with wider sociological knowledge comes further understanding of the nature of that humanity, and the need of varying treatment according to race and nation.

The forward surge of social enthusiasm which marked the close of the eighteenth century, finding such fierce expression in the French Revolution, such strong realization in the American one, assumed humanity to be all one thing. "The Rights of Man" applied to every man; all men were said to be "born free and equal," our high-souled Abolitionists held that the Negro differed from the white "only in the color of his skin."

The Great War has shown us, lit by that world conflagration, the deep, wide, lasting vital difference between races. Race-consciousness is increasing rather than decreasing, it is rising and moving more portentously than ever. The stir among Africans, the uprising in India, the sudden emergence of Japan, the huge efforts toward a more conscious national power in China, China with her mighty intellect and with immeasurable resources, all this does not bear out the innocent claim of "Liberty, Equality and Fraternity," which visualizes a world of brothers.

The study of the world must now turn on an understanding of races and their relative degree of advancement, with far-reaching views as to a fair division of the earth among them, *not* based on "the pressure of the population." An earnest German once told me that Germany must have more land on account of that pressure. I asked him if he meant that the surface of the earth should be apportioned according to the fecundity of races—and he thought of Russia and was still.

If that were any rule by which to judge, glorious France ultimately would be ousted by any tribe in Africa, for instance; and we Americans justly deprived of our country by fecund foreigners. The pressure of population has been too long a standing excuse for war. When pacificists gather together to seek the cause of war, does any one mention babies? It seems hard to recognize babies, unlimited babies, as a ceaseless cause of war, but any one who can count—both years and people—can see it. With all its lamentable accompaniment of license and misbehavior, an intelligent limitation of a population to the resources of a country is one of the most essential requirements for any hope of world peace.

This new century of ours, still gasping from its hideous baptism of blood, has immanent possibilities of swift improvement. If our so ostentatiously revolted youth would outgrow their infantile delight in "self-expression," playing with their new freedom as a baby does with its fingers and toes, and see their real power, their real duty, things would move.

This is the woman's century, the first chance for the mother of the world to rise to her full place, her transcendent power to remake humanity, to rebuild the suffering world—and the world waits while she powders her nose. . . .

Much, very much of what I have worked for has been attained. Far more is waiting to be done. There is need of new teaching, of ethics that a child can understand, of religion which requires no swallowing of baseless dogmas, and which shall fill the soul with hope and purpose of human happiness here, for all of us, instead of morbid anxiety for a posthumous hypothesis of personal immortality.

I keep on teaching, preaching, lecturing, writing, as opportunity offers. If I live ten years more there is room for considerable good work yet. *Here's hoping!*

CHAPTER XXI

THE LAST TEN

NEARLY ten years since writing this book—which ended in hoping. For nine of them I remained in the old house in Norwich.

As to books, I wrote a species of detective story, at least unique, called *Unpunished*. No takers. "I find your characters interesting," said one "reader." "That is not necessary in a detective story." Evidently it is not, but I have often wished it was.

There are two copies of this afloat, buried in manuscript heaps of some agent or publisher. The trouble is that after a year or so I forget their names.

I wrote my *Social Ethics* over and over. That, I hope, will be printed with *Human Work;* social economics and social ethics—on those two I would rest my claim to social service.

Human Work was recently read by a New York publisher. He was surprised to find how few alterations were required, and said he would be glad to reprint it "if conditions. . . ."

As to lecturing—that market has declined before the advance of the radio. I had hoped for some hearing in my native state, where I had spoken in quite recent years; but when I offered my services to that invaluable association, The League of Women Voters, undertaking to lecture for them anywhere in the state, for expenses only, the total result was one engagement in a neighboring town, audience of ten. Also I had not unreasonably expected to be heard in the Connecticut College for Women, only some twelve miles from Norwich. After so many years of work for the advancement of women, with a fairly world-wide reputation in that work, and with so much that was new and strong to say to the coming generation, it seemed to me a natural opportunity. It did not seem so to the college. Once, for the League of Women Voters, I spoke in their hall—never otherwise.

My happiness in Norwich was in my garden, with Houghton as always, and with a few beloved friends.

There were that admirable minister and more admirable man, Alexander Abbott, and his dear family; and Edwin Higgins—Houghton's close friend and, in time of need, most efficiently mine—and his family. A near neighbor and unfailing comfort, giving restful companionship, was Miss Elizabeth Huntington, and there were others, pleasant and kind.

In January, 1932, I discovered that I had cancer of the breast. My only distress was for Houghton. I had not the least objection to dying. But I did not propose to die of this, so I promptly bought sufficient chloroform as a substitute. Human life consists in mutual service. No grief, pain, misfortune or "broken heart" is excuse for cutting off one's life while any power of service remains. But when all usefulness is over, when one is assured of unavoidable and imminent death, it is the simplest of human rights to choose a quick and easy death in place of a slow and horrible one.

Public opinion is changing on this subject. The time is approaching when we shall consider it abhorrent to our civilization to allow a human being to die in prolonged agony which we should mercifully end in any other creature. Believing this open choice to be of social service in promoting wiser views on this question, I have preferred chloroform to cancer.

Going to my doctor for definite assurance, he solemnly agreed with my diagnosis and thought the case inoperable.

"Well," said I cheerfully, "how long does it take?" He estimated a year and a half. "How long shall I be able to type?" I asked. "I must finish my *Ethics*." He thought I might be quite comfortable for six months. It is now three and a half years and this obliging malady has given me no pain yet.

Then came what was pain—telling Houghton. He wanted an expert opinion, and we got it. No mistake. Then, since I utterly refused a late operation, he urged me to try X-ray treatment, which I did with good effects. He suffered a thousand times more than I did—but not for long. On the fourth of May, 1934, he suddenly died, from cerebral hemorrhage.

Whatever I felt of loss and pain was outweighed by gratitude for an instant, painless death for him, and that he did not have to see me wither and die—and he be left alone.

I flew to Pasadena, California, in the fall of 1934, to be near my daughter and grandchildren. Grace Channing, my lifelong friend, has come out to be with me. We two have a little house next door but one to my Katharine, who is a heavenly nurse and companion. Dorothy and Walter, her children, are a delight. Mr. Chamberlin, my son-in-law, has made the place into a garden wherein I spend happy afternoons under an orange-tree—the delicious fragrance drifting over me, the white petals lightly falling—in May! Now it is small green oranges occasionally thumping.

One thing I have had to complain of—shingles. *Shingles*—for six weeks. A cancer that doesn't show and doesn't hurt, I can readily put up with; it is easy enough to be sick as long as you feel well—but *shingles!*

People are heavenly good to me. Dear friends write to me, with outrageous praises. I am most unconcernedly willing to die when I get ready. I have no faintest belief in personal immortality—no interest in nor desire for it.

My life is in Humanity—and that goes on. My contentment is in God—and That goes on. The Social Consciousness, fully accepted, automatically eliminates both selfishness and pride. The one predominant duty is to find one's work and do it, and I have striven mightily at that.

The religion, the philosophy, set up so early, have seen me through.

[On August 17, 1935, Mrs. Gilman fulfilled her intention to end her life as her malady advanced. The letter, left by her, was a part of the text of this final chapter of her autobiography, beginning: "Human life consists in mutual service," and ending "I have preferred chloroform to cancer."]

INDEX